Arts and Crafts Activities Desk Book

Joyce Novis Laskin

Illustrated by Ginger Apuzzo Gherardi

Parker Publishing Company, Inc.   West Nyack, N.Y.

PRINTED IN THE UNITED STATES OF AMERICA
ISBN-0-13-048769-4
B & P

Dedication

TO MY HUSBAND, MOTHER, FATHER AND CHILDREN

Acknowledgements

The author would like to express her deepest thanks to the following persons for their dedicated assistance:

Selma Zatzkin Novis
Richard S. Laskin, M.D.
Ginger Apuzzo Gherardi
Rubi Roth
Gloria G. Kempner
Elizabeth Phelps Pyle
Audrey Mark

A Word from the Author

Most every teacher knows the potential of creative art for firing young imaginations. Early in my career, I learned how the addition of a little paint, paste and crayon, to even familiar classroom fare, could suddenly metamorphose a whole new learning adventure. However, despite my strongest wish to ignite young creativity, I was often discouraged by the lack of available materials, or time. I found I was not alone. The constant search for new, enriching materials and techniques seemed to transcend the experience of most classroom teachers. Hence, this book.

Arts and Crafts Activities Desk Book is unique because each lesson serves a dual purpose. Not only does an activity develop expression in the child; it may also be used to launch, culminate, enrich or supplement some important curriculum concept. An entire chapter is devoted to such areas as animals, nature, community helpers, the human body, space science, clothing, food, music and dance—and more! Here, art can help the child learn how and why he grows, where foods come from, about texture and clothing, to interpret dance—even how to make movies.

For practically every aspect of the curriculum you will find an applicable lesson, precisely detailed, and geared to the ability of your age group. With a tenacious respect for your time (or lack of it), each lesson provides an on-the-spot checklist of materials, a section of motivational and background information, and clearly written and numbered procedural steps with an accompanying step-by-step illustration. At the end of each activity you will also find creative ideas for display and follow-up activities, as well as time saving tips.

Remember, whether you choose a lesson to underscore a concept, decorate the room, create a costume, or brighten the day with a dash of whimsey, this book was written for you to use flexibly. Take as much as you wish from each lesson's many suggestions, or add a personal touch of your own. Most of all, enjoy it!

Joyce Novis Laskin

Contents

The Community
and Its Helpers

1

There is, perhaps, no better way to have children learn about their community and the people who serve it than by recreating its places and personalities in a classroom. This chapter contains activities which add both interest and fun to community study programs. They are designed to help orient the child to his surroundings, and to develop a better understanding of the interpersonal relationships of community life.

To help youngsters understand the importance of cooperation on the community level, many of the activities in this chapter are group experiences. Each child's individual project can be a contribution to a larger class activity.

Since these activities are not complex, the youngster has an opportunity to develop his handling of basic art materials such as paste, glue, scissors and paint. Emphasis, in this first chapter, also centers on classroom management. Children must realize that proper care of materials, and organization, have an important bearing on the success of both individual and group projects.

Though the activities in this chapter are sequentially designed, they may be used individually or adapted to other curricula as needs dictate.

MILK CONTAINER MODEL OF THE COMMUNITY

MATERIALS

1. milk container
2. square of paper, pre-cut to fit the bottom of the milk container
3. tempera paint, diluted with liquid soap detergent and water
4. crayons
5. scissors
6. masking tape
7. rulers
8. pencils

BEFORE YOU BEGIN

Your class will, no doubt, be excited about building a model of the community. You may find that each child has several ideas concerning what he would like to make. Of course, not everything in the community can be included in the project. "What places in the community are most important to you and your family (post office, supermarket, dime store, church)?" "Where do you have the most fun?" List the children's responses on the board. "Where will we put our model?" "Will we use a table or the floor?" Show the class the materials with which they will work, so that they may plan adequately and not overcrowd the allotted space. When the basic plans have been completed, let each child choose one of the listed structures on the board as his particular model. Each child may make more than one model, depending on available time and space.

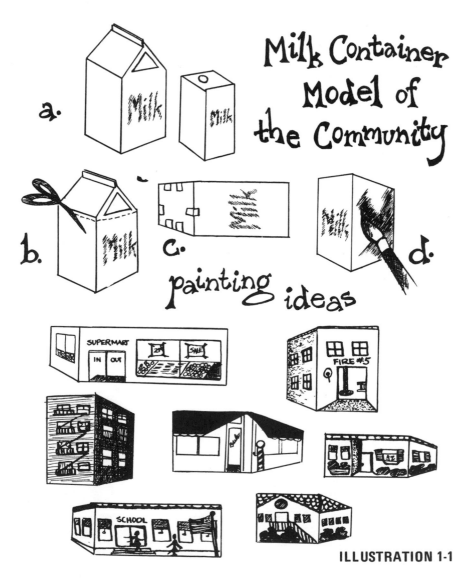

ILLUSTRATION 1-1

PROCEDURE (Illustration 1-1)

1. Remove the top of a milk container by cutting around its upper rim. (steps a & b)
2. "Now, look at the container." "Does it resemble the shape and size of the building you wish to represent?" "Will it be used horizontally or vertically?" Some containers will have to be cut down. Have each child decide what changes he will need to make. Using a pencil and straight edge, let the child mark off the amount he wishes to remove. "Remember, you will cut from the open end of the container, so make your changes from there." Emphasize, to those who use their containers vertically, that the open end will be the bottom, or base, of the model.
3. Provide a pre-cut square of paper for those who want to use containers horizontally. Use masking tape to secure the paper square to the open end of the container. Children are now ready to paint. Tell each child to choose a basic background color for his model and begin. While this color dries, discuss how the model details will be applied. "What are some of the features we notice about the building at first sight—its color, a flag outside, large windows?" Reassure the class that they need not include every detail; just the ones that distinguish the building as being different from others around it. (steps c & d)
4. Paint in the desired detailed features of the model. Provide an assortment of colors for this. Plastic ice-cube trays will eliminate confusion. Fill some sections with paint and others with water. Leave other sections empty for children to mix their colors. Allow one ice-cube tray for each table of four to five children.
5. Place the models on a large table, or piece of mural paper on the floor, so as to reproduce the local community. Use plastic toy cars, buses, and trees, brought in from home to complete the project.

WHAT THE CHILDREN CAN DO AFTERWARD

1. Let each child add his own model to the community replica. He might prepare a short talk about the structure, explaining its location and function in the community.
2. Invite another class for a "Guided Tour of Our Town." Children may take turns explaining their models to the other group.
3. Perhaps the model could be displayed in the school lobby or library. If this is possible, number each structure and have the class make a corresponding chart to identify each building.

RELAX WITH TIME SAVERS

1. Pre-cut additional squares of paper well in advance of the lesson.
2. Pre-mix the paint with a solution of liquid detergent and water. This process will enable the paint to adhere to the waxy milk container surface.

3. Mix and store the paint in empty liquid detergent bottles with locked tops. These containers will prevent spillage and breakage.

4. Spread newspaper on tables before starting to paint. Set up painting stations, at the appropriate time, in back of the room. Have each youngster complete the initial painting job at the table corresponding to his respective project color.

5. While the painted models dry, appoint a helper to collect the paint dispensers and put them away.

6. Choose a second helper to fill and distribute ice-cube trays of paint for final detail painting.

SPOOL DOLL HELPERS

ILLUSTRATION 1-2

Spool Dolls

MATERIALS

1. wooden spools
2. white glue
3. tempera paint and brushes
4. scraps of colored paper
5. scissors

BEFORE YOU BEGIN

Children will enjoy making small dolls representing the community workers about whom they are learning. Explain to your class that dolls will be made from ordinary empty spools. Advise them, at the start of the unit, to bring these in from home. You should thus have an abundant supply by the time you are ready to begin this activity. Spools may vary in size, and an assortment may be used for each doll. Encourage children to experiment by placing one spool on top of another before they glue. Imaginative spool personalities will emerge if time is taken to plan out each doll ahead of time.

PROCEDURE (Illustration 1-2)

1. Have children select an assortment of spools. Three spools usually produce a good size doll and are easily manipulated during the first attempt. (steps a & c)

2. Glue the spools together and allow them to dry thoroughly. (steps b & c)
3. Paint the details. If three spools are being used, paint a hat (if required) and facial features on the top spool. Paint limbs and costume details on the remaining spools. If desired, cut small pieces of construction paper from scraps. Paste additional decorations (badges, buttons, or the like) to the doll. These scraps may also be used, in place of paint to make hair and limbs. (step d)

WHAT THE CHILDREN CAN DO AFTERWARD

1. Dolls may be added to the milk container community model to bring the town to "life."
2. Let the children paint a scene inside a shoe box, relative to the roles of the dolls they have created. Place these spool personalities inside the boxes and display them along the window sill, or on a table in the corner of the room.

RELAX WITH TIME SAVERS

1. Spread newspapers on tables before gluing. Choose a helper from each table for this task.
2. One bottle of glue will adequately serve a table of four to five pupils. It may be applied quickly, straight from the bottle. Collect glue bottles when children have finished using them.
3. A plastic ice-cube tray, filled with an assortment of paints will also be sufficient for one table. The first child at a table to finish gluing should prepare paints in this fashion.
4. Advise the class to let one color dry thoroughly before applying a second. This will eliminate running and facilitate handling. Paint one side of the spool at a time.

TOY TRAIN

MATERIALS

1. box from a roll of waxed paper or aluminum foil
2. sheet of shirt cardboard
3. tempera paint, diluted with liquid detergent soap
4. pencil
5. aluminum foil (optional)
6. stapler
7. scissors

BEFORE YOU BEGIN

Ask the children to do some research about trains before you begin this activity. Your school library should have many books on the subject. Youngsters will enjoy sharing their reading about the many types of trains which carry people and freight to places far and near. Display these books around the room, permitting the children to look through them in their spare time. Some might be willing to bring in a few of their electric trains for group discussion.

On the board, list the types of trains about which your class has learned. You may choose this to be a group activity; with some making passenger cars, and others working on a variety of freight trains. If so, let the groups meet once for a planning session. Have each child decide the type of car he will construct. Before you begin, choose helpers to distribute paint, paste, and other necessary materials.

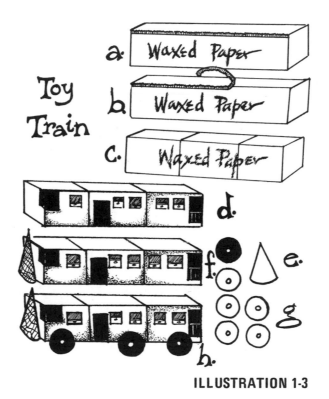

ILLUSTRATION 1-3

PROCEDURE (Illustration 1-3)

1. Tear the serrated edge off the box and discard it. Caution the children to handle the metal strip by its end. (steps a & b)
2. Section off the box in pencil, to produce the effect of several cars. (steps c & d)
3. Cut a "pie wedge" from cardboard. Staple it to the box to make the front end of a locomotive. (steps e and f)
4. Paint the box, using the penciled lines as a guide in making multicolored box cars. (step d)
5. Cut wheels out of cardboard. These may be painted or covered with aluminum foil. Staple them in place. (steps g & h)
6. If desired, use aluminum foil, instead of paint, to make windows and doors.

WHAT THE CHILDREN CAN DO AFTERWARD

1. Set up a railyard on a large table. Let each group explain the type of train it has contributed.
2. Use some of the trains in a model of the community to represent the local station.
3. Ask that each child write a short explanation about his creation on a 3″ x 5″ card. Display the trains and cards on a table, or along a window sill.

RELAX WITH TIME SAVERS

1. Group the children so that there are no more than four or five to a table. This will facilitate class management, whether the activity is to be an individual or group experience.
2. Place all materials needed in the center of each table. A stapler and a plastic ice-cube tray of assorted paint colors can easily be shared by each group.
3. Spread newspapers on the tables before starting to paint.

FIRE ENGINE

MATERIALS

1. aluminum foil or plastic wrap box
2. stapler or paste
3. scissors
4. tempera paint, diluted with liquid soap detergent
5. pencils
6. small jar caps
7. paper fasteners

BEFORE YOU BEGIN

A trip to the local firehouse would be ideal preparation for this activity. Firsthand experience will give youngsters lasting impressions of fire engines. Have the children notice the details of these engines and equipment. Their queries will, no doubt, be answered by the firehouse guide.

If a trip is not possible, use library books and toy models as a basis for group discussion.

Advise the class to bring in empty foil boxes, several days in advance of the lesson.

PROCEDURE (Illustration 1-4)

1. Remove the serrated edge from the box and discard it. (step a)
2. Remove the entire top flap of the box and *save* it. (step b)
3. Cut off approximately 2″ from one end of the box. This piece will form the driver's portion of the fire engine. (step c)

ILLUSTRATION 1-4

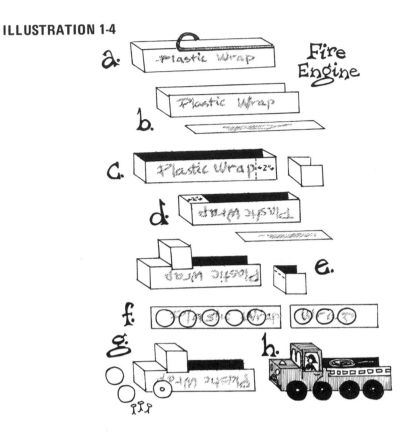

4. Cut all *but* 2″ from the bottom portion of the box. The remaining section will form the motor portion of the engine. (step d)
5. Staple or paste the driver section in back of the motor section, as shown in the illustration. Trim with scissors to make the two pieces fit securely. (step e)
6. Using small jar caps, trace wheels on the box top flap and cut them out. (steps f & g)
7. Attach the wheels to the engine with paper fasteners. This will enable the model to move. (step g)
8. Paint the body of the fire engine red. When dry, add other details (ladders, hoses, tools). (step h)

WHAT THE CHILDREN CAN DO AFTERWARD

1. Make a firehouse from an empty carton. Display fire engines in and around the firehouse.
2. Have each child write about his fire engine on a file card and display it, along with fire engine, on a table in the room.
3. Use engine models in the community display, where appropriate.
4. Make a bulletin board mural, tracing the route of a fire engine to a fire. Instead of drawing engines, tack models to the bulletin board where needed.

RELAX WITH TIME SAVERS

1. Have a helper walk around room with a wastebasket so that children may discard the serrated box edge as soon as it has been removed.
2. Mark off areas to be cut in pencil, before handing out scissors.
3. Mix the paint with liquid soap in empty soap squeeze bottles. Set up painting stations, with a container of red paint at each. Have the children apply red paint in these areas.
4. Supply a variety of paints in ice-cube trays for detail painting.

MINIATURE MAILBOX

MATERIALS

1. milk container
2. scissors
3. pencil
4. masking tape
5. red, white and blue paint, diluted with liquid soap detergent
6. brushes
7. ruler

BEFORE YOU BEGIN

Correlate this activity with a study about the post office. Here is a simple way to culminate a lesson, involving little time for completion.

If possible, take a walk with your class to the nearest mailbox and observe its characteristics (color, shape, lettering).

Demonstrate the procedure to be followed before handing out necessary materials. With very young children, repeat the procedure along with the class as they cut out and fold containers into a mailbox shape.

PROCEDURE (Illustration 1-5)

1. Cut off the top and bottom of the milk container. (step a)
2. Draw a horizontal line, four inches from the base, on two opposite sides of the container. These sides will later form the rounded edges of the mailbox. (step b)
3. Using the horizontal line as an upper limit, draw an arc from left to right on one of the container sides. Repeat this procedure on the second lined side. (step c)
4. Cut around these arcs discarding the remaining upper portions of the sides of the container. The unpenciled sides of the container will remain as two long flaps. (step d)

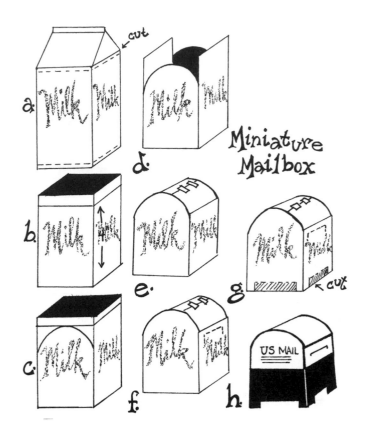

Miniature Mailbox

ILLUSTRATION 1-5

5. Overlap these flaps so that the top of the mailbox is even with its rounded sides. Tape the flaps down to secure them in place. (step e)
6. Draw a small letter opening, and cut it out on three sides. (step f)
7. Make legs by cutting small rectangles from each of the four sides at the base of the mailbox. (step g)
8. Paint the mailbox with red and blue paint. When dry, add details with white paint. (step h)

WHAT THE CHILDREN CAN DO AFTERWARD

1. Make a bulletin board display. Have each child address an envelope to a member of the class, including zip code, return address, etc. Emphasize the proper manner of addressing letters. Tack this envelope with the child's mailbox to the bulletin board.
2. Use mailboxes, where appropriate, in the community model suggested at the beginning of this chapter.
3. Tack the mailboxes, where needed, to the "Where We Live Bulletin Board," suggested in this chapter.

RELAX WITH TIME SAVERS

1. Do not hand out scissors until the children have finished marking the arcs on the sides of the container, and the rectangles at its base. If errors are made, they can easily be erased before cutting.

2. One roll of masking tape should be sufficient for a table of children. They may take turns using the roll when it is needed.
3. Mix the paint with liquid detergent well in advance of the lesson. Test the mixture on a milk container to be certain it will adhere properly. Use empty detergent squeeze bottles to mix paint, and use them as dispensers. Pour the paint into plastic ice-cube trays, to be distributed to tables when needed.
4. Spread newspaper on the tables before starting to paint.
5. Make certain the containers have dried thoroughly before lettering is added.

MODEL AIRPORT

MATERIALS

1. large sheet of mural paper
2. felt-tipped marker
3. assortment of small boxes in a variety of sizes and shapes (toothpaste boxes, small foodstuff boxes, round paper fastener boxes)
4. cylindrical oatmeal box
5. paste
6. paint
7. scissors

ILLUSTRATION 1-6

BEFORE YOU BEGIN

A trip to the airport would be ideal background for this project. If, however, it is not feasible, have the class learn as much as possible about the airport through group discussions, film strips, books, and the like. Discuss its many features, such as traffic circles, parking areas, terminal buildings, and hangars. Plan out the structures and areas to be included in the model, and write these items on the board. Divide the class into groups. Some children may work on the aerial view, while others construct representative buildings and create airplane hangars.

Explain that imaginations are to be used; the model needn't be an exact replica of the local airport. Children should use the knowledge gained through research, as well as their ingenuity, in constructing these models.

Groups should meet for a planning session. Show the class the materials with which they will be working. Circulate from group to group during the planning session, to help youngsters decide the exact layout of the airport and the types of buildings they will include.

PROCEDURE (Illustration 1-6)

1. Ask the group working on the aerial map to draw it on the blackboard first. Give guidance as the children proceed with this task. Once a blackboard sketch has been completed it may be copied, in pencil or chalk, on mural paper. The finished outline may then be gone over with felt-tipped marker.
2. Distribute an assortment of boxes to the groups that will work on terminal buildings. Children should experiment with these, piling one upon another to create interesting structures. The resulting box buildings may be pasted together once youngsters have been given ample time for experimentation.
3. Show the children how to make airplane hangars from oatmeal boxes. Remove box tops and bottoms. Cut the remaining cylindrical portions in half lengthwise. Two hangars will be formed from each box.
4. Paint the buildings and hangars with tempera paint.
5. When dry, have the children place their models on the aerial map.
6. Use plastic toy planes, cars, trucks, to complete the model.

WHAT THE CHILDREN CAN DO AFTERWARD

1. Place the model on a table in front of a bulletin board. Use the bulletin board to make a sample arrival and departure schedule.
2. Number the different areas of the model (place a 1 on the parking lot, a 2 outside the terminal building, and so on) to indicate the step by step procedure to be followed in taking a plane trip. Make a corresponding chart with numbers to explain these steps—(1.) park car, (2.) have baggage tagged outside terminal, and so on.
3. Learn about the functions of various airport workers. Ask each child to select one type of worker and present a talk to the class, indicating on the model the area in which this individual would perform his duties.

RELAX WITH TIME SAVERS

1. Separate the various groups into working areas where they may meet and discuss plans, before handing out any materials.
2. The groups which work on buildings should decide, in advance, how many of these structures they will need. Distribute boxes to "builders" once planning is completed.
3. Use empty jar caps for paste. Have a child fill several caps and distribute one to every group of 4-5 youngsters.
4. Set up a painting station in the back of the room, spreading tables with newspaper. Have an assortment of paints and sufficient brushes for approximately four children. All will not be ready to paint at the same time. Once the paste on box structures has dried, children may come to the painting area to decorate their models. Permit no more than four children to paint at one time. Instruct each child to wash his brushes for use by the next person.
5. Provide a table, covered with newspaper, on which to place painted buildings for drying.

WHERE WE LIVE BULLETIN BOARD

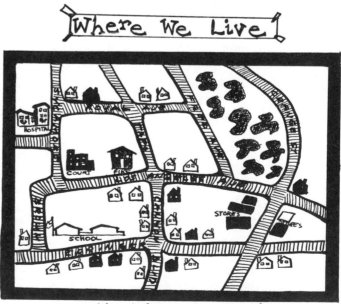

MATERIALS

1. green bulletin board paper
2. felt-tipped marker
3. heavy white drawing paper
4. crayons
5. scissors
6. rulers

ILLUSTRATION 1-7

BEFORE YOU BEGIN

This bulletin board suggestion need not be related to a complete study of the community. Here is an excellent way to erase some of the early-in-the-year insecurities of children who must walk to school. This activity will orient them to where they live in relation to the school, as well as to other members of the class. Present too, is an opportunity to introduce map study. Discuss the concept of direction with your class. Draw a key on the board indicating north, south, east and west. The map should be drawn on the blackboard before being tried on the bulletin board. Sketch in the local school and some of the major roads and boulevards in the vicinity. Help children discover which of these are north, south, east or west of the school. Write in the names of streets on which children live on a separate section of the blackboard. Then, ask youngsters to come up to the board, one at a time, to draw in these streets. Let the class contribute suggestions for improvement as classmates draw in these lines. Once the map has been completed on the board to satisfaction, the activity may proceed.

PROCEDURE (Illustration 1-7)

1. Cover the board with green paper.
2. Select a group of children to start copying the blackboard map on to the bulletin board, using light pencil and rulers. Be certain to include a key showing directions. Permit one small group to work on the map for a while, then call another to continue, until each child has had an opportunity to work on the project.
3. While these groups work, have the rest of the class color and cut out pictures of their houses on white drawing paper. Ask children to write their names and house numbers, clearly, on some part of the cut-out home.
4. When the map has been properly copied on the bulletin board, have new groups of children trace the penciled lines with felt-tipped marker, and write in the street names.
5. Select a child to draw a picture of the school on the appropriate street.
6. Request that each youngster come up to the bulletin board with his cut-out house, find his street, and staple the house to its proper place. Be certain the addresses are numbered in the correct sequence. Numerical progression, as well as the existence of odd and even numbers, can be correlated with this activity.

WHAT THE CHILDREN CAN DO AFTERWARD

1. Each child, using a pointer stick, can explain where he lives, indicating the direction his house lies from school. Let him trace the shortest walking route from home to school.
2. Review safety practices about crossing streets. You could have the class draw in traffic signals, marking the correct crossing areas.
3. Invite other classes to see the map. Your group can acquaint these visitors with some of the things they have learned.

4. Pretend there is to be a party at someone's home. Ask children to give verbal directions, without the use of a pointer stick.

RELAX WITH TIME SAVERS

1. Put paper on the bulletin board well in advance of the lesson.
2. Each child will want to work on the bulletin board map, so assign individuals a group number. Children are to come to the bulletin board only when their numbers are called.
3. Before the first group begins work, distribute materials the class will need for the house pictures. Group number one may start map work once the class has quietly settled down to drawing their houses. This latter part of the activity can be done independently by most children, freeing the teacher to supervise the bulletin board groups.
4. Emphasize neatness. Encourage pupils to take their time. "Each home or apartment house should be as attractive as possible."
5. Use rulers to pencil in streets on maps. Children can then trace these lines, using felt-tipped marker.

COMMUNITY HELPER HATS

MATERIALS

1. headbands, cut from 20" long by 1" wide strips of construction paper, in an assortment of colors (use a paper cutter for this)
2. visors, cut from 7" in diameter semicircles of colored construction paper
3. assorted 12" x 18" sheets of colored construction paper
4. paste
5. scissors
6. pencils
7. aluminum foil and a variety of scraps of colored construction paper for decoration

BEFORE YOU BEGIN

Play-acting is almost a natural activity for children, especially when they are learning about people who play an important role in their lives. "Who would you like to be; a policeman, a doctor, a baker?" Tell children that they will have an opportunity to "dress up" as their favorite community characters by making simple hats.

Discuss the types of hats worn by various workers in the community. If possible, have pictures available for the children to see. Of course, it would be best to have one or two real samples on hand. Talk about the many shapes of these hats. "Which ones are very high?" "Which are worn flat against the head?"

Show children the materials with which they will work. Pre-cut long strips of paper for headbands, and semicircle visors in advance. Permit each child to choose one strip, a semicircle (if necessary) and a sheet of colored construction paper, all in corresponding colors. Make one or two sample hats as the class watches. They may begin once they are thoroughly acquainted with the procedure.

ILLUSTRATION 1-8

PROCEDURE (Illustration 1-8)

1. Using pencil, have each child draw the basic shape of his hat on the 12″ x 18″ piece of construction paper. Supervise the work, reminding the class to think about the actual size and shape of the hat being made. Cut out the hat shape. Tell youngsters to save the left-over scraps and place them in a "scrap box" in front of the room. Distribute 20″ headbands. (steps a & b)
2. Color in the headband and hat background with crayons. (steps a & b)
3. Use scraps of construction paper and foil for additional decorations. Aluminum foil, with construction paper, may be used for badges, a doctor's head mirror and buttons. Paste these decorations to the hat. (step b)
4. Paste the cut-out hat piece to the inside edge of the headband. (step d)
5. Fold the upper edge of the visor down about 1/4″ (demonstrate this to the class). Run a thin coat of paste along this fold, and attach it to the inside, lower edge of the headband. (steps c & d)

6. Instruct the children to come up to your desk, one at a time, with their hats. Fit each child's hat to his head by stapling the two headband pieces together. (step e)

WHAT THE CHILDREN CAN DO AFTERWARD

1. Group four or five children together. Ask each group to put on a short skit, showing how community helpers they represent help residents.
2. Schedule a "parade" through several other classrooms, each child wearing his hat. Ask each youngster to prepare a sentence or two, describing his hat and the functions of the person who wears it, to be recited for "parade" viewers.
3. Write a class poem about community helpers. Invite other groups to a recitation. Hats are costumes.
4. Have class members write short reports about the helpers they've chosen, to be presented to the class. These reports should emphasize whatever safety regulations that community helper would want children to remember.

RELAX WITH TIME SAVERS

1. Pre-cut strips of paper and semicircles well in advance.
2. Place a scrap box in front of the room. Have small cut-out sheets of aluminum foil available in the same place.
3. Select a class helper from each table to come up for paste. It is suggested that you collect and save the tops from food jars for use as paste receptacles (tops of instant coffee jars are good for this purpose). Each helper can spoon enough paste for his table into a jar cover. Children may use small folded pieces of scrap paper to take individual amounts of paste. Left-over paste should be spooned back into paste jar and the cover receptacle saved for future use. This procedure eliminates unnecessary "traffic" in the room and limits waste.
4. Have a class helper walk around the room with a basket at the end of the lesson, so that tiny left-over bits of scrap paper can be discarded. Larger scraps may be returned to the box in the front of the room for later use in other activities.

COMMUNITY WORKER PICTURES

MATERIALS

1. magazine and/or newspaper pictures depicting a variety of working people (policemen, construction workers, businessmen, doctors, and the like)
2. drawing paper
3. scissors
4. paste
5. crayons

BEFORE YOU BEGIN

Show pictures of working people to your class, asking children to consider the type of work in which the individuals portrayed are involved. "What are some clues that we get from the picture?" "What does a man carrying a briefcase suggest to you?" "Does a certain kind of hat tell you something?" Encourage your group to observe these "clues," and bring in similar pictures from home magazines and newspapers.

Emphasize that some community helpers pictured in these clippings may also be reminiscent of workers with different roles. "A man in a white uniform could, among other things, be a barber, a doctor, or dentist." Instruct youngsters to keep these factors in mind when seeking pictures.

ILLUSTRATION 1-9

Community Workers

PROCEDURE (Illustration 1-9)

1. Cut out a figure from a magazine or newspaper. Discard remainder of the clipping.
2. Tell the children they will soon paste the figure to a piece of drawing paper. First, a scene will be drawn around the cut-out, illustrating the type of work in which the person is involved.
3. Ask the children to place the cut-out on paper and decide the type of picture

to be drawn. They may change their minds, since pasting will not be done until all drawing is finished. Encourage the class to "fill up" the paper.
4. Paste the figure to the desired place on the drawing.

WHAT THE CHILDREN CAN DO AFTERWARD

1. For use on a bulletin board, mount drawings on colored construction paper and write a label to describe the illustrated worker.
2. Tell each child to write a short story or poem about the worker he has chosen. Tack it, with its picture, to the bulletin board.
3. Use pictures as covers for work folders about community helpers.
4. Have the children share their pictures with class members. Let the class comment, suggesting different roles in which the cut-out figures could have been portrayed.

RELAX WITH TIME SAVERS

1. Have extra pictures on hand for those who do not have access to magazines. Some youngsters may be able to provide several pictures, and should be encouraged to do so.
2. Have a helper walk around room with a wastebasket, so that scraps may be discarded. Scissors, too, can be collected once the class has finished cutting.
3. Place a jar of paste in front of the room. When ready, children can paste figures to pictures at this station.

OAK TAG BRIDGE

MATERIALS

1. 18" wide x 12" long sheet of oak tag
2. pencil
3. ruler
4. scissors
5. paint or crayons

BEFORE YOU BEGIN

Many young children have difficulty understanding the relationship between the arithmetic they learn in school, and its application to true life situations. This lesson may provide them with firsthand clarification.

Ask youngsters if they have ever driven over a bridge. All have probably done so at one time or another. Ask them to describe the types of bridges they have seen. Some children will talk of very complex bridges, while others may describe a simple wooden bridge crossing a pond in a near-by park. Explain that a great deal of planning is involved in bridge construction; it is important that engineers measure accurately and draw out the design before work is begun. You might say, "Today we are going to make some simple bridges. However, we, too, are going to do some careful measuring and planning so that our bridges will be safe." Prepare a sample beforehand, and show it to the group. Open its folds, enabling the class to see its basic shape.

Review the distinguishing characteristics of squares and rectangles with your group. It is suggested that some of these shapes be drawn on the board with chalk and ruler before starting the activity.

Refer back to the sample bridge, helping children to discover that it was made by drawing a rectangle over a square. Have the group watch and listen as you draw the basic bridge pattern on the board once. Reassure your class that you will demonstrate it again as they work on individual projects.

PROCEDURE (Illustration 1-10)

1. Place a sheet of oak tag so that the 18″ width of the paper is parallel with the top of the desk. (step a)
2. Draw a 12″ square. The top and bottom of the paper itself will form two sides of this square. Have the children mark off edges of the square with dots, by measuring in 3″ from each side of the paper. Place a dot at each point. Connect these dots lightly in pencil, to form the sides of square. (step b)
3. Measure 2 1/2″ down from the top of two opposite sides of the square. Mark these points with pencil dots and label them A and B respectively. (step c)
4. Measure 2 1/2″ up from the bottom of these same two sides, and mark with dots. Label them C and D respectively. (step c)
5. Draw an 18″ line, across the paper through points A and B. Draw a second line through points C and D. These lines form the width of the bridge pattern. (step d)
6. Cut out the corner sections. (steps d & e)
7. Fold up line AB. Do same with line CD. These flaps will form the bridge's sides. (step f)
8. Fold down sides AC and BD. These flaps will form the ramp of the bridge. (step g)
9. Color the bridge with crayon or paint it with tempera.

WHAT THE CHILDREN CAN DO AFTERWARD

1. Use this lesson in conjunction with an arithmetic unit on measurement or geometry. Children can make a large scale "blue print" of the bridge on blue oak tag, marking in all its necessary measurements. Tack this "blue print" to the bulletin board, displaying individual bridges on a table beneath the diagram.
2. Discuss driving safety and the importance of road lines, emphasizing that bicycling regulations are the same as those for automobiles. Few children understand why some roads have double lines, dotted lines and so on. These details could be included in the bridge models. A short explanation of road markings might be written on a file card and displayed along with the models.

ILLUSTRATION 1-10

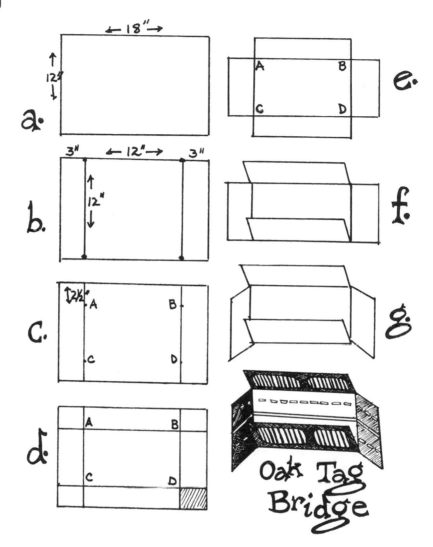

3. Use some bridges, where appropriate, in the community model suggested earlier in the chapter.
4. Bridges can be used during free play periods with toy cars and trucks.

RELAX WITH TIME SAVERS

1. Cut sheets of oak tag well in advance of the lesson.
2. Children should listen and watch the introductory lesson and demonstration before being permitted to take out rulers and pencils.
3. Repeat the procedure on the board as children work. Circulate throughout the room after each major step to insure that the procedure is well understood. Refer back to the sample bridge, so that the class may relate their diagrams to the finished product.

4. Clean up scraps and collect scissors before decorating models.
5. Spread newspaper first, if paint is being used.

Special Activities

The following suggestions are regarded as special activities because of their adaptability to many classroom situations. They will add significant interest to both your room and current area of study. With little care, permanent year to year use can be derived from these structures.

WALK-IN CITY

MATERIALS

1. large appliance cartons, or paper product packaging cartons
2. pencils
3. scissors or mat knife
4. paint and brushes
5. masking tape

BEFORE YOU BEGIN

What child wouldn't like to have his own skyscraper to play in? A visit to your local appliance store or supermarket should provide enough necessary boxes for your class to build one or more play buildings. Quite easily, children can construct an apartment house, supermarket, skyscraper, or any of a dozen city structures. The basic materials are large cartons and imagination.

Help youngsters decide what building or buildings they would enjoy making. You might want to draw some pictures first. Then, the entire group can decide which details to include in the model. List the steps to be followed on the board, and divide your class into groups. Each one will be responsible for a particular step.

PROCEDURE (Illustration 1-11)

1. Cut away flaps from one end of the carton. This end will be the building base.
2. Draw a door with pencil, making certain it is both tall and wide enough for a child to walk through. Draw in windows. (steps a and b)
3. Using a mat knife or scissors, cut out the door on two sides, and fold it back on the third. If desired, cut openings for windows (this is advisable if children are to play inside). (step b)
4. To make a skyscraper, stack smaller boxes on top of a larger box. Use masking tape to hold these boxes in place. (step a)

5. To make a house; separate two adjacent sides from an extra carton and tape this entire section, in triangular form, to a larger, bottom carton. (steps c & d)
6. Have one of the appointed groups paint the building a background color. When it has dried, another group can add details.

WHAT THE CHILDREN CAN DO AFTERWARD

1. Write a poem on large chart paper about the building and display it next to the structure.
2. Invite other classes for guided tours through the "city."
3. Build a model of the school for display in the lobby.

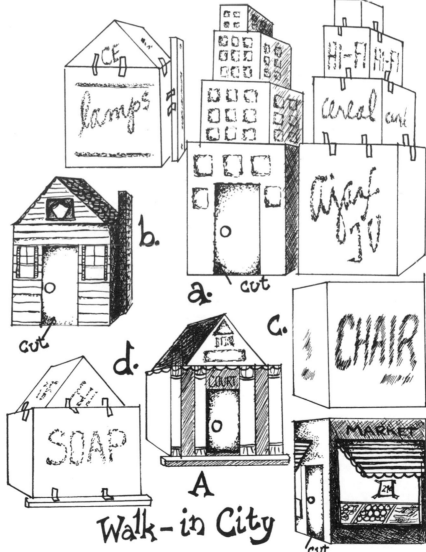

ILLUSTRATION 1-11

4. Use the model as a permanent play-house.
5. Find out about the people who work in the created buildings. Let children play-act the roles of these individuals.

RELAX WITH TIME SAVERS

1. Eliminate conflict by assigning each child in a given group a particular job. A child in group one might hold the boxes steady, while another tears masking tape for a third to use in securing the boxes for the skycraper.
2. Spread newspaper beneath the carton before beginning to paint.
3. Permit the background paint to dry thoroughly before applying details.

NEWSPAPER SCULPTURE SPATIAL ENVIRONMENT

MATERIALS

1. sheets of newspaper (use entire double sheet; do not cut on fold)
2. pencil
3. masking tape
4. paint (optional)
5. varnish (optional)

BEFORE YOU BEGIN

Tell children they are about to build a "fun sculpture." It can be almost anything they would like it to be, and probably larger than anything they have built before! With this introduction, youngsters will be eager to find out more about the activity and begin.

The purpose? Here is an excellent opportunity for youngsters to work together toward a group goal, and plan cooperatively. The outcome will also develop a better understanding of proportion between themselves and things around them. Besides, it's fun.

Demonstrate the process by which the newspaper is rolled for the sculpture. Make one or two samples before distributing materials.

PROCEDURE (Illustration 1-12)

1. Place a pencil flat against one corner of a sheet of newspaper. Begin to roll the paper, diagonally, around the pencil, keeping one of its ends exposed for easy removal. (steps a & b)
2. Continue to roll until the opposite end of the paper is reached. Tape this end to the rest of the roll to secure it in place. Permit each child to make several such rolls. (step c)
3. Divide the class into small groups. Have each group take turns attaching the

ILLUSTRATION 1-12

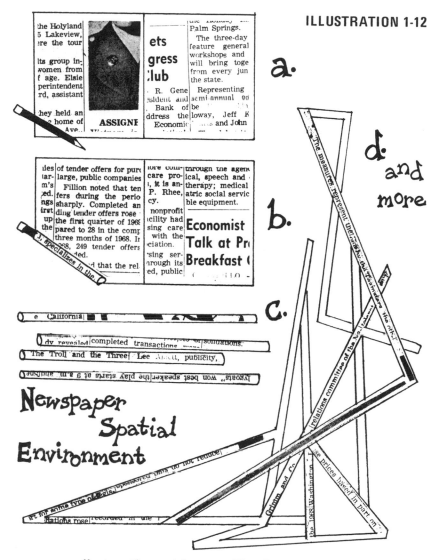

a.

b.

c.

d. and more

Newspaper Spatial Environment

paper rolls together with tape. The first group will have the task of building the "foundation" of the structure. Subsequent groups will have to plan their additions so that the structure remains steady. (step d)

4. The sculpture may be painted and/or varnished when finished.

WHAT THE CHILDREN CAN DO AFTERWARD

1. Upon completion of the activity, request that each child write a short story about the structure, explaining what it is and its function.
2. Use the structure as a permanent "holiday sculpture." At the appropriate time, have the children make decorated paper cut-outs (Christmas trees, valentines) and attach these to the sculpture with string.

RELAX WITH TIME SAVERS

1. Push back the tables and chairs before rolling paper. For freedom of movement this work should be done on the floor.
2. One roll of tape is sufficient for three to four children. Have each child tear off several tape strips before starting to roll his paper. Attach torn pieces, by their ends, to any convenient object. The child will then have tape on hand when it is needed and be spared the frustration of having his paper unroll while securing pieces of tape.
3. You may desire that the class complete another activity, with minimum distraction, while a particular group works on the sculpture. Therefore, chose an unobstructed area in the back of the room where children may attach their paper rolls.

Bonus Ideas

1. Make an Indian or colonial village, and compare the model to your own local community.
2. Create "international" spool dolls. Correlate these with a study of the United Nations.
3. Adapt the fire engine suggestion to a study of antique engines and methods of fire control.
4. Convert the "Where We Live Bulletin Board" into a milk container model, having each child make a milk container replica of his house. Place homes on a large piece of paper on the floor and paint in the appropriate streets.
5. Construct a classroom suggestion mailbox from half-gallon milk containers.
6. Make Pilgrim hats and Indian headbands for a Thanksgiving Day program.
7. Build a walk-in city of the future.

The Animal World

2

Whether you're teaching about birds, jungle animals, fish, or farmyard friends, you will find here a creative activity to correlate with your animal study program. The activities in this chapter offer an opportunity for self-expression by adding an imaginative touch to learning.

This chapter's emphasis on collage techniques is intended to improve the child's ability to paste, cut-out, and plan attractive arrangements. Many lessons, in addition to providing artistic experiences, are adaptable to play-acting, creative writing, and story telling. Some ideas are purely whimsical and fun, while others require some prior research. In any case, youngsters will enjoy experimenting with a variety of art materials.

PLAY DOUGH FARMYARD

MATERIALS

1. *Play Dough Recipe* (enough for eight children) Combine 2 cups of cornstarch and 4 cups of baking soda in a saucepan. Slowly mix in 2 1/2 cups water. Add a twist of lemon. Cook mixture over a slow flame for several minutes. Stir constantly until it reaches a dough-like consistency. Allow the dough to cool. Turn it onto a wooden board and knead until workable as clay.
2. variety of simple sculpturing tools, such as pencils and toothpicks
3. tempera paint
4. varnish (optional)
5. bowl of water for each table

BEFORE YOU BEGIN

Utilize picture books, movies and filmstrips about barnyard animals prior to this lesson. If at all feasible, heighten enthusiasm with a visit to a farm. Subsequent class discussion should emphasize the physical aspects of animals, as well as their farm functions. Though school age children can certainly discriminate visually between a cow and a horse, difficulty in sculpting may be encountered if distinguishing characteristics have not been pointed out. Some sample questions might include; "What are some of the things a cow and horse have in common?" "How are they different?" "Which farmyard birds have long necks?" "Short necks?" Such compelling observation will result in increased understanding, plus plausible farmyard sculpture.

Eliminated here is the heartbreaking disappointment of a child, who, after working hard, views his project cracked or broken in the kiln. Though play dough will have to be prepared in advance; it may be wrapped in plastic, refrigerated over night, and used the next day at room temperature. It has a smooth consistency and is easily manipulated.

PROCEDURE (Illustration 2-1)

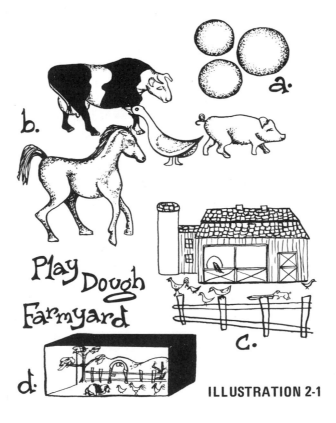

Play Dough Farmyard

ILLUSTRATION 2-1

1. Shape a variety of farm animals from the dough, keeping hands moist while working. Use sculpturing tools to add such details, as eyes, mouth, feathers. Permit each child to make several different animals, or a "family" of barnyard creatures. Continually remind youngsters to think about each animal's distinguishing characteristics. Advise them to take time, and to include as many of their observations as possible. (steps a & b)
2. Allow the sculptured animals to harden for at least 24 hours. Hardening time will vary according to size.
3. Paint the animals. Urge your class to permit the first coat of paint to dry before adding other colors for detail. (step b)
4. If desired, varnish the finished products. Spray shellac is easiest to apply. However, clear nail polish is an available and inexpensive substitute.
5. Arrange the animals around a toy barnyard, or inside shoebox dioramas. (steps c & d)

WHAT THE CHILDREN CAN DO AFTERWARD

1. Create a barnyard display in your room. Place the finished animals on a table covered with colored construction paper. Children can add plastic farm houses, barns, and fences brought in from home to complete the project. Similarly, the milk container activity, described in the previous chapter may be utilized to construct miniature buildings.
2. Make individual dioramas. Ask the class to bring in shoeboxes from home. Paint the inside of each box with an appropriate scene, and place the animals inside.
3. Ask the children to write creative or informative stories about their animals.
4. Use sculptured animals as gifts.

RELAX WITH TIME SAVERS

1. Prepare the dough well in advance of the lesson. If cooking facilities are available in your school, you might wish to involve the children in this cooking and measuring experience. Since the clay will have to cool, prepare it early in the day for use the same afternoon.
2. Mold the clay into several equal sized balls, one for each table. Wrap each portion securely in plastic until it is ready for use.
3. Place a small bowl of water on each table so that hands may be moistened as children work.
4. Provide a safe area where models can harden.
5. Spread newspaper on each desk before sculpting, and again before painting.
6. Distribute assorted colors of paint in plastic ice-cube trays.
7. If breakage should occur, simply repair broken sculpture with white glue and allow it to dry thoroughly.

PAPER BAG PETS (Illustration 2-2)

ILLUSTRATION 2-2

MATERIALS

1. small lunch size paper bag
2. newspaper
3. string
4. tape
5. construction paper scraps
6. paste
7. ribbon

BEFORE YOU BEGIN

Pets are a favorite topic of discussion among children. Easily encouraged to talk about their animal friends, youngsters are eager to answer to: "What do your pets look like?" "How are they cared for?" "Why is your pet so special?"

Tell the class they are about to make some animals using ordinary paper bags; they may fashion real pets, or others they might like to own.

PROCEDURE

1. Stuff 1/3 of the bag tightly with crumbled newspaper to form animal head. Approximately two sheets of paper will be required.
2. Gather the bag at the base of the "head" and tie it securely with string.
3. Stuff the remainder of the bag with newspaper and tape the bottom of the bag closed.
4. Cut eyes, ears, nose, mouth, and feet from construction paper and paste these in place.
5. Tie a colorful ribbon around the animal's neck.

WHAT THE CHILDREN CAN DO AFTERWARD

1. Ask the children to write informative paragraphs about their "pets," indicating the kinds of foods they eat, and general aspects of pet care. Tack these reports to a bulletin board, and display the paper pets on a near-by table.
2. Write creative stories or poems about the animals and display them as suggested above.

3. Make paper bag animals for Christmas gifts. Children might wish to donate them to sick youngsters at a local hospital.
4. Use these pets along the window sill, some facing in, others out, for both passers-by and class visitors to admire.

RELAX WITH TIME SAVERS

1. Choose helpers to hand out scissors, paper bags, sheets of newspaper, and string. One ball of string can be shared by a table of 4-5 children.
2. Stuff and tie the bags before distributing paste, construction paper, and ribbon.
3. Make certain that the string is tied tightly about animal "neck."
4. Place an assortment of construction paper scraps in the center of each table. Children may help themselves.
5. Select a helper from each table to get paste. Use empty jar covers as paste receptacles for each table.
6. At lesson's end, collect all usable scraps and save them for future activities.
7. Have paste helpers return any unused paste to the jar and then wash paste receptacles.

PAPER BAG ZOO MASKS

MATERIALS

1. paper bag—large enough to fit over child's head
2. 9" x 12" construction paper
3. tissue paper, scraps of construction paper, crepe paper, material scraps, and other collage materials
4. paste
5. scissors
6. crayons
7. masking tape

BEFORE YOU BEGIN

Children have a natural curiosity about animals they've seen at the zoo. Enthusiasm will be heightened with these whimsical masks.

Permit youngsters to share stories about visits to the zoo, encouraging vivid descriptions. Provide pictures and books for your class to study before they begin their masks. Fairy tales and songs about animal favorites can be included in preparation for this lesson. Children should try to associate a "personality" with animals they recreate. Emphasize that the masks are for fun, encouraging flights of fancy in this direction.

Request paper bags from home, several days in advance. Don't rush; two or three sessions may be necessary for completion. Additional time is well spent, for the greater detail, the more extraordinary the results.

Before handing out materials, demonstrate the procedure for cutting out masks.

PROCEDURE (Illustration 2-3)

1. Cut slits on each side of the paper bag so that it fits securely over child's head and does not tear at the widening shoulder portion. Use masking tape, on the inside of the bag, to reinforce these slits. (step a)
2. Fold the construction paper in half lengthwise. Draw half the shape of the desired animal's head on the fold. Make this drawing as large as possible. Remind your class that, though they will draw and cut on only half the mask, the features will appear on both sides of the animal face when mask is cut and unfolded. (step b)
3. Cut out the mask and keep it folded. Make a second fold, from the top of the animal's head, 1/4 of the way down the mask. (step c)
4. Cut out a semicircle (or any other shape) for eyes on this second fold (do not cut into center fold of mask when making eyes). (step c)
5. Cut out a nose and a mouth from the center fold. (step c)
6. Open the mask and paste it to the paper bag. (step d)
7. Cut eyes, nose, and mouth openings in the bag to correspond with those on construction paper mask.
8. Add characterizing facial features with crayon. (step d)
9. To further make the animal face interesting and whimsical, paste collage materials around construction paper mask. (Example—to make a lion, cut long, thin strips of yellow crepe paper and paste them around the head to form a mane. Curl the strips around a pencil, if desired. Add a large crown, cut from aluminum foil.) (steps e & f)

WHAT THE CHILDREN CAN DO AFTERWARD

1. Ask the librarian to assist the children in finding narratives about their respective animals. Group youngsters accordingly and ask them to prepare a skit based on one of these stories. Completed masks are their costumes.
2. Use the masks for an assembly circus program. Produce animal acts. Employ songs and poems, original if possible, to use as background music.
3. Use the masks as Halloween costumes.
4. Compose a song about animals. Each child might work on a separate verse about the animal he represents.

RELAX WITH TIME SAVERS

1. Demonstrate the procedure once or twice before handing out materials. Carefully supervise children as they cut out mask features.
2. Use empty jar covers as paste receptacles. Choose a helper from each table to fill these covers whenever they are nearly empty. Children may secure individual amounts of paste on scraps of paper from these covers.
3. Provide a box of scrap materials in front of the room. When ready, the children may

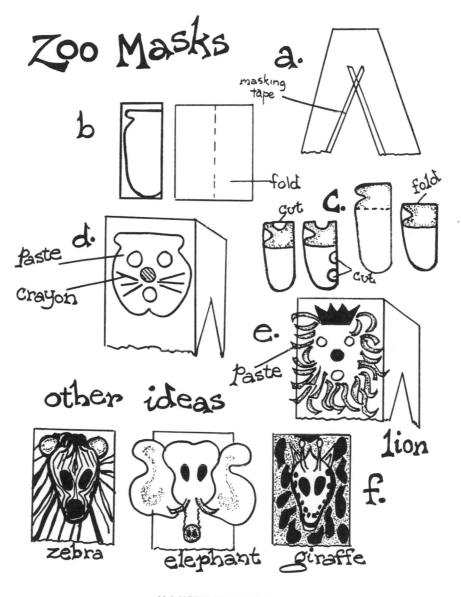

ILLUSTRATION 2-3

choose their own collage materials. Limit the number of children permitted up at a given time.

4. Place newspaper on all desks before pasting to facilitate clean-up.
5. Select a helper to circulate about the room with a wastebasket, collecting newspaper and small scraps. A second helper should collect the larger scraps for storage.
6. Left-over paste should be returned to paste jars. Paste receptacles should be washed and saved.

WALLPAPER ANIMALS (Illustration 2-4)

ILLUSTRATION 2-4

MATERIALS

1. wallpaper scraps (or paper
   from magazines)
2. paste
3. construction paper
4. scissors
5. black crayon

BEFORE YOU BEGIN

It is likely that many in your class have experimented with paper geometric shapes, using them to create both realistic and abstract pictures. This activity is an interesting variation. Children delight in using this wallpaper or magazine scrap approach to create attractive animal personalities. At the same time they will be learning more about common shapes.

Have some pre-cut wallpaper and a flannel board available as geometric shapes are reviewed. Demonstrate how these can be combined to produce animal representations. Permit children to make some sample animals on the flannel board, as the class watches.

Youngsters tend to use circles and ovals almost exclusively, if not otherwise directed. Guide them to experiment with an assortment of shapes, and indicate that any animal may be designed. Such instruction will produce a variety of results for children to later observe and discuss.

Rulers and other measuring devices need not be used. The figures should be cut out free-hand. It is wise, however, to stress care and neatness in cutting for best results.

PROCEDURE

1. Cut an assortment of different sized shapes from wallpaper to form parts of the animal's body.
2. Paste these shapes to a sheet of 9" x 12" construction paper. Encourage the children to experiment by placing these pieces together before pasting.
3. Add details (eyes, mouth, paws, horns) with a black crayon.

WHAT THE CHILDREN CAN DO AFTERWARD

1. Ask each child to show his picture to the class, describing the figures used. Or, have the class observe the picture and explain the utilized shapes.
2. Make an attractive display by tacking these wallpaper animals to a bulletin board.
3. Cut out the animals and use them individually in a class mural.
4. "Frame" each picture by pasting it to a larger sheet of construction paper. It may then be brought home for hanging in a child's room.
5. Wallpaper animals make attractive greeting cards. Use them on get-well cards, invitations, and holiday greetings.
6. Compile an animal study folder. Wallpaper pictures make excellent covers.
7. Make the animals "double-faced" for use on mobiles.

RELAX WITH TIME SAVERS

1. Do not hand out materials until the introductory lesson has been completed.
2. Place an assortment of wallpaper scraps on each table, so that children may help themselves.
3. Provide time for youngsters to experiment with shapes before asking helpers to hand out paste.
4. Use jar covers as paste receptacles for each table.
5. At the activity's end, discard any small scraps. Collect the larger, usable pieces for future collage activities.
6. Select a helper to collect jar covers for washing and storing.

TISSUE PAPER ANIMAL COLLAGE (Illustration 2-5)

BEFORE YOU BEGIN

Discovering the many effects to be achieved with tissue paper as a collage material is the primary purpose of this lesson. Demonstrate the possibilities by crumbling, shirring, cutting and twisting the paper, then pasting it to a sheet of drawing paper. You might wish the children to indulge in this experimentation, prior to proceeding with the activity.

Encourage the youngsters to make any type of animal they wish; jungle creatures, domestic pets, birds, and the like.

ILLUSTRATION 2-5

MATERIALS

1. heavy drawing paper
2. sheets of tissue paper in an assortment of colors
3. pencil
4. scissors
5. paste

PROCEDURE

1. Draw an animal shape, in pencil, on a sheet of tissue paper and cut it out.
2. *Tear* openings for the eyes, nose and mouth.
3. Paste the shape to the drawing paper.
4. Imaginatively decorate the animals with scraps of tissue paper, by crumbling, tearing, twisting and folding it, to achieve as many effects as possible.

WHAT THE CHILDREN CAN DO AFTERWARD

1. Tack the collages to a bulletin board for an interesting room display.
2. "Frame" the collages by pasting them to larger sheets of colored construction paper. These may be brought home and used as wall hangings.

RELAX WITH TIME SAVERS

1. Choose helpers to distribute the drawing paper and scissors.
2. A child from each table should spoon paste into empty jar covers for use by his table.
3. Place sheets of tissue paper on a desk in front of the room. Permit children to come up, by tables, to select two or three color choices. Each child's scraps may be shared by others in his group for decoration.
4. Place newspaper on desks before pasting.
5. Have one child circulate about the room with a wastebasket to collect scraps.
6. Have the paste helpers return any unused paste to jar, then clean the paste receptacles for future use.

BIRD HELMETS

MATERIALS

1. colored crepe paper sheets (approximately 20" x 36")
2. manila paper (10" x 36")
3. pencil
4. stapler
5. construction paper scraps
6. paste

BEFORE YOU BEGIN

Children, especially those not residing in wooded or tropical environments, have little knowledge of the vast variety of bird life which exists throughout the world. You will have to rely on filmstrips, movies, and picture books to increase understanding and launch this activity. A trip to the zoo's bird buildings is always an exciting addition to this study.

Encourage the children to find out as much as possible about not only the brilliantly beautiful, but common birds as well. Fire imaginations with: "What kind of bird would you like to be?" "Why?" "What part of the world would you inhabit?" "If your feathers were wild, bright colors, would this be advantageous?" "Why are a bird's eyes located on the sides of his head?" With this combination of imagination and anatomical awareness, children inevitably produce a splendid aviary.

PROCEDURE (Illustration 2-6)

1. Make a basic cut-out pattern of a bird's head on the manila paper. Use the entire 10" x 36" paper as a guide for pattern size. (step a)
2. Fold the crepe paper in half lengthwise. Using a pencil, outline the pattern on the folded crepe paper. (step b)

ILLUSTRATION 2-6

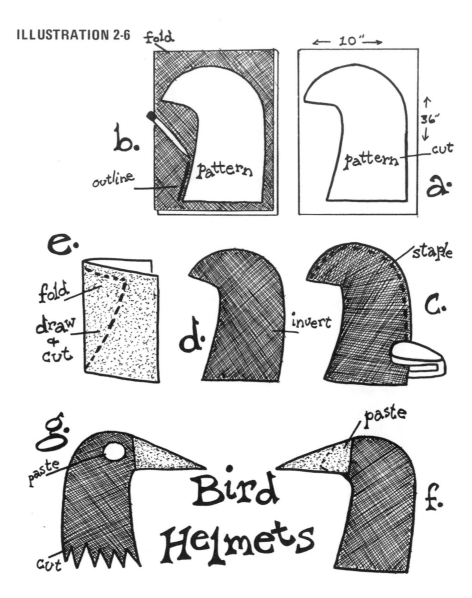

Bird Helmets

3. Cut out the crepe paper outline—you should have two pieces.
4. Place the cut-out pieces together, the right sides of crepe paper facing inwards.
5. Staple a "seam" around the head, leaving an open seam at the neck. (step c)
6. Invert the crepe paper helmet, so that the seam is on the inside. (step d)
7. Fold a piece of construction paper in half and draw a beak shape on the fold. (step e)
8. Cut out the beak. Do not cut on the fold. (step e)
9. Open the cut-out beak. Overlap and paste the beak on each side of the bird's head, just above the open seam. (step f)
10. Cut eyes and other detail features from construction paper and paste them in place. Be certain to put a "face" on each side of the helmet. If desired, add colorful plumage. (step g)

11. Make shaggy cuts on the bottom of the helmet. (step g)
12. To wear, slip mask, helmet style, over the child's head, and tape at neck to hold in place. Running a draw string, with yarn, around the neck of the helmet is an alternate method of securing it in place. The child will be able to see through the open seam.

WHAT THE CHILDREN CAN DO AFTERWARD

1. Ask each child to wear his helmet as he tells the class about the bird he represents.
2. Make up a play about "bird people" from other planets. Helmets are costumes.
3. Most birds like to sing, so, collect or write appropriate songs for an assembly production. The library may have records of bird calls which could be added to the presentation.
4. Use the helmets as Halloween masks.

RELAX WITH TIME SAVERS

1. Prepare the patterns in advance if you work with very young children.
2. Supervise the youngsters as they staple the helmet parts together. Be certain they are working on the correct side of paper.
3. Distribute at least two staplers to a table for children to share.
4. Ask youngsters to try on their helmets before decorating them. Walk around, helping, to insure proper fit.
5. Distribute an assortment of construction paper scraps to each table. Children may help themselves.
6. Select a helper from each table to get paste. Use empty jar covers as suggested in previous activities.
7. Select a helper to circulate about the room with a wastebasket at the end of the lesson. Make certain that loose staples, as well as tiny scraps, are discarded. Collect larger paper scraps for use in future activities.

BIRDS IN NESTS

MATERIALS

1. excelsior
2. medium-thick solution of flour and water
3. small sponges
4. aluminum foil
5. squares of tissue paper in assorted colors
6. white glue
7. paint
8. toothpicks

BEFORE YOU BEGIN

Spring is an ideal season for this activity, since children can actually observe birds as they gather nesting materials. If any in your class have found an abandoned nest, have it brought to school for study and display. If possible, take a walk with your group and watch for birds building nests. Use such field trips to observe birds as they care for their young. These experiences, so wonderful to children, should be part of your study unit.

Allow two or three sessions to complete this lesson. The steps involved, though quite simple, require ample drying time.

PROCEDURE (Illustration 2-7)

1. Form the excelsior into the shape of a bird's nest. (step a)
2. Using a small sponge, coat the nest with a solution of flour and water. Be certain that the entire nest is well coated. *Do not saturate.* This solution will hold the nest together. Allow the dampened nest to dry over-night. (step b)
3. Shape a family of birds out of aluminum foil. Eggs may be made, too, if desired. (step c)
4. Using white glue, cover the aluminum foil birds with colored tissue paper. Overlap the sheets of paper until there is no trace of foil. Allow the birds to dry. (step d)
5. Paint in the details (eyes, feathers, beaks). (step e)
6. Place the birds in the nests. To secure in place, insert one end of a toothpick into the straw nest, and pinion each bird to the opposite end of the toothpick. (steps f & g)

WHAT THE CHILDREN CAN DO AFTERWARD

1. Have each child choose a particular bird family (robin, crow, and so on). Ask that an informative paragraph be written on a file card to accompany each project. Display the nests and cards on a table in the room.
2. Make miniature nests. Prop a large tree branch in a corner of the room on which to set the nests.
3. Find out how to make bird houses. Use nests and houses as part of a display entitled "How Our Native Birds Live."

RELAX WITH TIME SAVERS

1. Spread newspaper on all the desks before starting this activity.
2. Provide a bowl, with just enough flour and water mixture for each table. Emphasize that only a small amount of the solution is needed. Pass out small sponges for application.
3. Provide a safe area where the nests can dry.

ILLUSTRATION 2-7

Birds in Nests

4. Cut tissue paper into workable squares (this will depend on desired bird size) before the lesson.
5. Clip these squares of paper together according to color. Children may select an appropriate packet of colored paper, depending on their respective bird choices.
6. Add painted details during a separate art period. This will permit both nests and birds to have dried thoroughly.
7. Distribute an assortment of paints in plastic ice-cube trays. Use lock-top detergent bottles as paint dispensers. Select a helper to re-fill these trays when they are empty, from these bottles.

CLOTHESPIN BUTTERFLIES

MATERIALS

1. clothespin with rounded head
2. sheet of crepe paper (approximately 7″ x 8″)
3. pipe cleaner
4. black paint (optional)

BEFORE YOU BEGIN

Here is an excellent, simple activity for very young children, to be correlated with your springtime unit. These butterflies are easily made and quickly completed. Youngsters may make several.

PROCEDURE (Illustration 2-8)

1. Paint the clothespin black, if desired. Allow it to dry before continuing the activity. (step a)
2. Gather the crepe paper in the center to form a set of "wings." (step b)
3. Insert "wings" through the clothespin opening. Instruct the children to push the paper tightly into the upper end of the clothespin opening to secure it in place. (step c)
4. Spread each wing by gently stretching crepe paper between fingers.
5. Twist a pipe cleaner around clothespin head to make antennae. (step d)

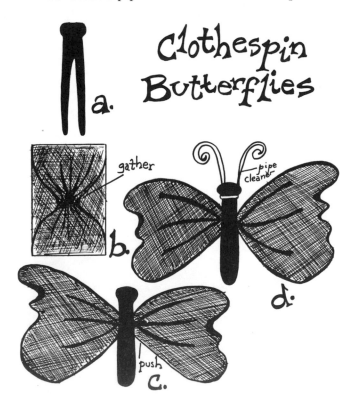

ILLUSTRATION 2-8

WHAT THE CHILDREN CAN DO AFTERWARD

1. Tack the butterflies to a spring mural bulletin board.
2. Place the butterflies on a line, stretched across room, as an attractive display.
3. Use butterflies as gifts.
4. Attach each butterfly to a narrow dowel stick with a thin piece of elastic, and use it as a "bobbing" toy.

RELAX WITH TIME SAVERS

1. Spread newspaper on the desks if clothespins are to be painted.
2. Permit the clothespins to dry before handing out other materials.
3. Cut crepe paper in advance of the lesson.
4. Circulate about the room as children fit the paper into the clothespin, giving help where necessary.
5. Remind youngsters to *gently* stretch the paper as the wings are adjusted.

EGG CARTON CATERPILLARS

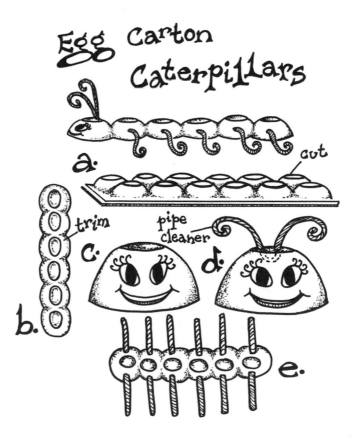

MATERIALS

1. molded egg cartons
2. scissors
3. paint
4. pipe cleaners

ILLUSTRATION 2-9

BEFORE YOU BEGIN

Tell the children they are about to make some "kooky caterpillars." Though they will bear little resemblance to the realities of nature, they will be fun to fashion. Adapt these decorative creatures to the creative aspects of your unit, as suggested in the "What the Children Can Do Afterward" section.

PROCEDURE   (Illustration 2-9)

1. Cut the egg cartons in half lengthwise. Each half will make one caterpillar. (step a)
2. Trim the edges of the carton so that it is even on both sides. (step b)
3. Paint the caterpillar a basic color and allow it to dry.
4. Add interesting details with contrasting paint colors.
5. Paint a "face" on one end of the caterpillar. Permit all paint to dry thoroughly. (step c)
6. Thread a pipe cleaner through each section of the caterpillar to form legs. (step e)
7. Thread a pipe cleaner through the top of the front egg section to form antennae. (step d)

WHAT THE CHILDREN CAN DO AFTERWARD

1. Write a class poem about caterpillars on chart paper. Tack the chart paper to the bulletin board and display the caterpillars on a table beneath.
2. Display the caterpillars along a window sill. Make colorful paper butterflies and tape them to the windows above.
3. Using two-way adhesive, tack these "crawling creatures" to a wall.
4. Use individual egg holders from cartons to make other "crawling creatures" and use them as part of a display.
5. Give the caterpillars as gifts to younger brothers and sisters.

RELAX WITH TIME SAVERS

1. Save time by cutting the cartons in half before introducing the lesson.
2. Spread paper before painting. Distribute the paint in plastic ice-cube trays. Instruct your class to permit the basic color to dry before adding details.
3. If necessary, have children use a pencil point to make tiny holes through which to thread the pipe cleaners.

PAPER PLATE FISH

BEFORE YOU BEGIN

Here is a quick art idea to use along with your marine life program. Request the children to do some prior research before introducing this project. Visit an aquarium, if possible, and have books and pictures of a variety of attractive fish on hand for children to study.

You can, of course, keep the activity strictly fun, encouraging the class to fashion imaginative and fancy fish.

ILLUSTRATION 2-10

MATERIALS

1. paper plate
2. colored construction paper and/or aluminum foil
3. scissors
4. stapler
5. paste

PROCEDURE (Illustration 2-10)

1. Cut a "V"-shaped mouth from the paper plate. (step a)
2. Color the paper plate, so as to give detail to the fish.
3. Cut tails and fins from colored construction paper, or foil, and staple them in place. (step b)
4. Cut a construction paper eye, and staple it in place. (step b)

WHAT THE CHILDREN CAN DO AFTERWARD

1. Make a marine bulletin board mural. Cover the board with blue paper, and tack the fish in place. Use various sized paper plates for this adapation. Cut grasses and other plant life from construction paper and paste them in place.
2. Ask the children to write creative stories about their fish. Tack the fish and stories to a bulletin board labeled "Fish Tales."
3. Ask the children to write a challenging math problem on reverse side of their fish.

Tack these to a bulletin board entitled "Fishy Numbers." During their free time, children may go to the display, copy a problem, and solve it at their seats. Provide an answer box near the display. Review problems at the end of each week, to see who "caught" the most fish.

4. Have each child write a paragraph about his fish. Paste this to the reverse side of a paper plate. Suspend the fish on a string from fixtures (or arrange on wire hangers) for informative mobiles.

RELAX WITH TIME SAVERS

1. Give a demonstration lesson before you distribute materials.
2. Provide a stapler for each group of children to share.
3. Keep a paste jar in front of the room. When the children are ready they can paste an "eye" on their fish at this station.
4. Since there will be time to make more than one fish, allow the children to take materials, as needed, from a designated station in the room.

INSTANT AQUARIUM

MATERIALS

1. corrugated carton or shoe box
2. yellow plasticine
3. black poster paint
4. heavy drawing paper
5. crayons
6. scissors
7. thin, stiff wire
8. pebbles and shells (or pasta in these shapes)
9. clear plastic wrap
10. stapler
11. green construction paper

BEFORE YOU BEGIN

At last, here is a worry-free aquarium! It requires no maintenence, and fish will not go hungry during vacations! In this "instant aquarium," any specie of fish, both real or imagined, can be included. Complete with fish and plant life, it is made of paper and other easily obtainable materials.

This can be an individual or group experience. Use a large carton if you choose to make a class tank. For individual projects, ask for shoe boxes from home.

Coordinate the project with studies of marine life, using books, movies, aquarium trips, and group investigation as background experiences. Permit the class to discuss the fish, flora and fauna to be included in the model. With final decisions listed on the blackboard, each child can pick his own fish for recreation.

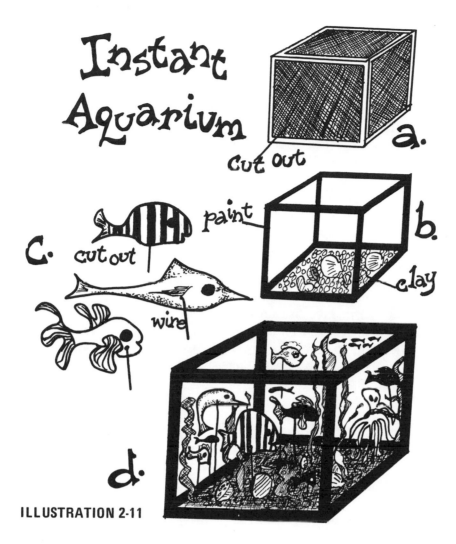

Instant Aquarium

a. cut out

b. paint — clay

c. cut out — wire

d.

ILLUSTRATION 2-11

PROCEDURE (Illustration 2-11)

1. To make the fish tank, cut out panels on all four sides of a carton or shoe box, leaving approximately 1 1/2 inch borders. (step a)
2. Paint the "tank" frame black. Paint both the inside and outside of the frame. The bottom of the tank need not be painted. (step b)
3. Allow the painted tank to dry.
4. Press plasticine on the bottom of the cardboard tank, to resemble sand. Sprinkle the plasticine with pebbles and small shells. (step b)
5. Draw, color and cut out an assortment of fish on heavy drawing paper. Remind the children to include features on each side of cut-out fish. (step c)
6. Thread one end of thin wire through each fish and secure the opposite end to the aquarium's plasticine base. (steps c & d)
7. Cut grasses from green construction paper and set these in the "tank" base. (step d)
8. Wrap clear plastic around the entire fish tank. Secure the plastic with staples and trim edges with scissors.

WHAT THE CHILDREN CAN DO AFTERWARD

1. Place a small number on each fish in the aquarium. Make a corresponding chart, identifying the fish.
2. Write reports about the fish which have been included in the model. Tack these reports to a bulletin board. Have the aquarium displayed near-by.
3. Have each child do research on one fish, then make a corresponding shoe box aquarium. Invite other classes to visit the display. Your class can act as host, giving lectures on group and individual projects.

RELAX WITH TIME SAVERS

1. Hand out drawing paper, crayons and strips of wire to the class. Most school age children can work on the fish independently.
2. Select one group to make a fish tank. Supervise their work, particularly as panels are being cut from the carton. The remainder of the class can fashion marine life.
3. Have each child come up individually to place his fish in the aquarium base.
4. Green construction paper, for grasses, may be taken when needed from a station in front of the room.

Special Activity

The mask suggestion described below is a versatile idea which may be used throughout the school year for many occasions. Eliminated here, is the need for elaborate costumes in plays, choral presentations, or impromptu role-playing. Both sides of the mask may be decorated, each for a different purpose. Later, strip the circus features described in this activity, and redecorate the mask to make story book characters. The possibilities are manifold, while materials and method are kept simple.

PEEK-A-BOO CIRCUS MASKS

MATERIALS

1. 12″ x 18″ sheet of heavy cardboard
2. tempera paint
3. scraps of colored paper, roving, material scraps, buttons, aluminum foil, and other collage materials.
4. paste

BEFORE YOU BEGIN

Discuss circus acts and personalities and list these on the board. Include the ringmaster, bareback riders, clowns, as well as animals in this listing. Let each child choose whatever animal or circus personality he wishes to represent.

Have a sample mask available for the class to inspect and model. Since children's faces will appear through these "masks," it will be necessary for them to exaggerate other distinguishing features of the particular animals or circus people they have chosen. "How can we make a clown, without drawing his face?" Certainly, a funny hair-do, comical hat, and large ruff would clearly indicate a clown's costume; high hat the ringmaster, and roving mane, the lion.

Pre-cut oval openings in advance of the lesson. Older children can do this themselves, given a pattern and pair of scissors.

ILLUSTRATION 2-12

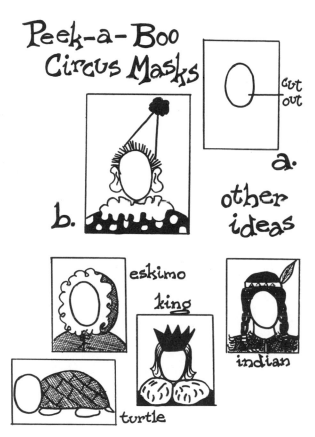

PROCEDURE (Illustration 2-12)

1. Make an oval shape, the size of a child's head in the center of the cardboard sheet. For best results, make one pattern and have others cut it out on a jig-saw. (step a)
2. Cut out the oval, thus leaving an opening in the cardboard for the face. (step a)
3. Paint the cardboard sheet a solid background color, and allow it to dry.
4. Draw an outline of a desired circus animal or personality around the oval opening. Paint in this outline and allow it to dry thoroughly. (step b)
5. Paste a variety of collage materials on and around the outline, making the mask as interesting and as lively as possible. (step b)
6. To wear, have the child hold the oval opening against his face.

WHAT THE CHILDREN CAN DO AFTERWARD

1. Collect or write poems and songs about circus characters. Use the masks as costumes for presentations.
2. Choose a youngster to narrate a circus story. Have others, holding up their masks, act out this narrative.
3. When not in use, tack the masks to a bulletin board for an interesting display.

RELAX WITH TIME SAVERS

1. Plan two sessions for this activity; one to complete painting, the other for collage work.
2. Spread the tables with newspaper before painting.
3. Place a different color jar of paint at each table. According to their color choices, have the children paint the background of their masks at these stations.
4. Provide plastic ice-cube trays with an assortment of colors (one tray for each table) for detail painting.
5. Have a box of collage materials on hand. It is advisable to ask children, at the start of the school year, to be on the look-out for interesting scraps. These should be brought in and placed in a class scrap box. This practice will insure a sufficient variety of materials for activities of this type.
6. Place a box in front of the room and permit children to come up, one table at a time, to select their desired materials.
7. Choose a helper to circulate about the room with a wastebasket to collect unusable scraps. Larger collage materials should be returned to the box for future use.

Bonus Ideas

1. Use the play dough suggestion to create a three-ring circus, complete with ringmaster, bareback riders, and clowns.
2. Make a pre-historic animal display with play dough.
3. Try making paper bag rabbits for Easter. Place them in baskets surrounded by colored eggs.
4. Use wallpaper animals to decorate wastebaskets, odds and ends cans, kitchen cannister sets, and painted tissue boxes. The above make beautiful gifts.
5. Make a variety of animal heads from paper plates and collage materials. Tack these to a bulletin board.
6. Make Indian and Pilgrim peek-a-boo masks for Thanksgiving, or early American studies.
7. Bird helmet patterns can be used to make knight and gladiator headgear. Cut swords and shields from cardboard and paint them to complete the costume.

World of Nature

3

Rocks, shells, and a plethora of seasonal foliage are surely nature's special gifts to young children. Class collectors enthusiastically tote these to school throughout the year, presenting the teacher with a set of problems; abundance needs storage, and breakage or loss is not always met with young courage. Among the lessons in this chapter are suggestions for preserving and utilizing nature's bounty, so that it may be enjoyed and remembered long after discovery.

The activities which follow also include a wide range of experiences and techniques, such as a variety of new effects to be achieved with paint, crayon, and collage. Each encourages the young artist to express his impressions of the world about him, adding profoundly personal accents to the fascinating observation of nature.

PAINT A SUNNY DAY

MATERIALS

1. painting paper
2. crayons
3. thin wash of yellow paint
4. small sponge

BEFORE YOU BEGIN

When balmy days make young minds stray from class work to daydreams of outdoor fun, don't despair. Here is an activity to combat lethargy. "What would you like to be doing toady?" Look for answers to fit the season. Chances are, children will dwell on baseball, beaches, ice cream and picnics. "How would you describe the flowers, trees and near-by pond on a sunny day?" Elicit a variety of responses.

Paint a Sunny Day

Andy

"Walking the Dog"

ILLUSTRATION 3-1

Following this discussion, ask the children to think about a scene or experience they associate with sunshine and warm weather. Tell them to recreate these memories in crayon, adding all details, except the sun. This will be applied last with paint.

PROCEDURE (Illustration 3-1)

1. Have the children crayon a "sunny day" scene. They must press down *hard* with their crayons as they work. Yellow crayon must *not* be used, since it will be lost when the wash of yellow paint is added.
2. Encourage the class to make their drawings as large and as colorful as possible.
3. When the crayon drawing is complete, "paint it sunny" by applying a thin wash of yellow paint across the entire paper with a sponge. The underlying picture will show through, as the paint will not adhere to the crayoned areas.

4. Children who wish to represent the sun as a physical body, may do so with an orange crayon, before applying paint.

WHAT THE CHILDREN CAN DO AFTERWARD

1. Write stories about these pictures for display on the bulletin board.
2. Write a class poem about "Sunny Days" on chart paper. Display this poem in the center of the bulletin board, surrounded by the pictures.
3. Use the finished pictures as scrap book covers.

RELAX WITH TIME SAVERS

1. Clear the desks before starting to work.
2. Remove the yellow crayon from each box before starting the picture.
3. Spread newspaper on each desk before applying paint to the picture.
4. Dilute yellow paint with water to obtain a thin wash, in advance of the lesson.
5. Distribute sponges and paint cups containing the yellow "water paint" *after* the drawings are completed. One paint cup can be shared by two or three children.

PAINT A STORM

"A Snowstorm"

ILLUSTRATION 3-2

MATERIALS

1. full color tempera paint
2. brushes
3. large manila paper

BEFORE YOU BEGIN

"What is a storm?" Encourage class to respond with vivid descriptions of storms they have encountered. "What did the sky look like?" "What were people doing?" "Were you gazing along city streets, or romping in country hills?" Some may have been on a plane, high in the clouds, or riding in an automobile. "In what way did the place make a difference?"

Talk about many storms. Sea and sand storms may be among the unfamiliar to many. Films on the subject can be shown before the activity is initiated.

Ask children to use class discussion, plus personal experience to create a storm with paint. Time taken for preliminary investigation will have been well spent, for youngsters will produce a variety of interesting and exciting storm creations.

PROCEDURE (Illustration 3-2)

1. Have each child select *one* type of storm as a subject for his painting. Remind the class to think back to group discussions and personal experience as they paint, including as many "storm" details as possible.
2. Hand out the paper, paint and brushes and have the class paint a storm. Encourage children to fill their paper completely.

WHAT THE CHILDREN CAN DO AFTERWARD

1. Have the children write poems about their paintings. Use both in a bulletin board display.
2. Ask the class to label paintings accordingly (Storm at Sea, City Blizzard) for use on the bulletin board.
3. Make a class mural, showing many types of storms.
4. Develop a "storm" vocabulary, including descriptive words for storms, as well as their names. Such a list might include words as cyclone, tornado, tempestuous, raging, and rampant. Have youngsters use these words to write expressive sentences about the finished class paintings.

RELAX WITH TIME SAVERS

1. Clear the desks of all materials not related to the activity.
2. Spread newspaper before painting.
3. Two youngsters can share a plastic ice-cube tray filled with assorted colors of paint. Some sections of the tray should contain water for cleaning brushes.

HAPPY TO KNOW YOU TREE

BEFORE YOU BEGIN

Identifying with a new group is a primary concern during those first bewildering days of a new term. Here is an easy and successful method to erase early-in-the-year apprehension, as children work together on this simple project.

The crimsoning and falling leaves of the coming season provide an exciting time to launch a fall study program of dual use. "What's happened to the trees?" "How have they begun to color?" Tell the class they are about to put their own leaves on a very unusual tree, belonging to no known specie. This "Happy to Know You Tree" may have leaves brightly hued and shaped according to the imagination.

ILLUSTRATION 3-3

MATERIALS

1. heavy painting paper or colored construction paper
2. tempera paint
3. pencil
4. brown roving

PROCEDURE (Illustration 3-3)

1. Have the children draw a free-form leaf with a pencil. The size of the paper, and leaf, will depend on the amount of available bulletin board space. Within this confine, make the leaves as large as possible. (step a)
2. If using painting paper, a solid colored background should be applied to the cut-out leaf. Allow the paint to dry thoroughly. (Of course, this step is eliminated if colored construction paper is used.)
3. On the center of the leaf, largely but lightly in pencil, the child should print his name. Remember the letters must be sized so as to be visible from the bulletin board. Avoid having the name get "lost" in the leaf's design. (step b)
4. Using a single color, paint in the letters over the pencilling.
5. Around the name, colorfully decorate with paint.
6. Dry the painted leaves.

7. Make a tree from brown roving. To form the trunk and branches, simply cut yarn into long strips and staple them close together, to the bulletin board. The tree can be as large as class space permits. (step c)
8. Staple the finished leaves to the roving branches. (step d)

WHAT THE CHILDREN CAN DO AFTERWARD

1. Write brief "Now You Know Me" autobiographies. Before each child attaches his leaf to the tree, he may read his "story."
2. The bulletin board, which includes the teacher's name, can also be labeled "Friendship Tree," "The Howdoyoudo Tree," or "The Hello Tree." Class aspirations during the coming year can be explored and a written resume placed on the bulletin board next to the tree.
3. Extra leaves, made by the quick and ambitious, can be used individually on classroom windows. Attach these with two-way adhesive.
4. Game: Let all the children concentrate on the tree. Ask a child, at a given signal to "pop out of his seat." Then, choose a second child to quickly find the standing classmate's signed leaf. Each child has a turn, until everyone has been identified, and names have been learned.

RELAX WITH TIME SAVERS

1. Have the children draw and cut out their leaves before distributing paint.
2. Spread newspaper on all the desks before beginning to paint.
3. Have the class temporarily put away their pencils when they are ready to apply a background color. Only when instructed, and the leaves have dried thoroughly, may the children again use their pencils to print their names.
4. Distribute the paint in plastic ice-cube containers; one tray to every four youngsters.
5. Assign a group number to each table. When called, that group may have a chance to work on the roving tree. Supervise this step carefully when working with very young children.

AUTUMN SPONGE PAINTING

BEFORE YOU BEGIN

A stroll outdoors, amidst autumn's brilliant colors, provides a wealth of inspiration for young artists. Back in the classroom, there should be a general sharing of the experience. Encourage discussion with a comparison of seasons, asking, "How is autumn different?" "Special?"

Use scrap paper to practice the sponge painting technique. Wiping the paint coated sponge clear across the paper is the simplest method. Shapes can be outlined by dipping the corner of the sponge into the paint, wiping off the excess, and "writing" with the edge. For textural effects, try lightly dabbing the sponge against the paper; an interesting perforated design will result. Don't discard those practice sheets! They result in frequently delightful free-form painting.

Once children have experimented with sponge painting, they are ready to use the technique to create an autumn scene.

ILLUSTRATION 3-4

Autumn Sponge Painting

MATERIALS

1. full color tempera paint
2. small sponges
3. large painting paper
4. small paint brushes

PROCEDURE (Illustration 3-4)

1. Hand out paint, sponges and paper, and have the youngsters do an "autumn" sponge painting.
2. Allow the paintings to dry thoroughly.
3. Distribute small brushes with which to add accentuating details.

WHAT THE CHILDREN CAN DO AFTERWARD

1. Attach the pictures, side by side, to a long sheet of mural paper. Each child should title and sign his work. Display the pictures by attaching the mural paper to the tack board above the blackboard.
2. Staple each picture to a larger sheet of colored construction paper and use it on the bulletin board.
3. Use the paintings as fall scrap book covers.

RELAX WITH TIME SAVERS

1. Spread newspaper before beginning to paint.
2. Place two plastic ice-cube containers of paint, plus small bowls of water for cleaning sponges, at each table.
3. Do not permit brush painting during the sponging process. Brushes must not be distributed until the sponge paintings have dried.
4. Select helpers to wash trays and sponges at the sink, as soon as the activity has been completed.
5. Have another child circulate about the room with a wastebasket to collect newspaper from the tables.

LAMINATED LEAVES

MATERIALS

1. assorted autumn leaves (still flexible, and not too dried out)
2. paper towels
3. two sheets of waxed paper (approximately 9" x 11" each)
4. warm iron

BEFORE YOU BEGIN

No crumbling here! Autumn's brilliantly hued flora is preserved indefinitely with the following simple process. Spared is the disappointment which comes when an attractive project disintegrates.

Your class will be eager to "show off" their leafy treasures, so guide discussion, with special attention to color, shape and leaf identification. Try arranging the leaves on desks; children will delight at the interesting and varied patterns which result. Continue this experimentation until the youngsters have created designs they wish to preserve. Additional materials may then be distributed.

Should laminations be intended for use on classroom windows, prepare the waxed sheets, cut to fit, in advance.

PROCEDURE (Illustration 3-5)

1. Press the leaves gently between paper towels to remove any surface moisture.
2. Have the children lay out their arrangements on the waxed side of the first sheet of paper. Encourage them to "try" arrangements, before deciding upon a permanent pattern. (step a)
3. Place a second sheet of waxed paper, waxy side inward, over the leaf design. (step b)
4. Using a warm iron, carefully press the two sheets together. The resulting melted wax will fuse the sheets of paper, preserving and securing the leaves in place. (step b)

ILLUSTRATION 3-5

Laminated Leaves

WHAT THE CHILDREN CAN DO AFTERWARD

1. Make somewhat transparent window displays by taping the laminations to panes. The brilliance of the leaves will be intensified as light shines through.
2. Staple the finished products to a larger sheet of construction paper and display these on a bulletin board.

RELAX WITH TIME SAVERS

1. Have the children work against a book, or sheet of cardboard, larger than waxed paper, to facilitate carrying the arrangements to the teacher for pressing.
2. As a safety measure, do not allow the children to handle the iron. If an ironing board is unavailable, place a blanket, covered with muslin or linen on an empty desk, and use this as an ironing surface.
3. Permit the children to "check" the leaf design after it is transferred to the ironing surface, making certain that the leaves have not slipped out of place. Sheets of waxed paper may be fused once the final finishing touches have been added.

ALUMINUM NATURE PLAQUES (Illustration 3-6)

ILLUSTRATION 3-6

MATERIALS

1. shirt cardboard
2. aluminum foil
3. assortment of leaves, flowers, petals, grasses, and seeds
4. white glue
5. spray shellac
6. clear plastic wrap
7. stapler

BEFORE YOU BEGIN

The following activity, intriguing, and informative of growing things, may be used during almost any season. On field trips, over the week-end, and on walks to school, children can collect seeds, flowers, leaves, and grasses to be shared by all.

List, identify, and discuss these contributions. Each aluminum foil plaque, employing several of the available nature samples, becomes bright, colorful and unusual.

PROCEDURE

1. Place the nature samples between two paper towel sheets to remove surface moisture.
2. Cover the front of the cardboard with aluminum foil. Overlap the edges on the reverse side, and staple, to secure in place.
3. Select an assortment of nature samples. Placing them on the foil covered cardboard, experiment until an attractive arrangement is decided upon.

4. Carefully apply a small amount of glue to the reverse side of each specimen and press it gently into its proper place.
5. Allow the glue to dry thoroughly.
6. Apply a thin coat of spray shellac to the entire plaque surface. This will give the specimens a sheen, and help prevent disintegration.
7. When the shellac has dried, wrap clear plastic tightly around the finished plaque and staple it in place.

WHAT THE CHILDREN CAN DO AFTERWARD

1. Tack the plaques to a bulletin board. Each child can list the contents of his creation on a 3" x 5" card. Display this card beneath the appropriate plaque.
2. Use the finished plaques as Mother's Day gifts. Place stick-on wall hangers on the back of each plaque so that it may be used as a wall decoration.
3. Using two-way adhesive, attach the plaques to windows.

RELAX WITH TIME SAVERS

1. Pre-cut sheets of aluminum foil in advance. Provide a stapler for each table of children to share.
2. Place a variety of nature samples on each table for individual selection.
3. Allow ample time for the children to plan their arrangements, before distributing the glue.
4. Spread newspaper before starting to glue.
5. Provide a glue dispenser for two or three to share. Dispensers with "controlled flow" tops are best. Caution the class to use the glue sparingly.
6. Set up a spray station in an unobstructed, well ventilated area of the room. Spread this table with newspaper. Supervise spraying, making certain to follow the directions on the can. Only a thin coat of shellac is necessary.
7. Have a few rolls of plastic wrap on hand at a separate station. The children, when ready, can tear off the required amount.

SPRING MURAL COLLAGE

MATERIALS

1. construction paper in assorted colors
2. tissue paper and other collage materials (cotton, excelsior, and so on)
3. stapler
4. paste
5. bulletin board paper
6. white chalk
7. crayons and/or paint

BEFORE YOU BEGIN

Most rooms require a face lifting when the last of winter's snow has melted. This decorative, three-dimensional bulletin board suggestion will brighten spirits and surroundings, as it welcomes spring.

Signs of the coming season should be listed on the board. Flowers, blossoms, birds, showers, butterflies, and sunshine will probably head the list of things to grace the collage. Since a basic mural scene will also be necessary, select a special committee for this task. While they work, others will be busy making items to be included.

Whether youngsters work alone or in groups, planning is the most important factor in developing an attractive room display. Once the children are aware of their specific roles in the project, demonstrate ways of cutting and pasting paper figures to produce a three dimensional effect.

PROCEDURE (Illustration 3-7)

1. Tack sheets of bulletin board paper in place. Green may be used on the bottom to represent grass, and light blue on the top to suggest sky. Of course, these areas may be painted instead.
2. Have one group of children design a basic background sketch, in white chalk, on the bulletin board. The layout should include bare trees, hills, sky, and perhaps a few houses (do not include any of the details listed on the blackboard in the background drawing).
3. Crayon over, or paint the completed chalk picture.
4. On colored construction paper, draw a variety of items to be included in the mural. Advise youngsters to make and cut out paper figures so that they are large enough when placed on the bulletin board mural.
5. Folds, as well as a variety of collage materials, make the items to be included three dimensional. Some suggestions follow (consult the illustration for sample ideas).
   a). *Tree*—Make a roving tree by stapling long strips of brown roving to the bulletin board to form a tree trunk and branches. Make the leaves from construction paper cut-outs. (steps a & b)
   b) *Leaves*—Cut the leaves from several shades of green construction paper. Overlap these when attaching them to the bulletin board. Some may be folded in half lengthwise. For a 3-D effect, paste only half of the folded leaf to the mural. (step b)
   c) *Flowers*—Cut a variety of flower shapes, adding contrasting colored paper to the centers of some with paste. On tulips, and similarly shaped flowers, utilize sharp folds. Paste these to the bulletin board in a "pop-up" manner. Other flowers can be made by simply crumpling tissue paper. Use separate strips of green construction paper to make stems and leaves. (steps e, g, h, j)
   d) *Birds*—Cut out bird shapes. Add the details with crayons or collage scraps.

Cut a wing from a separate piece of construction paper. Attach only one end of the wing to the bird, allowing the remaining portion to "flap." (step c)

e) *Butterflies*—Decorate a basic butterfly shape. Cut it out, and fold up the wings. Attach only the center portion of the butterfly to the mural, allowing the wings and antenna to stand out. (step f)

f) *Clouds*—Use cotton balls. (step i)

g) *Nests*—Paste excelsior, or fine egg noodles to tree branches. (step d)

6. Have the children come up to the mural collage in small groups, to attach their creations. The use of paste or a stapler will depend on the construction of each contribution. Guide decisions, with special focus on the desired 3-dimensional quality.

ILLUSTRATION 3-7

WHAT THE CHILDREN CAN DO AFTERWARD

1. For a hall or lobby display, design a collage on an extra long sheet of mural paper.
2. Encourage impromptu tunes about the season, or have the class write poems.

RELAX WITH TIME SAVERS

1. Prepare the bulletin board with background paper well in advance of the lesson.
2. Provide white chalk for children working on the mural lay-out. Errors can easily be dusted off.
3. Spread newspaper on the floor if the mural details are to be gone over with paint.
4. Provide a sufficient assortment of construction paper, collage scraps and crayons for each table. Also distribute jars of paste and a stapler.
5. Ask the children to come up to the mural, one table at a time, to add their contributions.
6. Have two helpers circulate about the room at the activity's end; one with a wastebasket to collect small scraps, another with a box to collect usable left-over materials.

EGG CARTON FLOWERS

MATERIALS

1. molded egg cartons
2. scissors
3. paint and brushes
4. green pipe cleaners
5. brown or green plasticine

BEFORE YOU BEGIN

Liven a dreary day with brightly colored flowers. Easy and fun to make, these egg carton arrangements may be fashioned by primary, as well as intermediate grade youngsters.

Show the class the type of egg cartons that will be needed, requesting that these be brought from home. One container may be shared by two primary grade youngsters, enabling each to create up to six flowers. Plan on the use of one entire carton per child in the intermediate grades.

PROCEDURE (Illustration 3-8)

1. Remove the top of the egg carton and save it. (step a)
2. Cut out the individual egg containers. These will form the basic flower shapes.

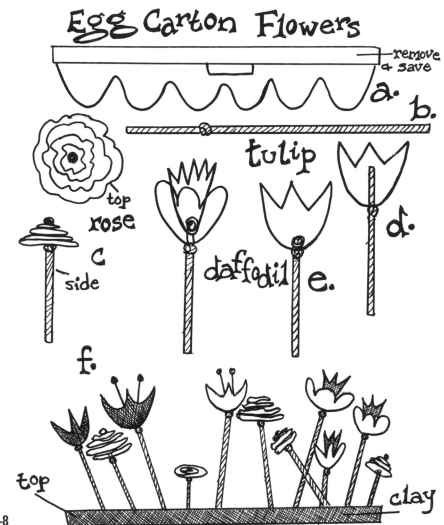

Egg Carton Flowers

ILLUSTRATION 3-8

Save the pointed egg sections which separate molded egg containers. These, too, may be made into flowers, or used as flower stamens.

3. Cut the flower shapes from these cut-out sections. Some children may find it easier, initially, to use the existing folds as guides for cutting. Some flowers will have several parts; advise youngsters that these extra pieces will be attached *after* they have been painted. There are many flower possibilities. Here are but a few suggestions:

a) Cut tulip points around the egg container. (step d)

b) Make daffodils by using one egg container, and one pointed section. Cut four petals from the container and invert the pointed section into the flower center. After painting, these parts are secured together with pipe cleaners. (step e)

c) Roses may be made by cutting rounded petals from two egg containers. Place one cut out shape inside the other, and attach, after painting, with pipe cleaners. (step c)

The possibilities are manifold. The children should be encouraged to experiment and evolve their own ideas.

4. Paint the cut-out flowers, as well as the egg carton cover. Allow both to dry thoroughly.
5. Place the flower sections together and attach them with green pipe cleaner stems. Make a knot 2/3 of the way up the pipe cleaner. Thread the flower through the *short* end of the pipe cleaner, up to the knot. The flower will be unable to slip. Twist the remaining short end into a small ball to further secure the flower in place. Pipe cleaners may also be used as flower stamens. (steps b & e)
6. Make a planter by filling the egg carton cover with plasticine. Insert the flowers in a decorative arrangement.

WHAT THE CHILDREN CAN DO AFTERWARD

1. Make a garden display along a window sill or on a large table.
2. Place the flower planters on a table beneath a bulletin board. Use the bulletin board for original poems about flowers or spring.
3. Learn about the art of flower arranging. Collect vases and bowls to plan individual displays.
4. Use the flowers as centerpiece gifts—a delightful idea for Mother's Day.

RELAX WITH TIME SAVERS

1. Complete all the cutting before starting to paint.
2. Clean up any scraps, and spread newspaper before painting.
3. Provide a plastic ice-cube tray of paint for two children to share. Each tray should contain an assortment of colors, as well as empty compartments for mixing colors and washing brushes.
4. Some children may require a pencil, with a sharp point, to make holes, before inserting the pipe cleaner stems.

ROCK CREATURES (Illustration 3-9)

ILLUSTRATION 3-9

MATERIALS

1. assortment of rocks and pebbles in a variety of sizes and shapes
2. white glue
3. paint and brushes
4. optional—assortment of collage materials (roving, felt and other material scraps, paper doilies)

BEFORE YOU BEGIN

Try a field trip for this activity. Pretending they are geologists, have your class gather an assortment of rocks, seeking "finds" with unusual shapes. These will be converted into a host of weird creatures and unusual animals. The specimens should be freed of any clinging soil, washed, and thoroughly dried.

Help the children identify their samples, providing books, and, if possible, commercially labeled rock collections. Select a few odd looking stones for the class to observe. "Look at the natural lines and texture. What does this rock shape suggest to you?" Young imaginations will conjure some astonishing animals and figures; rock formations suddenly resemble facial features, animal markings, even feathers!

Providing time for all to handle and experiment with the samples, show how two or more stones can be joined to form "creatures." Go lightly with paint! Details and collage decoration should merely define the already present lines and rock textures.

PROCEDURE

1. Wash and dry the rocks.
2. Use white glue if more than one rock is required. Press the glued rocks together firmly, holding for a few seconds. Allow them to stand until the glue has dried. Pebbles, for eyes, nose, or feet can be applied using the same procedure.
3. Add distinguishing features with paint. Allow ample drying time.
4. If desired, rock creatures may be embellished with collage materials, such as roving hair, paper doily skirts, and fancy button "suits."

WHAT THE CHILDREN CAN DO AFTERWARD

1. Group creatures into appropriate families (e.g., The Granites, Mr. and Mrs. Quartz). Or, have children create whimsical names for their fantastic families (The Groggles, The Flameran Clan).
2. Ask each child to exhibit his work, explaining how the innate form of the rock helped determine his invention.
3. Make individual dioramas from empty shoe boxes and use them as background for the completed rock creatures.
4. Use the rock creatures as paperweights; an excellent gift idea for Father's Day.

RELAX WITH TIME SAVERS

1. Spread newspaper before starting to glue.
2. Use "controlled flow" glue dispensers.
3. Allow ample time for the children to select their rock samples. Since some youngsters may find special rocks which they want to use and keep, provide an additional assortment of stones from which others can choose.
4. Distribute paint in plastic ice-cube containers. One tray should suffice for a table, as only a minimum amount of paint is required.
5. Be certain that the paint and glue have dried before adding any collage decoration. Place an assortment of these materials on each table.
6. To facilitate clean-up, have two helpers circulate about the room at the activity's end; one with a wastebasket, another with a scrap box for usable materials.

SHELL DESIGNS (Illustration 3-10)

ILLUSTRATION 3-10

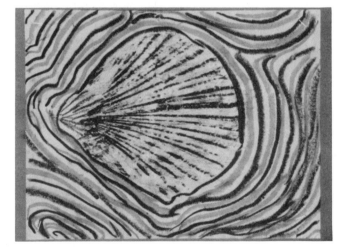

MATERIALS

1. thin drawing paper
2. medium-large size sea shell, with contour lines
3. two crayons in contrasting colors.

BEFORE YOU BEGIN

Much classroom chatter at the start of the new term abounds with tales of summer and vacations. With encouragement to bring "holiday treasures," including shells, from home, effervescence can be channelled into an informative, artistic lesson.

Identify samples, noting shapes, colors and markings. For this activity, use shells with definite contour lines (the deeper the furrows, the better). Do a sample shell design for the class to see before initiating the lesson.

PROCEDURE

1. Place the shell on a desk, contour side upward. Spread the drawing paper over the sea shell, holding it in place with the thunb and forefinger of one hand.
2. Select a crayon and color over the paper-covered shell surface. The contoured texture of the shell will be reproduced.
3. Using the same color crayon, trace around shell to define its outline.
4. Select a second crayon, in a contrasting color. Interchanging crayon colors, draw complementary contour lines around the shell outline. For most interesting effects, add contrasting lines one next to another.

WHAT THE CHILDREN CAN DO AFTERWARD

1. Staple the designs to a sheet of colored construction paper, and display them on a bulletin board, along with compositions about summer fun.
2. Use the display suggested above as a backdrop for seashells, arranged on a near-by table.
3. Have each child do some research, then identify his shell.
4. Begin a permanent class shell collection.

RELAX WITH TIME SAVERS

1. Provide a table of well displayed shells for individual selection.
2. It is helpful to first have the children experiment with contrasting crayon colors on scrap paper. Drawing contour lines, similar to those used in the activity, will enable them to make wise color decisions, enhancing the design. The remaining crayons in the box should be stored out of sight once a color decision has been made.

Special Activity

A movie camera, willingness to attempt the unusual, plus imagination, equal enriching excitement for sixth graders. Proud to be a part of this venture, youngsters can indeed produce a simple cartoon-type movie.

The following film sequence, animating seasonal changes from fall to winter, has been chosen for its inherent contrasts. Children can vividly visualize crimsoning, falling leaves, barren trees, and the onset of winter's white wonderland.

Don't be discouraged by seemingly lengthy directions. The planning activities in "Before You Begin" section, though time consuming, help produce enviable results.

ILLUSTRATION 3-11

FALL TO WINTER ANIMATION

MATERIALS

1. bulletin board paper; green for bottom in fall scene, white for bottom during winter scene, and light blue for top, to represent sky.
2. construction paper
3. scissors
4. crayons
5. two-way adhesive, or masking tape, curled so as to adhere to two surfaces.
6. can of commercially prepared spray snow
7. sheet of black cardboard for black-out scenes
8. 8 mm camera with color film, and, if possible, a cable release
9. tripod

BEFORE YOU BEGIN

Even parents will enjoy getting into this one! If there's a camera bug Dad belonging to someone in your class, invite him to talk, on a child's level, of course, about camera mechanics. A class hobby may very well stem from here!

Explain that a moving picture is simply a series of "stills," in which gradual changes, filmed in rapid succession, give the effect of motion. Of course, movement in this project will not be as smooth as a Hollywood production. Time lapse sequences, if available through your school film library, will help children acquire a better perception of the type of film to be produced.

Following preliminary discussions about films in general, plan out scenes on chart paper, or a reserved section of the blackboard. One suggestion is to write "fall" on the top of the board, and "winter" at the bottom. Ask the children to visualize the key stages marking seasonal changes, using responses to evolve an outline similar to that illustrated in the Procedure section. To produce realistic films, emphasis should be on the typical and obvious changes.

Step two requires groups of children to do the following;

1. prepare a basic bulletin board scene, showing a house, tree, grass and sky.
2. draw, color and cut out appropriate decorations to be added during the filming, as detailed below.

Guide group work, with special attention to cut-outs; they should be large enough to be visible from the bulletin board.

PROCEDURE (Illustration 3-11)

I. Preparing the Bulletin Board

a. Staple the background bulletin board paper in place, using light blue to represent the sky and green to represent the grass. A sheet of white paper, to replace the green during the snow sequence, should be readied in advance.

b. Measure a distance of 4-6 inches from edges of the bulletin board paper. Draw a border lightly in pencil. To keep unrelated objects well outside viewing area, cut-outs used in the film should not extend beyond this border.

c. A multi-branched tree is made from strips of brown construction paper, stapled in place. A colorful house completes the background scene.

II. Preparing the Cut-Outs—   Draw, color and cut out the following;

a. pumpkins, many leaves, from green, orange, brown and yellow construction paper. Crayon in the veins of leaves.

b. bird shapes: some sitting, others flying

c. an assortment of squirrels in standing and running positions.

d. figures of children, standing and tumbling

e. a snowman, covered with cotton. Cut out and save, construction paper eyes, mouth, nose and pipe, to be added during final scene.

Place two-way adhesive, or curled masking tape, on the back of each cut-out.

III. Making the Film —Discuss these general rules with your class;

a. The camera will be permanently set up on a tripod to encompass the viewing area. If possible, a cable release will be utilized.

b. Two children at a time may work at the bulletin board during the filming. Pair off youngsters, giving each couple a number. Calling these numbers at spaced intervals will give all an opportunity to participate.

c. To avoid a disoriented, jerky effect, only one major figure, (animal, child, or bird) may be moved at a time.

d. Demonstrate how to move the cut-out objects about the bulletin board *slowly*. For example, it may take 6-8 changes in position to show a squirrel running down a tree. To effect motion, each progressive movement must be small. Individual changes in the position will be filmed at 1/2 to 1 second time intervals.

e. As soon as the placement of a cut-out is made for filming, children must move completely out of the camera's range.

f. Black-out cardboard, between scenes will be moved from left to right across camera. Black-outs will provide a transition between major scenes.

g. The actual camera handling should be done by the teacher only. (A cable release, however, will enable youngsters to do some camera work.)

The procedure for filming is explained in double outline form. Part A details the suggested sequence, complete with necessary cut-out items, and directions for their placement. Part B contains specific filming guidelines.

FALL TO WINTER ANIMATION

PART A OUTLINE SEQUENCE	PART B FILMING GUIDELINES

I. *FALL SCENE*

A. Set up the background scene, complete with a large tree covered with leaves, birds, a house surrounded by grass, and one squirrel, high in a tree, another on the ground.

B. Change the position of the squirrel, so that it moves slowly down the tree, approximately two inches at a time, until it reaches the ground.

C. Have a second squirrel, on the grass, ascend the tree, two inches at a time.

D. Black-out

II. *MID FALL SCENE*

A. Prepare this scene by separating several leaves from the tree, and attaching them sideways to various areas of the bulletin board, as if they were blowing in the wind. Place pumpkins outside the house.

B. Show leaves progressively falling to the ground and blowing off the tree. Start with a few, placed a short distance from the tree, working up to many leaves, scattered about the bulletin board. In this sequence, several leaves may be moved concurrently.

I. *FALL SCENE*

A. Film this introductory scene for approximately six seconds.

B. Film each change in the squirrel's position using 1/2 second time lapses. Approximately six sequences will be necessary for completion.

C. Film as described above.

D. Have a child *slowly* move a sheet of black cardboard across the camera lens. *Stop filming. Prepare the next scene.*

II. *MID FALL SCENE*

A. Film the background scene for five seconds.

B. Film each progressive change at 1/2 second intervals.

II. *MID FALL SCENE (cont.)*

C. Have one child move an "acorn" slowly from the tree to the ground, 2" at a time. A second child continues to separate leaves from the tree until it is almost bare.

D. Black-out

II. *MID FALL SCENE (cont.)*

C. Film the falling acorn at 1/2 second intervals, until it reaches ground. The continued movement of leaves should be filmed along with the falling acorn.

D. *Film black cardboard moving slowly from left to right across lens. Stop camera.*

III. *COMING OF WINTER SCENE*

A. Prepare a background scene. Remove the blowing leaves, retain some on the ground. Remove the pumpkins sitting birds, and squirrels.

B. Show birds "flying south," by introducing them, one at a time, from the upper periphery of the bulletin board. Move them, in flocks, two inches at a time, progressively across the viewing area, until they have "flown off" the board.

C. Spray small amounts of snow, lightly over the bulletin board. Simultaneously, remove the leaves from the ground, until it is bare.

D. Black-out

III. *COMING OF WINTER SCENE*

A. Film this for about five seconds.

B. Film each progressive movement of flying birds at 1/2 second intervals. Approximately five sequences will be required for completion.

C. Film these progressive changes in the scene at one second intervals.

D. *Move a sheet of cardboard across the lens. Stop camera. Prepare the next scene.*

IV. *WINTER SCENE*

A. To prepare this scene, remove all leaves from the bulletin board. Replace the green background paper with white, and place a Christmas decoration on the door of the house. Add cut-out children around the snowman shape. Show other children tumbling in snow.

IV. *WINTER SCENE*

A. Film winter scene 5 seconds.

IV. *WINTER SCENE (cont.)*

B. Gradually spray the board with increased amounts of snow, until the effect of a heavy snowstorm is achieved. Pay special attention to the roof and tree branches. At the same time, film figures of children moving around snowman and/or tumbling in snow.

C. Add features (eyes, pipe, nose) to the snowman, one at a time.

D. Attach a "Seasons Greetings" sign to a dowel stick.

IV. *WINTER SCENE (cont.)*

B. Film each change in position at 1/2 second time intervals.

C. Film each addition at 1 second intervals.

D. Move the sign slowly across the camera lens. Film this for 5 seconds.

WHAT THE CHILDREN CAN DO AFTERWARD

Make a "soundtrack," using a tape recorder. This can be a documentary narration, explaining seasonal changes, or a poem written by the class. Invite other groups for a viewing, or use the movie as part of an assembly program.

Bonus Ideas

1. Paint a "snowstorm" (see the first two chapter suggestions). Use discussions about storms as a basis for the crayon pictures. Paint over, using a thin wash of white paint. Or, use streaks of white paint to achieve the effect of wind-blown snow.
2. The "Happy to Know You Tree" can become a "Do You Read Me Tree" to perk up a limp vocabulary lesson. After decorating the periphery of his leaf with a crayon, ask that an interesting or unusual word be printed in its center. Give the class several days to look up the definitions, to be discussed later in the week.
3. Kindergarteners will enjoy the "Color Tree." Have them choose a sheet of colored construction paper, and cut a free-form leaf shape. The teacher then writes the leaf color clearly on the leaf and attaches it to the tree. The children will soon develop a sight, color vocabulary.
4. Paint abstract sponge designs.
5. Make laminated designs, using grasses and flowers, as well as leaves.
6. A 3-D Santa Claus bulletin board can be achieved with padded cotton costume trim, added to a construction paper Santa. Paste small boxes, individually wrapped with Christmas paper, to the board. Enclose "gifts" in a fishnet "sack," draped over Santa's shoulder.
7. Attractive leaf designs may be achieved, using the procedure outlined for shells.
8. "Film" a favorite story. Narrate with tape recorder.

Stitches, Scraps and Haute Couture

4

When a maverick caveman thonged two skins of a different species together, because of whim, originality, or just because there wasn't enough of one kind to go around, he inadvertantly seeded haute couture!

Since finery is nothing without good grooming, the lessons that follows will deal with both. Texture, design, weaving, and sewing, all touched upon, can easily serve the double purpose of developing unusual class projects. For example, after experimenting with fundamentals of weaving, groups can go on to make their own looms for original rug design. It's only a short step from one to the other.

Our main purpose, however, is to develop an interest in personal appearance. While children are fashioning mod accessories and playing couturier in "Puppet Parade," they will, hopefully, be encouraged to look to their own clothes and grooming.

TEXTURE RUBBING HUNT

MATERIALS

1. newsprint
2. crayons

BEFORE YOU BEGIN

Covering a raised surface with paper, then rubbing with pencil until an embossed design shows through, has been schoolboy fun for many years. Why not use this familiar pastime as an exercise in texture?

Though materials and procedure are deceptively simple, the experience has several purposes. As interest joins with the development of observational skills, children become aware of everyday things about them, which they've never really examined or "seen." Slow learners, expecially, are helped by this fundamental approach. And, when considering the relation of texture to fabric, clothing, and design, the activity becomes a "must."

Texture Rubbing Hunt

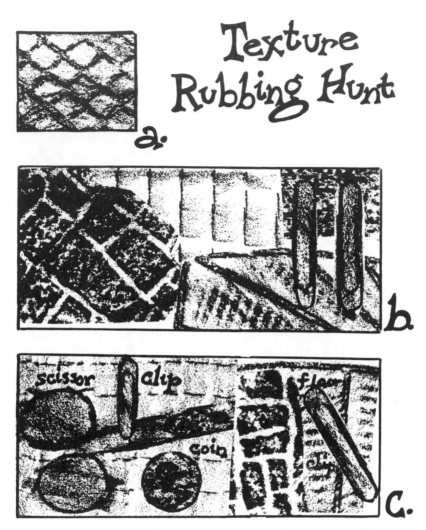

ILLUSTRATION 4-1

As a preliminary step, play a game of "guess what." Pair off children, assigning one the role of guide, the other "follower." At the teacher's signal, the "follower" will close his eyes, while his "guide" slowly, and carefully leads him about, directing his hand over such schoolroom textures as grills, switchplates, doorknobs, tile, drapes etc. No talking here! Children should concentrate on the feeling experience. At a second signal, partners reverse roles and repeat the experience.

Later, discuss "follower's" sensations—responses are varied, and frequently humorous. "Did you 'see' what you were feeling?" Let the class describe the textures they encountered, and list these on the board (hard, soft, rough, prickly, nubby).

By this time, there should be no doubt about what is meant by texture. Now, with a sheet of paper, and some crayons, the most ignored schoolroom object can be avidly explored.

PROCEDURE (Illustration 4-1)

1. Hand out newsprint, and let the children select two or three crayons, in contrasting shades.
2. Permit the youngsters to explore the classroom for textures. Place the paper over a given area (tile, erasers, grates) and gently rub it with crayon until a portion of the paper is filled. Go elsewhere in the room, embossing a second texture. Proceed until the paper is covered with an assortment of rubbings. (steps a & b)

3. Children may go through their pockets for additional textured items. For unusual results, combs, keys and coins can be rubbed into the design, and superimposed over existing patterns. (step c)
4. If desired, label each section of the rubbing.

WHAT THE CHILDREN CAN DO AFTERWARD

1. Before labeling, have each child hold his rubbing before classmates, quizzing them for identifications of the objects used.
2. Prepare a texture vocabulary chart to share space with the rubbings on the bulletin board.

RELAX WITH TIME SAVERS

1. Demonstrate the rubbing technique in advance, leaving an approximate one inch border around the paper. Emphasize that rubbings should not go beyond this marginal line. This will save walls and furniture. The border may be trimmed later, should it become smudged or sloppy.
2. Eliminate shoving and confusion by starting the groups in assigned areas of the room. Have the children move in a clockwise direction at five minute intervals.

TEXTURE COLLAGE

ILLUSTRATION 4-2

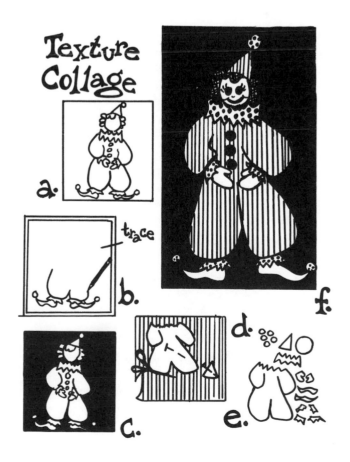

MATERIALS

1. shirt cardboard
2. pencil
3. tracing paper
4. paint and brushes
5. straight pins
6. assorted fabric scraps
7. paste

BEFORE YOU BEGIN

Collage, a natural successor to texture rubbing, provides a lesson in fabrics the easy way. Whether it is used for primary or upper grades, the resulting wall hangings are original looking, and worthy of display at home or in school.

Well in advance of the lesson, set the class on a home fabric safari. While collected samples are going into a class scrap box, examine the materials to note texture and content (wool, silk, synthetic). "Is anyone wearing clothes made from a material similar to this one?" Let the children handle these fabrics as comparisons to their own apparel are being made. For added identification, complete a fabric chart, giving the name of the material (cotton, crepe, linen, silk) and its origin (animal, plant, synthetic).

By touching, sight acquires new dimension. As in the previous activity ("texture rubbing"), sensory experience is used to inspire the child to learning. Developing such perception is encouraged by a "feel box." Place a variety of samples in a cardboard carton, through which a hole has been punched. Have each child thrust his hand in, grope about, then select one of the hidden fabrics. Amongst the host of the ordinary, expect as many bizarre replies to: "How does it feel: soft? nubby? smooth?" "What kind of cloth is this?"

Though emphasis has been on apparel, the collage you are about to make needn't be aimed at couture design. Landscapes, people, cities, as well as wierd and fanciful animals can, and do, emerge.

PROCEDURE (Illustration 4-2)

1. Draw a desired shape or design on the cardboard, avoiding tiny details. (step a)
2. Transfer the drawing to tracing paper. (step b)
3. Paint a background color around the cardboard drawing. *Do not paint over the drawing.* (step c)
4. While the paint dries, prepare patterns for the fabric cut-outs. These are made by cutting the traced paper drawing into appropriate pattern pieces; one piece for each part of the drawing. Explain that the fabrics will be used in place of crayon to fill in drawing. Cut out pattern pieces for every new "color" and "shape" as dictated by the drawing. (step d)
5. Next, choose an assortment of fabric samples. Encourage the selection of a variety of textures. Pin the pattern pieces to the desired material scraps, and cut them out. (step e)
6. Remove the patterns from the cut-out fabrics.
7. Paste the cut-out fabric pieces to the corresponding sections of the drawing. The picture should be entirely covered when all the pieces have been pasted in place. (step f)
8. If desired, or necessary, outline the completed collage with a dark crayon to add definition to the design.

WHAT THE CHILDREN CAN DO AFTERWARD

1. Use the texture collages as permanent wall decorations. Attach stick-on picture hangers to the pictures and give them as gifts.

2. Tack the pictures to a bulletin board, as part of your clothing unit display.
3. Ask each child to list the fabrics in his collage, citing their origins. Display the list alongside the collage.
4. Cut out figures from the cardboard sheets (do not paint the cardboard background in this case) and use them to design a fabric mural.

RELAX WITH TIME SAVERS

1. Prepare materials in advance; tracing paper should be cut to fit cardboard sheets, pins should be attached to individual scraps of paper or fabric, and a painting station, complete with water and brushes should be ready in the rear of the room. Avoid crowding when materials are selected, by providing two or three boxes of fabric samples in different corners of the room.
2. Each child, when ready, may paint the cardboard background color at an appropriate station. Provide a place for projects to safely dry.
3. With patterns complete, each youngster may select several material swatches, and a sheet of straight pins. Encourage the class to share left-over scraps amongst their neighbors. Such sharing eliminates "traffic" in search of added materials.
4. Pins should be returned, attached to their small paper sheets. Make certain that pins are cleared from all the desks and the floor.

PAPER WEAVING

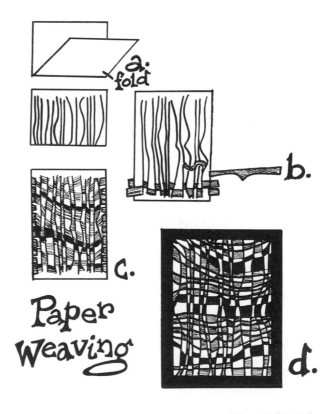

MATERIALS

1. construction paper in an assortment of colors
2. scissors
3. paste

ILLUSTRATION 4-3

BEFORE YOU BEGIN

Since children of all ages take to weaving almost naturally, this project will require little explaining. Approach the ancient craft with an eye to coordinating manipulative skills and young imagination. "How did people make their clothes?" "What types of materials were used?" Movies and filmstrips will certainly underscore the striking improvements wrought by our modern day technology.

Teach too, about various looms and their functions, introducing weaving's three "W's": warp, weft, or woof. As youngsters work on creations, have them refer to these terms. They'll love using those odd words!

PROCEDURE (Illustration 4-3)

1. Fold one sheet of construction paper in half. (step a)
2. For the "warp," cut several slits across the fold, towards the edge of the paper. Leave an approximate 1″ border at the top (it is best to have younger children pencil in this border beforehand). Slits needn't be evenly spaced or equal in width. In fact, the combined use of curved, slanted, and straight edges produces a varied, unusual result. (step a)
3. Cut the "woof" long enough to stretch across the loom, from assorted colors of construction paper. Again, these may be irregular and vary in width. Though some may wish to stick to only two or three hues, thus achieving a patterned effect, multi-colored combinations are, in fact, limitless. (step b)
4. Start at the bottom of the paper, weaving the first strip over, under, and over warp, from one edge of "loom" to the other edge. Reverse the procedure with the second strip, weaving under, then over. Continue to weave until the loom is filled. (step b)
5. Paste down the edges of the woof strips to one side of the woven paper. Fold down, and paste the border edges to this same side of the finished product. (steps c & d)

WHAT THE CHILDREN CAN DO AFTERWARD

1. Use these woven creations on a bulletin board, along with compositions about weaving which trace the early history of the craft.
2. Decorate empty containers with paper weaving and use these as odds and ends jars. Give them as gifts.
3. Weave serapes using extra large sheets of construction paper. To wear, drape serape over one shoulder, and pin, or tape the sides in place.
4. Spray the woven paper with shellac, for use as a class party placemat.
5. Make a cylinder out of the woven creation and use it as a paper lantern.

RELAX WITH TIME SAVERS

1. Place assorted colored sheets of construction paper on each table. Children may select one color for the "loom" and share the rest for cutting paper strips.

2. Distribute paste in empty jar covers. Select a helper from each table for this task. One paste receptacle may be shared by three or four children, using folded scraps of paper to obtain necessary amounts for personal use.
3. Ask a class assistant to collect unusable scraps in wastebasket.

WOVEN RIBBON PURSE

ILLUSTRATION 4-4

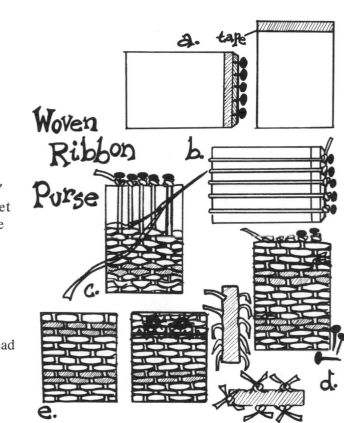

MATERIALS

1. corrugated cardboard, approximately 6" x 8" (flaps from supermarket cartons, cut to size, are excellent)
2. tape
3. straight pins
4. strong cotton string
5. yarn needle
6. ribbon
7. sewing needle and thread
8. scissors
9. snaps
10. fabric for lining purse, optional

BEFORE YOU BEGIN

You can depend on the lassies to whip up enthusiasm for woven purses, matched to their favorite outfits. As for the boys, they always have problems finding proper gifts for the ladies. With definite recipients in mind—Mom, Grandma, Sis—lads also take easily to this handiwork.

Refer to the concepts discussed in "paper weaving" and review these with your class. In demonstrating the procedure, stress the importance of a firm, close weave. Cardboard looms should be completed, and the weaving technique introduced, as part of a regular art lesson. Once mastered, the children may complete the process during their free time.

One note of caution—special instruction should accompany the removal of the completed purse from the loom. The over-zealous are bound to have spirits, tempers, and projects unravel, without such supervision.

PROCEDURE (Illustration 4-4)

1. Cover one 6″ edge of cardboard with tape. Stick an uneven number of straight pins, downward, and vertically through this taped edge, at approximately 1/4″ intervals. The pointed tips of the pins will be buried between the thickness of the cardboard sheet. (step a)
2. Tie the warp string securely around the first pin at the top of the loom. Carry the string down one side of the cardboard, around the bottom, and up the reverse side of the cardboard, wrapping it around the second pin at the top of the loom. Continue to wind the thread in this manner, until the entire loom is filled. End the warp by knotting the string around the last pin. (step b)
3. Thread the ribbon through a yarn needle. Starting at the bottom of the cardboard loom, weave the ribbon around the entire loom—front and back. Make certain that each piece of ribbon is long enough to weave around the loom at least once. Knot the loose end to the next piece of yarn. *Remember—each line of ribbon must be woven firmly and closely against preceding line.* (step c)
4. Remove the pins. Cut along the top of the loom to separate the warp string and create a purse opening. The resulting loose ends should be tied together; join each string with the one adjacent to it. Be careful *not* to tie these ends so as to re-close the purse opening. (step d)
5. Invert the purse to its right side. Turn down the top edge about 1/2″, and hem with a needle and thread. Sew snaps along this edge in order to close. (step e)
6. If desired, make a lining and stitch it to the inside of the woven purse.

WHAT THE CHILDREN CAN DO AFTERWARD

1. Make a comb and/or eyeglass case to match the purse.
2. Give the ribbon purses as Christmas or Mother's Day gifts.
3. Use the purse to preserve a favorite charm, or other item to be kept scratch-free.

RELAX WITH TIME SAVERS

1. Complete the looms before handing out other weaving materials.
2. Prepare individual packets of pins, attached to a piece of paper, or fabric. When not in use, they should be returned in the same manner.
3. Distribute a ribbon box for each table to share. Each strip of weft should be long enough to fit around the loom at least once.

CREATIVE BURLAP STITCHERY

MATERIALS

1. 9″ x 11″ sheet of construction paper
2. chalk

3. fixative
4. 9″ x 11″ piece of burlap
5. multi-colored yarns
6. yarn needle
7. straight pins
8. scissors

BEFORE YOU BEGIN

The sooner youngsters understand how to manipulate a needle and thread, the quicker they'll learn good grooming. Older children should certainly be able to handle the repair of open seams, hanging hems, and dangling buttons. Creative stitchery offers a painless, enjoyable method of learning the chore of simple sewing. Objections of lads who balk should be met with reminders of crusty boatmen who mend their own sails.

Focusing on both the functional and decorative aspects of their own clothing, children can consider the following: "Is Suzie's dress lovely because of the pattern and embroidery?" "What about style?" "Do buttons hold Johnny's shirt closed?"

To practice, hand out a needle, some thread and a few squares of cotton cloth. Then demonstrate several basic sewing stitches. Begin by making a knot—small and tight. Then go on to hemming, back, running, blanket, chain, satin and cross stitches. These are quickly mastered. When a child's first attempts tangle, encourage and guide him showing how shorter lengths of thread are easier to cope with.

Follow these practice sessions with chalk drawings. These should be carefully planned, and completed, before sewing materials are distributed.

PROCEDURE (Illustration 4-5)

1. Supply a sheet of construction paper and white chalk and ask the children to design a pattern or picture. Chalk errors will quickly dust off. The final drawing should be sprayed with a fixative, before sewing, to prevent smudging. (step a)
2. Have each child contemplate his completed drawing to determine which stitches will best be suited to the design. Help your class make these decisions. For a clearer idea of how the finished product will look, sketch these stitches on the picture, using chalk.
3. Pin the construction paper picture to the burlap. (step b)
4. Using assorted yarn colors, proceed to sew through the construction paper drawing and attached burlap. Focus attention on the outline of the design using simple, neat stitches. (The picture will be "filled in" once the construction paper has been lifted from the fabric.) (step c)
5. Make certain that all aspects of the drawing have been outlined in yarn. Then, remove the pins and carefully tear away the paper, lifting it gently from the burlap backing. Supervise this step. (step d)
6. Fill in the open spaces of the design with appropriate stitches. Satin stitches fashion leaves, while chain stitches make interesting flowers. The possibilities are many and class ideas should be shared and discussed. (See "some stitches" in illustration.)

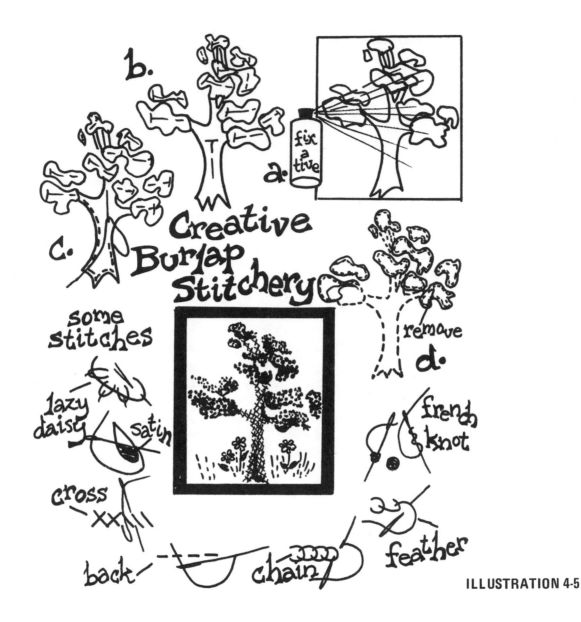

ILLUSTRATION 4-5

WHAT THE CHILDREN CAN DO AFTERWARD

1. For wall hangings, roll the top and bottom edges of the completed picture on to long dowels, and glue these in place. Tie a piece of string to each end of the top dowel and suspend it from a nail in the wall.
2. Glue the burlap to stiff cardboard to make pictures, suitable for framing.

RELAX WITH TIME SAVERS

1. Provide individual packets of pins, attached to small sheets of paper. These should later be returned, in the same manner, to prevent loss.
2. Distribute an assortment of yarns to be shared by each table.

3. Show the children how to attach the needle to the burlap when it is not in use. Stress the importance of preventing pins and needles from being lost around the room.

4. Use one color yarn, wherever that color is required, before selecting another. This prevents small bits of unusable yarn from accumulating and eliminates waste.

DESIGN A PAPER FABRIC

ILLUSTRATION 4-6

MATERIALS

1. large sheet of drawing paper
2. crayons
3. scissors
4. construction paper

BEFORE YOU BEGIN

You can expect sassy stripes, Indian designs, and merry circles to flourish when children muster ingenuity for these colorful paper abstracts. Recalling what has been learned about texture, weaving and stitching, ask your class to crayon fabric drawings. The "cloth," it may be explained, will later be used to produce "in fashions" for the K-6 set.

Remind children to press down hard on their crayons for best results. Combat finger fatigue, and hasten to complete patterns, with occasional breaks. Many teachers prefer to begin the activity as a regular art lesson, stopping well before the first signs of restlessness, and resuming work during a free period. Styling wardrobes from the completed paper designs may be initiated as a separate art lesson.

PROCEDURE (Illustration 4-6)

1. Distribute the drawing paper and crayons.
2. Ask the class to design "fabrics" with their crayons. Remind the children to press down hard on their crayons and to fill in the entire paper. (step a)
3. Each completed drawing should be folded, and cut into several equal parts, or "fabric squares." Squares should be large enough to "show off" a representative portion of the total design. (step b)
4. Display the cut-out squares of "cloth" on a table for all to see. Each child may select any two or three designed sheets (except his own). From these choices he will cut his own original clothing styles. Provide colored construction paper for those who want to coordinate solid colors with patterned paper. Draw clothing designs on the reverse side of the paper "fabric." (step c)
5. Cut out and paste the finished costume to a sheet of construction paper. (step d)

WHAT THE CHILDREN CAN DO AFTERWARD

1. Turn the selection of "material" samples into an arithmetic lesson, with a fabric shop. Label the squares with price tags, choose sales people, and supply the "customers" with play money for their purchases. With pocketbooks involved, albeit fake, selections are done with thought and discrimination. After a formal review of decimals, the use of the dollar sign, and linear measure, ask children to write out problems related to their retail experience, for the entire class to solve.
2. Concoct newspaper ads for "kiddie originals," with descriptions of style, available sizes, "fabric" content and price, accompanying the sales pitch.
3. For a bizarre display of designs, try pasting cut-out squares in a random pattern on a large sheet of mural paper. Display this on the bulletin board, suspended from the ceiling as a room divider, or use the patchwork to liven up a dreary hall.
4. Instead of cutting up sheets, use them whole, backed with construction paper frames, for a bulletin board display.

RELAX WITH TIME SAVERS

1. Inspect crayon boxes for tiny crayons which will soon be used up, before the child has begun his design. Any diligent designer would surely "erupt" if his "most important color" was suddenly gone.
2. Call children by tables to make their fabric selections.
3. Pass out jar covers filled with paste when creations are ready to be placed on construction paper. One such receptacle serves 4-5 children, and may be re-filled, if necessary, by each table helper.

PUPPET FASHION PARADE

MATERIALS

1. liquid detergent bottles
2. wheat paste and water solution
3. newspaper
4. string
5. scissors
6. paint
7. fabric scraps, crepe paper, colored tissue paper, buttons, and any other suitable collage materials
8. yarn
9. paste
10. needle and thread
11. masking tape
12. shellac
13. black glove, when needed

BEFORE YOU BEGIN

All the newly learned artistry of design, as well as concepts of texture and simple sewing techniques, come into play with the making of these puppets. Staging a fashion show for the benefit of an audience is a thought met with such lively welcome, that every young puppeteer will over-extend himself to present the best, most fashionable puppet ever!

Results are unique, especially if each step is given a bit of extra care. When carefully executed, this plastic bottle and papier-maché method produces beautifully sturdy puppets which can double as dolls, and last for years. Have a selection of appropriately shaped containers as examples of what the children are to bring in from home.

Before demonstrating the papier-maché technique, try to have puppet samples as they would appear in several stages of completion. Add to the fun of papier-maché, having children squeeze it through their hands, describing its texture. Then, watch excitement rise as wheat paste and bottles metamorphose into paper people. Try to aid children during their initial attempts at forming proportionately shaped figures.

Obviously, this is not a one lesson project. Papier-maché and paint must dry before the puppets are dressed. Meanwhile, costumes should be planned and materials gathered. Details will depend largely on age level and individual abilities. Primary grade children should stick to pasting all decoration—it's the easiest, fastest method. The more adept costumier, will enjoy making patterns, sewing and, perhaps, embroidering. Demonstrate costuming techniques; show how the paper as well as the fabric can be draped, sewn, decorated and applied to the puppets. Actual styles, however, should be left to the whims of young couturiers. Mod, odd, formal, or casual, these puppets will long be remembered as a highlight of the school year.

PROCEDURE (Illustration 4-7)

1. Cut and remove the bottom of the detergent bottle. (step a)
2. Looking at the front of the bottle, try to imagine the human shape. Both the head and the arms must be added from papier-mâché, while the legs can be cut from the lower half of the bottle. To make the legs properly spaced, and in proportion, draw an inverted "V" on the bottle as a cutting guide. Once certain of the correct leg proportion, cut along the pencilled "V". (step b)
3. Leaving the upper "torso" intact, cut a panel from the back of the bottle. This opening must be wide enough to accommodate a child's hand, and enable easy manipulation of the puppet. (step c)
4. Make the puppet's head and neck from one sheet of newspaper, torn in half. Fold one of these two halves in half, and cut on the fold. The original sheet of paper is now divided into 1/2 + 1/4 + 1/4 sections. (step d)
5. To form a neck, take one of the 1/4 size sheets of newspaper and fold it into thirds. Roll the folded paper tightly, securing it at the end with a piece of tape. (step e)
6. Crumple a 1/2 size sheet of newspaper to form the head. (step f)
7. Place the "head" on top of the "neck" roll, and cover the head shape with the remaining 1/4 size piece of paper. Gather this over the neck, tying it securely in place with string. Now, place the paper neck over the detergent bottle neck, and tie, and tape it in place. (steps f & g)
8. To form the arms, gather and shape "clumps" of paper, and tape them in place. Trim the arms to a proper length. (step g)
9. You are now ready to prepare the papier-mâché. First, cut many sheets of newspaper into long strips. Make a batter-like mixture by combining wheat paste with water. (step h)
10. Cover the entire puppet shape with newspaper strips, which have first been dipped in the wheat paste and water solution. *Caution children not to close off the back opening as they cover the doll.* (step i)
11. Allow at least two days for the puppets to dry and harden.
12. Paint on all the details, except the clothing and hair.
13. Shellac the painted puppets and let them dry.
14. Selecting a variety of fabrics, papers and collage items, children may now fashion appropriate costumes for their puppets. Provide paste, needles, and thread. Some may choose to prepare patterns in advance, fitting these to the puppet, before sewing the outfit. The exact costuming methods will depend on individual capabilities as well as the type of costume that is designed. Yarn hair should be glued in place. Try varied styles (long, straight, braids). (step j)
15. When "parading" puppets, black gloves may be worn, if necessary, to completely conceal the puppeteer's hand.

ILLUSTRATION 4-7

WHAT THE CHILDREN CAN DO AFTERWARD

1. When puppets are complete, give a fashion show, inviting parents and other classes to the event. Advertise the event with posters and personal invitations to guests. Ask each young designer to prepare a description of his creation, to be presented at the showing. Don't worry about an elaborate stage; a large table, turned horizontally on its side, and gaily adorned with crepe paper, is all that is needed, should a more professional looking theater be unavailable. Don't forget background music! The ambitious will want to select a variety of tunes to match styles. "Rock" can usher in a mini-skirted girl, or mod boy puppet, while waltz music may be used to announce those long, flowing evening gowns.

2. Appoint several children as newspaper fashion critics to take notes and report "fashion trends" for a class, or school newspaper.

3. Observe and discuss how clothes are advertised in newspapers and magazines. Ask each child to write an ad for his finery, giving himself a trade name.
4. When not in use, puppets may be suspended from dowels on wooden stands and used as show dolls.
5. Fit the puppets over small jars and bottles to cover unsightly odds and ends containers.

RELAX WITH TIME SAVERS

1. Cut strips of newspaper for pâpier-maché in advance.
2. Cover tables with newspaper before distributing materials.
3. Form the puppet's head and add the arms before handing out pâpier-maché solution. Check that the head, neck and arms are well secured to the bottle; that the back opening is wide enough to envelop a child's hand, and that the legs are cut out in proportion to the size of the doll.
4. Allow two bowls of wheat paste and water mixture for each table to share.
5. Supervise the class as the dolls are coated with newspaper strips. These should be applied evenly and smoothly.
6. Remember that drying time will vary. Have a painting station ready in the back of the room where children may paint their dried puppets.
7. Facilitate the selection of materials by having all of the fabric and paper scraps neatly stacked for quick recognition. Call children by tables to choose their needed materials.
8. Provide a box of decorative buttons and collage scraps for each group to share. Needles and assorted colored thread should be made available to those requesting them.
9. Choose table assistants to distribute paste in empty jar covers.
10. Emphasize the need to be thrifty with materials; small pieces of fabric should be cut from the edge, not the center of the sample. Usable scraps, often hard to come by, should be stored and saved for future activities.

MOD BELTS

MATERIALS

Belt I — Webbing and Rings
1. upholstory webbing
2. 1 inch curtain rings
3. yarn and needle
4. fabric glue

Belt II — Pipe Cleaners and Rings
1. 1/2 inch eyelet curtain rings
2. pipe cleaners, cut into 1 1/2 inch pieces
3. key ring

BEFORE YOU BEGIN

Only a child's special knack for invention is needed to transform ordinary hardware into "groovy" belts and baubles.

ILLUSTRATION 4-8

With parental help, and permission, youngsters invariably furnish an assortment of "finds" from Dad's workshop, Mom's sewing basket, and of course, their own private junk drawers. Contributions (to be shared) should be gleaned over a period of weeks to insure a sufficient supply.

Before long, a treasure of curtain rings, chains, spools, nuts, and bolts will accumulate. If many of these items differ from the above suggested materials, all the better. Most youngsters, finding the procedures outlined here a snap, will be eager to dream up a variety of belts and matching accessories.

One important reminder—if these belts are to be used as gifts, find out necessary waist sizes in advance.

PROCEDURE (Illustration 4-8)

Belt I — Webbing and Rings

1. Cut the webbing to the desired belt width and waist size.
2. Fold back the edges at each end of the belt and glue them in place. (step a)
3. Thread a needle with a desired colored yarn.
4. Sew the curtain rings, one next to another, along the entire length of the webbing belt. Some may choose to encase the circumference of each ring with buttonhole stitches. However, just two stitches, placed at opposite sides of each ring, will firmly hold it in place. (step b)
5. Gather long strands of yarn together and make tassels at each end. (step c)

6. To wear, place the webbing belt around the waist. Thread the tasselled yarn through the end rings and tie the yarn so that the belt fits securely around the waist. (step d)

Belt II — Pipe Cleaner — Ring

1. This belt is made by linking eyelet curtain rings with 1-1/2 inch pieces of pipe cleaner. Show the children that each 1/2 inch "link" contains a small (eyelet) circle, and a larger one. Thread a piece of pipe cleaner through the small circle of one ring, and around the larger circle of the next ring. Twist the pipe cleaner tightly to join the two links. (step e)
2. Continue the above process until the belt fits comfortably around the waist. To close the belt, place an ordinary key ring through the first and last link. (step f)

WHAT THE CHILDREN CAN DO AFTERWARD

1. Make a variety of belts and matching costume jewelry to be worn in a class fashion show.
2. Sell these accessories at a fund raising school fair.
3. Give the belts and bangles as gifts.
4. Turn pictures into household "boutique" items, by gluing the curtain rings around a simple wooden frame.

RELAX WITH TIME SAVERS

1. Sort hardware in advance, placing each item in a separate box for easy recognition. Place several boxes on each table for the children to share.
2. Have a selection of yarn, needles, webbing, felt strips. and assorted colored pipe cleaners in front of the room. Call children up by tables to select additional materials.

BUTTON PICTURES

MATERIALS

1. shirt cardboard
2. fabric (any patterned or solid fabric)
3. assorted buttons
4. white glue
5. rickrack, optional

BEFORE YOU BEGIN

Scads of buttons are needed here, so launch an early collection drive. Geared to all age levels, this activity is strictly for fun. Kindergarteners can design simple pictures, while older children may expand the idea to make mosaics.

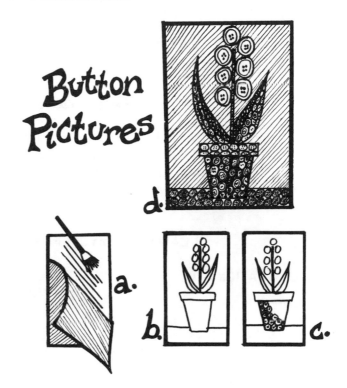

ILLUSTRATION 4-9

PROCEDURE (Illustration 4-9)

1. Glue the fabric to the cardboard, securing the edges to its reverse side. (step a)
2. Experiment with an assortment of buttons, placing them on and about the fabric until a satisfying design or picture is outlined. Almost any subject (people, animals, still life, flowers, houses) may be used. Once the outline is complete, fill in the picture with many, many buttons. (steps b & d)
3. When pleased with the arrangement, glue these buttons into place, one at a time. (step c)
4. If desired, rickrack may be used as a decorative trim.

WHAT THE CHILDREN CAN DO AFTERWARD

1. Write whimsical poems about the creations.
2. Attach a stick-on wall hanger to the back of the cardboard and give the button picture as a gift.
3. Use the pictures for a bulletin board display.

RELAX WITH TIME SAVERS

1. Pre-cut the fabric to fit the cardboard in advance of the lesson.

2. Distribute small bottles of white glue with "controlled flow" tops; one per child, if possible.
3. Provide a box containing a wide selection of buttons for each table to share.
4. Using small amounts, demonstrate how glue should be applied to each button. If used in excess, smearing will result, and mar the finished product.

Special Activity

For pre-schoolers and kindergartners only! Make this special poster once, and use it year after year—children take as much pleasure in its use as they do in construction. Naturally, new groups may wish to add touches of their own. If so, simply strip the old decoration, and update the project to suit new tastes.

"I CAN DO IT MYSELF" POSTER (Illustration 4-10)

ILLUSTRATION 4-10

MATERIALS

1. extra-large sheet of oak tag
2. child model
3. pencil
4. felt-tipped marker
5. discarded children's clothing
6. shoelaces
7. paste
8. crayons
9. scissors

BEFORE YOU BEGIN

To a kindergartner, "independence" is the ability to button, zip, snap and tie. To the teacher, "happiness" is when all her charges have mastered these skills. Advice to the weary: try this poster idea before the overcoat and snow season. With practice, all should catch the homeward bus on time—zippers zipped and boots buckled.

Most children love to costume dolls. Somehow, the same skills which frustrate young fingers as they lace and tie, become great sport when applied to play. Tell the youngsters they will make a life-size "doll," which they will dress in "real" clothes.

First, choose a child model and pencil an outline of his figure on oak tag. The procedure outlined below for dressing the poster doll is just one of many possibilities. With an assortment of clothing samples on hand, leave the final attire combinations to your class's fancy. Many will want to add manly ties—even cufflinks. It may be necessary to placate feminine demands for equality with a second poster; this one appropriately bedecked with bangles and bows.

To facilitate the visualization of the costume, tape the clothing in place until a choice is make. Once a decision is reached, complete the activity as a small group experience. No more than three or four children should work at one time, when pasting clothing to the poster.

PROCEDURE

1. Ask one child to lie down on a sheet of oak tag, with his arms and legs spread slightly. Select two more youngsters to draw his outline lightly in pencil.
2. Hold up the outlined shape for the class to observe. As an aside to the general purpose of this lesson, discuss body proportions. Many will be helped with future figure drawing if the length of arms and legs, placement of shoulders, size of hands and so on are discussed now. As you talk, add definition to the outlined shape with a felt-tipped marker.
3. Choose several children to crayon in facial features, hands, and shoes.
4. Display the available clothing samples, helping the class decide how the figure should be dressed. Concentrate on items with buttons, snaps, hooks and zippers.
5. Cut the clothing to fit the model. Usually, *front halves* of shirts and slacks can be used with minimum trimming.
6. Clothing can now be pasted to the figure. Use paste sparingly, avoiding "lumps" beneath the surface of the clothes. Be particularly careful about "practice areas" (buttons will not button if button holes have been firmly pasted to oaktag!).
7. Thread shoelaces through holes which have been punched at the instep of each "shoe."

WHAT THE CHILDREN CAN DO AFTERWARD

Have the children practice their dressing skills on the model as a regular free time activity. Make lists labeled "I Can Tie," "I Can Button." As each child masters a new skill, add his name to the appropriate list.

RELAX WITH TIME SAVERS

1. Group the children in advance; some to add crayon features, others to paste. Assure all of an opportunity to work on the poster.
2. Cut out the necessary pieces of clothing beforehand.
3. For attractive results, remind the children to press hard with their crayon when adding the detail features.
4. To insure that paste will be applied sparingly, distribute individual amounts on small scraps of folded paper, or on tongue depressors.

Bonus Ideas

1. When texture rubbing combines with simple sewing, you can expect original and unusual creative stitchery. Substituting chalk for crayon, make rubbings on construction paper. Spray with fixative. Pin the completed design to burlap and sew, using the techniques suggested in "creative stitchery."
2. Intermediate grade children are quite capable of reed weaving. Read and learn some history of the craft. If appropriate materials are available, fashion simple mats and baskets.
3. With assistance from the shop teacher make a simple rug loom. What a boost to class prestige, when the originally designed rug is proudly displayed in the main lobby or front office!
4. Putting newly acquired skills to practical use, make kitchen aprons for the ladies, and shop aprons for Dad's helpers. Using easy to follow apron patterns, learn to read and carry out pattern directions.
5. Stitch together felt decorator pillows for a family den or bedroom. adorn these pillows with fancy embroidery or appliques.
6. Learn to sew as did the pioneer children; try making samplers. The truly creative will surely want to invent their own sayings.
7. After stitching burlap, as suggested in "creative stitchery," sew up the sides, add a draw string, and you've made a purse.
8. Dress pâpier-maché puppets in traditional foreign costumes. Add zip to United Nations studies with an international fashion show.
9. A simple gift suggestion; make purse-sized sewing kits. First draw a pattern to be cut in duplicate, from colorful felt. Inside this "packet" stick a needle, safety pin, and small card wound with assorted thread.
10. Like early American settlers, experiment with the local berry crop for dyes (if all fails, there is always commercial fruit juice). What to do with the brew? Try tie dying.
11. Use texture collage to make abstract wall hangings. In addition to fabrics, use sandpaper, screening, and pieces of wood.
12. Cover odds and ends containers with burlap stitchery.
13. Puppet show "book reports" add novelty to a frequently dull classroom routine. Make those tales come to "life" with pâpier-maché puppets, dressed in the roles of favorite characters.
14. Substitute hard candy with hole centers for hardware, and make "delicious" mod belts.

What's Cooking?

5

As a classroom art media, foods have a special niche all their own. In this chapter, we have adapted the many areas of food study and appreciation to lessons which are suitable to young connoisseurs at all elementary grade levels.

Along with countless other edibles, vegetables, spices and pasta have a way of igniting a sometimes listless area of the curriculum so that it sparks with animation. Prove this by trying "Pasta Plaques," "Spice Collage," and "Vegetable Printing."

Tapping creative resources is also a way of persuading the young to try foods previously blacklisted on their menus. Surely, curiosity and interest in vegetables are aroused with "The Pushcart," "Bean and Seed Mosaics," and "Gourd Creatures." The transition from paper, paint and paste, to tongue and palate is natural. So, don't be stunned if your classroom soon becomes a bustling gourmet center.

THE PUSHCART

MATERIALS

1. crayons
2. long strips of construction paper
3. drawing paper
4. stapler
5. scissors
6. felt-tipped marker
7. pencil
8. toothpicks
9. background bulletin board paper.

BEFORE YOU BEGIN

Ask any chef, and he'll say good cooking begins in the supermarket. Even the young can learn the art of choosing firm tomatoes and crisp salad greens. Sharpen

ILLUSTRATION 5-1

observational skills, whet appetites, and end the "conspiracy" against vegetables with an excursion to the green grocer. Then, try this bulletin board idea.

Unfortunately, many youngsters are familiar with common fruits and vegetables only as they come canned or frozen. They'll be somewhat amazed to discover that those peas in pods, prickly pineapples, artichokes, fresh green beans, and peculiar looking gourds are the same as the contents of cans which line mother's cupboard.

Funny shapes, with matching names to roll on one's tongue; "rhubarb," "chicory," "avocado," "escarole," and "mango," will delight young shoppers. Buy some fresh produce, explaining how it is sold; some by the pound, others by the bunch, and head. Class selections involving cash will surely be made with thoughtful care.

After returning to the schoolroom, the purchases should be displayed for handling and study. Slice open and investigate the layers inside.

Now let's get on with making rosy, juicy fruits and vegetables to "sell" from our old fashioned fruit stand. Recalling their own market experience, encourage children to draw their "produce" deliciously, capturing their original, vivid colors. Remember too, that to a green grocer, an apple is not just an "apple"–it can be a Delicious, MacIntosh, Rome, Green, or Golden apple. Each is different in color or shape. Avoid turning out tiny looking or vague lumps. For a lush look, have the harvest "life-sized."

Make sure the market doesn't turn into a one or two item display. "More peppers, please." "Isn't anyone going to grow some potatoes?" "How about onions!" Once children are absorbed drawing their stock to trade, select several youngsters to decorate bulletin board pushcart.

PROCEDURE (Illustration 5-1)

1. Distribute the drawing paper, crayons and scissors, Ask the children to draw, color and cut out a variety of fruits and vegetables. (step a)
2. Cover the bulletin board with background paper. In pencil, draw the frame of an open vegetable cart, complete with a canopy and wheels. Have the children gaily decorate the completed drawing with crayons. (step b)
3. Cut thin strips of construction paper, long enough to stretch across the width of the cart. These strips are then stapled in place, forming compartments or "pockets" to hold the paper fruits and vegetables. (step c) Make certain to staple the strips along the bottom and side edge only–do not close off the slots (or pockets) at the top edge.
4. Ask the children to come to the fruit stand, one at a time, identify their crayoned produce, and insert it into a slot on the bulletin board pushcart. Keep each new variety in its own special section; apples with apples, peppers with peppers and so on. (step d)
5. Write the produce names and their respective prices on small squares of paper, to be called "markers," and attach these to toothpicks. Insert each marker in its proper pocket. (step e)

WHAT THE CHILDREN CAN DO AFTERWARD

1. Learn to identify produce by playing "market." Have the children take turns being a "vegetable man." As classmates ask for a particular fruit or vegetable, it's his job to find and sell it. Use the opportunity to judge cost; is 6 for 25¢ the same as 5¢ apiece? Each "vegetable man" should suggest other items carried, stressing price and quality, so that the class may learn how salesmanship encourages extra sales.
2. Have the children write practical arithmetic problems, based on the marketing experience, for the class to solve.

RELAX WITH TIME SAVERS

1. Place the background paper on the bulletin board and cut out the construction paper strips in advance. The latter may later be trimmed to fit the cart.
2. Provide extra drawing paper in front of the room. When needed, children may help themselves.

FRUIT AND VEGETABLE WREATH (Illustration 5-2)

ILLUSTRATION 5-2

MATERIALS

1. colored chalk
2. heavy drawing paper
3. oaktag
4. paste
5. fixative

BEFORE YOU BEGIN

Harvesting done, Thanksgiving heralds, and another Christmas is about to begin. To add to the joy of these seasons, gather fruits and vegetables into a wreath of myriad colors. For motivational tips, borrow "The Pushcart" activity format. Remember to save and store this creative project for future decorative use.

PROCEDURE

1. Pass out the drawing paper. Using assorted colored chalk, have children draw a variety of brightly hued fruits and vegetables. Make these life-sized.
2. Spray the chalk drawing with fixative.
3. Cut out each individual fruit or vegetable.
4. Draw and cut out a large wreath shape from a sheet of oaktag.
5. Call children, two or three at a time, to paste their contributions to the wreath. Place cut-outs close together, with emphasis on contrasting color combinations. Continue pasting until the entire wreath is filled.

WHAT THE CHILDREN CAN DO AFTERWARD

1. Tape the wreath to the classroom door. Add a sign "We Welcome the Fruits of Autumn."

2. Learn traditional harvest songs.
3. Use the wreath as decoration for a "Food Unit" bulletin board.

RELAX WITH TIME SAVERS

1. Have two or three children share a box of chalk.
2. Keep a supply of extra drawing paper in front of the room. Children may help themselves.
3. Place a can or two of fixative spray in front of the room. When all drawing has been completed, children may apply fixative at this station.
4. Have the children wash their hands of all chalk residue before attaching the chalk cut-outs to the wreath. Use an applicator stick when applying paste to the back of the cut-outs.

TISSUE PAPER FRUITS

ILLUSTRATION 5-3

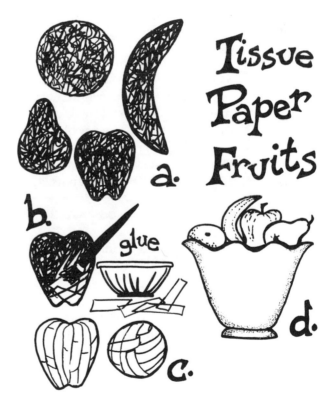

MATERIALS

1. aluminum foil
2. tissue paper—assortment of bright colors
3. polymer acrylic medium or white glue, diluted with water
4. brushes
5. pipe cleaners
6. spray shellac, optional
7. paint, optional

BEFORE YOU BEGIN

A little ingenuity and a lot of tissue paper can brim a cornucopia with fruit forever. Even Mom will agree, this centerpiece is elegant enough to proudly grace her dining table.

Begin with a selection of real fruits for children to handle, noting their shapes in detail. Try with eyes closed, too; enabling children to "feel" will help them sculpt later. They will discover that some apples are "bumpy," top and bottom. Others are rounder. A pear becomes a combination of a small triangle atop a circle. "What about bananas?" "They curve, don't they?" Keep samples available as the class works; some children may require additional comparisons.

Diluted white glue may be substituted if a polymer acrylic medium is unavailable. The latter has the advantage of producing a sturdier product, containing its own glaze, and being water resistant. Where paint is to be applied, go lightly. The brilliance of the tissue paper, made slightly translucent by the acrylic medium, provides sufficient color. Variations may be achieved by overlapping different shades of tissue paper. Therefore, painted strokes, when used, should merely convey subtle shadings and, perhaps, detail.

PROCEDURE (Illustration 5-3)

1. Distribute the aluminum foil. Have each child model three or four life-sized fruits. (step a)
2. With a brush, apply a small amount of polymer acrylic medium, or diluted white glue to the surface of the aluminum foil fruit. Cover the fruit with tissue paper. Work a small area at a time, overlapping the paper, smoothing it, and applying new amounts of glue when necessary. Continue to shape the tissue paper sheets as it is worked over the aluminum foil. Several tissue paper sheets may be applied. (steps b & c)
3. Allow the foil and paper objects to dry.
4. If desired, paint on the details. Let the fruits dry.
5. Insert pipe cleaner stems. (step d)
6. If glue and water has been used, coat each fruit with spray shellac.

WHAT THE CHILDREN CAN DO AFTERWARD

1. Ask each child to bring in a bowl or basket from home. Arrange the fruit decoratively and give to mother as a centerpiece display.
2. Make and donate the fruits as centerpieces for a PTA luncheon or other school functions.
3. Sell fruits at a school fund raising event.
4. Attach a thin wire to each fruit, and suspend it from the ceiling, or use it as a Christmas tree decoration.
5. Use fruits in a class fruit market display. These may be "bought" and "sold" as part of an arithmetic lesson.

RELAX WITH TIME SAVERS

1. Complete the aluminum foil sculpture before distributing additional materials. One roll of foil should serve four to five children.
2. Spread newspaper before gluing and again before painting.

3. Pre-mix glue and water, and distribute the mixture in paint cups; one cup for two children to share.
4. Provide an assortment of colored tissue paper sheets for each table. Cut these down to reasonable size beforehand.
5. Set up a painting station in the back of the room. Those who wish to add painted details should complete this job in the specified area.
6. The teacher should spray fruits with shellac in a well ventilated section of room. Allow the fruits to stand, untouched, until they have dried thoroughly.
7. Appoint two or three assistants to collect and wash the brushes.

BEAN AND SEED MOSAICS

ILLUSTRATION 5-4

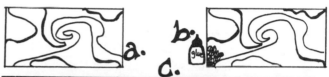

MATERIALS

1. sheet of stiff cardboard
2. white glue, brushes for applying
3. assortment of packaged seeds and dried beans (pumpkin seeds, lentils, barley, Indian corn, pinto beans, split peas)
4. spray shellac
5. sheet of newspaper
6. pencils
7. cupcake tins

BEFORE YOU BEGIN

Combine a handful of beans and a smidgen of seeds with flights of fancy—you'll come up with intriguing mosaics. At the same time, launch an introduction to the methods of food preservation among American Indians and pioneers. These very beans are exactly like those used in the old days to stave off hunger during lean winters; to many they meant survival. Even today, where fresh vegetables are unavailable, people depend on such foods. Perhaps you can plan an eat-in soup lunch, prepared, of course, from dried beans (canned soup, chosen for its use of legumes may be substituted).

Request that dried foods be brought from home. Explain that these will be used to make pictures, called mosaics. "Has anyone ever seen a mosaic?" Chances are many have; on floors, church murals, tables and wall hangings. Have a picture or sample on hand. It won't take children long to understand that a mosaic is made by simply placing bits of some material (usually tiles) close together to form a design or picture. Today's mosaics, of course, will be made of beans and seeds.

After the dried foods are examined and identified, drop a few and let them fall in a random pattern on a sheet of paper. Ask one or two children to experiment making a simple picture (beans and seeds shouldn't overlap). Armed with a variety of seeds, beans, free choice, and jumping imaginations, children are now ready to cook up some mosaics of their own.

PROCEDURE (Illustration 5-4)

1. Distribute an assortment of beans in cupcake tins—one tin for every two or three children to share. Spread newspaper. By lifting the paper and spilling the enclosed beans, scattered bits can easily be returned to their respective containers without waste.
2. Pass out a sheet of cardboard and pencils. Ask the children to draw anything they please. Though given full freedom of design, caution your class to avoid many tiny shapes in this first attempt. Too much detail may produce undefined results for those unfamiliar with the technique. For beginners, faces, animals, trees and abstracts emerge pleasingly. (step a)
3. Once drawings are completed to satisfaction, distribute glue and an assortment of lentils and seeds.
4. Work one small section of the drawing at a time. Allow the glue to sparingly flow over a given area, spreading it evenly with a brush. Place the desired beans or seeds, one next to another, over the glued portions of the cardboard drawing. Small bits, such as split peas, can be sprinkled over a desired section. The excess is then shaken from the cardboard to the newspaper, then returned to the cupcake tins for re-use. (step b)
5. Make certain to cover the entire cardboard—drawing and background. (step c)
6. From time to time, each child should view his work from a distance to judge what colors or minor changes are needed.
7. Coat the completed mosaic with spray shellac, and let it dry thoroughly.

WHAT THE CHILDREN CAN DO AFTERWARD

1. Do research, then write reports which tell how people survived by preserving foods.
2. Apply stick-on picture hangers to the backs of the cardboard and give the mosaics as gifts.

3. Have each child hold up his mosaic for the class to observe and discuss. "How many different beans and seeds were used?" "What are their names?"
4. Use the completed mosaics as a bulletin board decoration.

RELAX WITH TIME SAVERS

1. If possible, use glue containers with "control flow" tops. Two to four children can share one bottle.
2. Distribute an assortment of beans and seeds in cupcake tins. Place boxes and packages of seeds and beans in front of the room with spoons, for those requiring re-fills.
3. Select a helper from each table to collect the brushes, wash them well, and store them for future use.
4. Help the children apply shellac. This job should be done in a well ventilated area of the room, according to the directions on the can.

VEGETABLE PRINTING

MATERIALS

1. vegetables and fruits (cut crosswise in thick slices) such as cucumbers, lemons, potatoes, celery, oranges, green peppers, and the like
2. paint and brushes
3. painting paper
4. newspaper
5. small kitchen knife

BEFORE YOU BEGIN

Hardly gastronomical, this menu will be remembered because, though it looks good, it's surely not for eating! A feast for the eyes, our salad is all fruit and vegetable. To enjoy, dab each ingredient lightly with paint, then deliciously print on paper. Make a weird fruit jungle, make a merry vaudeville of vegetable clowns, but make them splendidly vibrant!

Demonstrate the printing technique by applying paint to a vegetable cross-section then pressing it against the paper. When making the first impression, blot off any excess paint on a piece of scrap, or newspaper to avoid blurred results. During the demonstration, have each child experiment with and exploit the possibilities of a different vegetable. The result: a blaze of line, shape, and color.

Note, two procedures are described for this lesson. The first reproduces the actual lines and shapes of the vegetable cross-sections. Procedure II, potato printing, provides an interesting, exciting variation.

lemon

onion

Vegetable
Printing

potato

carrot

ILLUSTRATION 5-5

PROCEDURE I (Illustration 5-5)

1. Spread newspaper on the desks before starting to paint.
2. Distribute paint, brushes, paper and a varied assortment of vegetables, sliced in thick cross-sections, to each each table.
3. Brush paint over the face of a cross-sectioned vegetable to be used for printing. *Cover the entire surface.*
4. Stamp the first print firmly on a sheet of newspaper. Add more paint, if necessary. Caution the children that if they press too hard with a vegetable, the result will be blurred and undefined.
5. Should the surface of the fruit or vegetable become worn, slice away the painted surface, exposing a new layer.
6. Allow the paintings to dry.
7. Fill in extra brush work by hand for added interest or meaning.

PROCEDURE II (Illustration 5-6)

1. Cut a large potato in half.
2. Using a small kitchen knife, whittle a pattern on the surface of the exposed potato cross-section (use both halves to make and print two patterns, if desired).
3. Apply paint and stamp as described above in Procedure I.

ILLUSTRATION 5-6

WHAT THE CHILDREN CAN DO AFTERWARD

1. Give the paintings imaginative titles.
2. Have each child hold up his painting and ask the class to guess which vegetables were used.
3. Tack the paintings to a bulletin board. Surround the border with crayoned and cut-out pictures of whole fruits and vegetables.
4. If possible, print on cloth using a fabric dye paint. Make a lively set of curtains for the room.
5. Decorate plain writing or note paper with vegetable prints.
6. Try printing on inexpensive, solid colored wallpaper. Use this as a backdrop for a play, or as a room divider.

RELAX WITH TIME SAVERS

1. Slice the fruits and vegetables large enough so that they may be comfortably held while printing.
2. Distribute paint in plastic ice-cube trays; one for every three children to share.
3. Do not permit young children to slice "worn" fruit layers—this is a job for the teacher.
4. Choose an assistant from each table to collect paint trays and brushes, wash them well and store them for future use.

SCULPT A "DINNER" (Illustration 5-7)

MATERIALS

1. Play-dough recipe (for eight children). Combine two cups of cornstarch and four cups baking soda in a saucepan. Slowly mix in 2 1/2 cups water. Add a few drops of lemon juice. Cook the mixture over a slow flame for several minutes, stirring constantly, until it reaches a dough-like consistency. Allow it to cool. Knead the dough on a wooden board, until it is workable as clay.
2. toothpicks, pencils, pens and other available tools for sculpting
3. paint and brushes
4. spray shellac, or clear nail polish—optional
5. small bowls of water
6. newspaper

BEFORE YOU BEGIN

Since that flat meatball was invented, Mothers have harrassed their young to "Eat properly . . . you can't live on hamburgers, french fries and soda pop!" In this day of enlightenment, many a youngster may quip back with " . . . protein, fat and carbohydrate." Usually, he knows it's not well-balanced, for indeed he's heard it enough. But, that kind of eating sure is fun. Very well, let's enjoy ourselves.

ILLUSTRATION 5-7

Move away from prosaic bulletin board "good eating habit" pictures by sculpting a dinner menu instead. There's no guarantee that this alone will incur a better sense of nutrition. However, if tied in with a sound introduction to basic food groups, and their relation to the three traditional meals a day, some of its importance might sink in.

Divide your class into three committees: "Breakfast," "Lunch," and "Supper." With the teacher's supervision, groups should meet to plan an assortment of appropriate menus. Each child will "prepare" one meal from the dough.

Since the "clay" takes several days to harden before painting, there is ample time to present these menus for class discussion.

PROCEDURE

1. Spread newspaper on the tables.
2. Distribute dough, small bowls of water, and sculpting "tools." Have each child mold his menu items from the dough, moistening hands, occasionally, from the available bowls of water. Remind your class to use sculpting tools to make these foods look real. Though models will be painted, the unadorned clay should resemble the food as closely as possible.
3. Allow the models to dry.
4. Paint the molded foods. Urge the children to permit the first coat of paint to dry before adding detail colors. Allow the models to dry thoroughly.
5. If desired, shellac the finished products, or coat them with clear nail polish.

WHAT THE CHILDREN CAN DO AFTERWARD

1. Give each child a paper plate on which to arrange his "meal." Food names, and their respective food groups, should be listed on a file card, and displayed with models on a large table.

2. Play "restaurant." Prepare written menus, choose waiters, and learn to order when eating out. Each committee could be responsible for a skit, portraying proper restaurant manners and the ordering of nutritional meals.
3. Arrange to have play-dough meals displayed in the school cafeteria for other classes to observe. Large posters, encouraging good eating habits, should accompany the exhibit.
4. "How far must meat, diary, and vegetables travel to reach us?" To show where food comes from, glue play-dough models to respective areas of a large bulletin board map of the United States.

RELAX WITH TIME SAVERS

1. Prepare the dough well in advance of the lesson; it may be wrapped in plastic, refrigerated over night, and used at room temperature the next day. If cooking facilities are available, you might wish to involve the class in this cooking and measuring experience. Clay must cool, so prepare it early in the day for use the same afternoon.
2. Mold the clay into several equal-sized balls—one for each table. Children can help themselves to necessary amounts.
3. Provide a safe area where models may harden.
4. Spread newspaper on the tables before sculpting, and again before painting.
5. Distribute assorted colors of paint in plastic ice-cube trays.
6. Should breakage occur, simply repair models with white glue and allow them to dry thoroughly before re-painting.
7. Choose table helpers to collect and wash brushes and ice-cube trays.

VITAMIN ART

MATERIALS

1. construction paper
2. paste
3. descriptive magazine and newspaper cut-outs (see explanation below)
4. scissors

BEFORE YOU BEGIN

Platoons of life-giving vitamins that nourish us as we dine are, unfortunately, only hazily understood and valued by the very young. First, learn which vitamins are inherent in natural foods. Then, with a single vitamin in mind, have the children dig through magazines and newspapers for representative clippings.

For example, let's take vitamin "A". It promotes growth, good vision, and helps keep one's skin normal. This can all be made visual with magazine pictures—eyes, in myriad colors and shapes, people in varying sizes, complexion ads, plus the

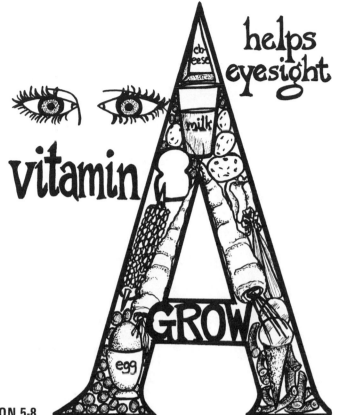

ILLUSTRATION 5-8

interspersion of words such as "skin," "tall," "short," and "growth." Vital to the story of "A", green and yellow vegetables, cheese and milk, must also be included. Where a desired food picture is unavailable, substitution of cut-out letters to spell its name can have a startling effect.

Forget the traditional poster look. Pasted materials may overlap, giving our friend the vitamin an eye-catching summation.

PROCEDURE (Illustration 5-8)

1. Distribute the construction paper, paste and scissors. Have the children cut out pictures, words and letters.
2. Place these cut-outs on a table. Before pasting, try some trial arrangements. The overall look should be informative as well as pleasing in pattern.
3. When satisfied with the arrangement, paste the cut-outs in place on a sheet of construction paper. Fill the entire paper.

WHAT THE CHILDREN CAN DO AFTERWARD

1. Use the pasted arrangement as a scrap book cover for a food unit.
2. Make vitamin charts, indicating vitamin functions and in what foods they are found. Display these charts and projects on a bulletin board.

3. Tack the pictures to a bulletin board as an informative decoration.
4. Write whimsical stories about Vitamin People and lands they inhabit (e.g., King "A" rules the mountain of butter and eggs; his army protects good vision).

RELAX WITH TIME SAVERS

1. Avoid sticky desks by spreading newspaper before pasting.
2. To keep cut-outs "neat" and "pressed," have the children place them between the pages of a book until they are ready for use.
3. Provide extra newspaper and magazines for those requiring additional items.
4. Paste, smeared on the front surfaces of the cut-outs will, of course, produce sloppy work. Keep hands mess-free by using applicator sticks to apply small amounts of paste at a time to the backs of the cut-outs.

CREEPY GOURDS

ILLUSTRATION 5-9

MATERIALS

1. gourds
2. paint and brushes
3. spray shellac
4. newspaper
5. pipe cleaners, paper clips, wires, pins

BEFORE YOU BEGIN

In the land of a child's fantasy, gourd people make most natural tenants. Grotesque as they may be in a natural state, imagination, paint, and humor often coax the gourds into unearthly, often incredibly funny caricatures.

Allow several days for the gathering of these gourds from home. As the class considers the collection of odd shapes, put them on the dream track with "If this gourd reminds you of somebody, or something somewhere . . . shhh, keep it a secret!" To lend to the sport, each gargoyled gourd should, when finished, be a special surprise. With all the children "doing their own thing," prepare for the zaniest gourd people parade ever!

PROCEDURE (Illustration 5-9)

1. Spread newspaper on the tables before starting to paint.
2. Using paint and brushes, have the children transform their gourds into whimsical creatures. Allow them to dry.
3. Insert pipe cleaners, wires, pins, and the like, to make antennae ears, and crazy hair-dos. Bend the paper clips, and insert them as feet in the bottom of the gourd (if the gourd wobbles, secure the clip with a small amount of clay).
4. Coat the finished product with spray shellac.

WHAT THE CHILDREN CAN DO AFTERWARD

1. Make up crazy names for the creatures and display, for fun, on a table in the room.
2. Write stories about gourd people giving them unlikely names and homes. Tack these on a bulletin board above the gourd display.
3. Give the gourds as gifts to mother for use as kitchen decoration, or give them to younger brothers and sisters.
4. Have a gourd play. Insert manipulating sticks in the bottom of each gourd and work it from behind a desk.

RELAX WITH TIME SAVERS

1. To avoid mix-ups, ask each child to write his name on the bottom of his gourd before bringing it to school.
2. Distribute paint in plastic ice-cube containers for every three children to share.
3. Set up a spraying station in a well ventilated area of the room where painted gourds may be varnished.

SPICE COLLAGE

MATERIALS

1. assorted bottles of spices and herbs (use products with perforated tops, if possible)
2. boxes of whole spices and herbs, such as cloves, cinnamon sticks, bay leaves
3. white glue and paint brushes
4. water
5. construction paper
6. pencils—optional

7. newspaper
8. cupcake tins and spoon

BEFORE YOU BEGIN

The tale of Christopher Columbus chronicles the search for spices from the exotic east. One can only imagine their importance, for they were used in medicine, perfume and flavoring. Yet, when asked to mention a few, or quote the uses of these aromatics, many a child comes up with a vague, "They have something to do with food." Columbus would have been aghast at such understatement! Hence, this spice collage.

A whole study to be remembered begins here. How many know that pepper and nutmeg come from the fruit? That a flower bud brings forth the clove? That cinnamon is a bark?

The very best way to appreciate the pungency, the perfume of spices, is to smell, feel, and taste. Underscore their roles by preparing a simple vegetable, first unseasoned, and then with savory additions. Watch for a class of connoisseurs as young tastebuds gain sophistication. If class cooking is not feasible, use labels from prepared food, and note the spice content on a class list—basil, cinnamon, ginger, nutmeg, oregano, thyme and scores more (as a language arts aside, notice how these words lend themselves easily to lessons in spelling syllabification and alphabetizing).

These spices, sprinkled on a sheet of paper produce some rather engaging abstracts. Of course, conservatives, desiring a definite "picture" may certainly make one. Most important, is the use of contrasting colors and varied textures. Parsley, placed next to some oregano leaves will show up poorly, as will the combination of peppercorns and whole cloves. When in doubt, children may, before gluing, sprinkle sparing amounts of each spice on paper to consider the effects. Minds changed, spices may easily be returned to a container for re-use. Demonstrate the latter procedure, cautioning against waste.

PROCEDURE (Illustration 5-10)

1. Place newspaper on tables, and distribute cupcake tins. Show how, by folding up the sides of the newspaper, and carefully pouring, the scattered spices can be returned to cupcake tins.
2. Hand out paper, brushes, white glue, water cups and an assortment of bottled and boxed spices and herbs.
3. Those desiring a "picture" in place of an abstract, should draw it in pencil on construction paper before receiving spices. (step a)
4. Work a small area at a time. Place a small amount of glue on a portion of the construction paper and spread it over a given area with a brush. Dip the brush in water occasionally to dilute the glue so that it will spread evenly. (step b)
5. Place the desired spices and herbs over the glued area. Those which pour easily may be sprinkled from bottles with perforated tops. Larger pieces, such as cloves, bay leaves and peppercorns should be added individually. (step b)

ILLUSTRATION 5-10

6. After each spice application, shake excess onto newspaper. Pour into cupcake tins and save. Accumulated spices in tins may later be spooned back into bottles.

WHAT THE CHILDREN CAN DO AFTERWARD

1. Make a class chart to indicate the spices used in this collage lesson.
2. Glue the construction paper design to a sheet of heavy cardboard for use as a wall hanging. Give it as a gift.

RELAX WITH TIME SAVERS

1. Those working on "pictures" instead of abstracts should complete a pencilled drawing before they're given spices and glue.
2. Provide as varied an assortment of spices as possible for each table to share.
3. One cup of water, and one cupcake tin serve three to four children.
4. Demonstrate how to apply glue without either saturating paper or leaving "globs." Use controlled flow glue bottles where possible.
5. Spoon spices from cupcake tins to bottles at the lesson's end.
6. Have a helper pass a wastebasket so that newspaper and debris may be discarded.

STILL—LIFE PLAQUES

MATERIALS

1. shirt cardboard—one sheet for cutouts, one for background
2. newspaper—torn into strips approximately 1″ wide and 5″ long
3. wheat paste and water solution
4. scissors
5. pencils
6. paint and brushes
7. scrap paper
8. spray shellac (optional)
9. old toothbrush

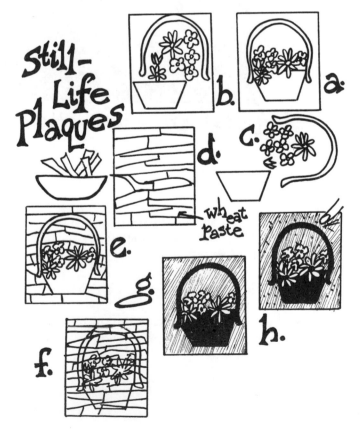

ILLUSTRATION 5-11

BEFORE YOU BEGIN

Asked to describe a "still life," most children will respond "fruits and bottles." This understatement may be clarified by explaining how the great masters created paintings by combining both the inanimate and commonplace. After gathering available pepper mills, casseroles, fruits, vegetables, flowers—even canned soup—have children "play" with these arrangements. Just a wee bit of thought can turn a dull collection of utensils into striking displays. Study these to discover what makes one juxtaposition stimulating, another tedious.

What we are about to do is paint, and antique, pâpier-maché still-life plaques for Mom's kitchen. Time and care is of the essence here, so make this a project for older children.

For those wishing to "test out" their ideas first, allow time for making "set ups" and preliminary sketches.

PROCEDURE (Illustration 5-11)

1. On scrap paper, sketch a still life. To complete the plaque, each item in this sketch must be individually re-drawn on cardboard and cut out. With this in mind, beginners should avoid too many small shapes and details. (step a)
2. Copy each item in the sketch on the first cardboard sheet. Remember to draw each individual shape proportionately. These shapes will later be cut out and pasted to the plaque, according to the initially sketched arrangement. If the sketch contained a bowl of fruit, the cardboard fruit should not be drawn larger than the bowl! (step b)
3. Neatly cut out the cardboard shapes. (step c)
4. Cover the front of the second sheet of shirt cardboard with newspaper strips that have first been dipped into a wheat paste and water solution. Apply these strips so that they overlap in a basket weave type pattern. The resulting surface should be textured, rather than smooth. (step d)
5. When the cardboard sheet has been completely covered, place the still-life cut-outs on the newspaper covered plaque, following the sketched arrangement. When satisfied with the placement, cover each cut-out with papier-maché and attach it to the cardboard sheet. (steps e & f)
6. Apply a final layer of newspaper to the plaque, molding it around the shapes. The still-life should acquire a three-dimensional quality. This raised effect may be further developed by simply shaping additional layers of papier-maché over the cut-outs. (step f)
7. Permit the entire plaque to dry thoroughly; this may take two or three days.
8. Paint the plaque colorfully. Don't rush this step—planning out the use of color is as important as the arrangement. (step g)
9. To antique: dip a stiff brush (toothbrush) into a solution of brown paint and water (make this solution very thin). Holding the brush several inches from the plaque, run your thumb over the bristles, spraying the "antiquing" over the entire still-life. Using a finger, rub some of the solution onto the edges of the plaque. *Don't over-do.* (step h)
10. Let the antiquing dry. Finish it with a coat of spray shellac.

WHAT THE CHILDREN CAN DO AFTERWARD

1. Attach stick-on picture hangers to the plaques and give them as gifts.
2. Collect prints of still-life paintings by famous artists for study and display; don't forget Van Gogh and Cezanne!

RELAX WITH TIME SAVERS

1. Complete the sketches and cardboard cut-outs before introducing pâpier-maché. As children work, cut newspaper strips and prepare the wheat paste and water solution.
2. Spread newspaper on desks before handing out pâpier-maché materials, and then again before painting.
3. Provide a bowl of wheat paste and water, plus newspaper strips to every table of five.
4. Have extra paper available. Choose a table helper to cut additional strips when necessary.
5. Find a safe area where the plaques may dry. Table helpers should clean and store the pâpier-maché bowls for future use.
6. Distribute paint in plastic ice-cube trays; one to every three children.
7. All antiquing should be done in one area of the room (two to three children at a time), under teacher supervision.
8. Shellac the plaques in a well ventilated area of the room.

PASTA IN ABSTRACT

MATERIALS

1. Assorted pasta shapes (rigatoni, shells, wheels, manicotti, lasagne, spaghetti)
2. white glue and brushes
3. shirt cardboard
4. scissors
5. paint and brushes
6. shellac—optional

ILLUSTRATION 5-12

BEFORE YOU BEGIN

In this day of art anything goes, including the use of spaghetti as a medium. All those marvelous rounds of rigatoni, shells, wheels, wavy and flat pasta combine here to produce original, if not weird, wall hangings.

Many days before the lesson, request that children bring in the most unusual boxed macaroni they can find. Since most artistic results depend on a diverse assortment, gleen everything from minute soup garnishes to mammoth manicotti.

PROCEDURE (Illustration 5-12)

1. Distribute cardboard, assorted pasta shapes, glue and brushes.
2. Have children begin by experimentally arranging pasta shapes on the cardboard to achieve a basic design. They may use the entire cardboard, or a smaller area. Any exposed cardboard will later be trimmed, leaving the sculpture only.
3. Using brushes for the pasting operation, glue the basic arrangement to the cardboard. Selecting an assortment of pasta shapes, "build up" sculpture to add interest and dimension. (step a) Each new addition should be held firmly in place with a finger until it has partially adhered. Avoid lifting the cardboard from the table until the sculpture is complete and somewhat "tacky." Unnecessary movement may cause pasta pieces to fall off.
4. Allow the glued sculpture to dry thoroughly.
5. Carefully trim the exposed cardboard with scissors so that only the pasta sculpture shows.
6. Decoratively paint the plaque. Let it dry. (step b)
7. If desired, spray the painted plaque with shellac. Let it dry.

WHAT THE CHILDREN CAN DO AFTERWARD

1. Attach stick-on picture hangers to the plaques and give them as gifts.
2. Ask each child to title his sculpture. Display it in school window cases.

RELAX WITH TIME SAVERS

1. Spread newspapers before gluing and again before painting.
2. Depending on the size and shape, distribute each variety of pasta in a separate box or cup. Ask that unused macaroni be returned to an appropriate container. Each table should receive a varied assortment.
3. Glue should be poured into small painting cups; one cup to be shared by two or three children.
4. Assist children as they trim the exposed cardboard, making certain the sculptured plaque has dried first.
5. Distribute paint in plastic ice-cube trays.
6. If projects are to be varnished, set up a spraying station in a well ventilated area of the room. Provide a place for the plaques to safely dry.
7. Repair any breakage with white glue. When dry, re-paint the damaged area.

Bonus Ideas

1. Make a giant sized "Food Album," using oaktag sheets as pages. Each page should have a theme (e.g., Vitamins: How They Help Us). Fill the pages using the approach suggested in "Vitamin Art." Committees may be chosen to complete each page.
2. Use the "Vitamin Art" suggestion to decorate kitchen cannisters (e.g., flour cannister might contain pictures of cakes, cookies, flour bags, and the letters F–L–O–U–R, cut from newspaper and magazines).
3. Sculpt attractive fruits and vegetables from the play dough recipe and give them as gifts.
4. The still-life plaque suggestion may be adapted to any holiday theme; an excellent project for Thanksgiving, Christmas, Father's Day, and so on.
5. For Indian headbands, paste bits of pasta, beans, and seeds to heavy paper or stiff fabric.
6. Kindergarteners love to string macaroni and paper scraps into colorful necklaces. To color pasta, dip it into food coloring—allow it to dry before stringing.
7. Use beans and seeds as "wampum" to teach the concept of currency.
8. Use those extra beans to make bean bags.
9. Plant and study lima beans as they grow.
10. Make papier-maché baskets for tissue paper fruits. Attach an inexpensive chain to the baskets, and suspend them from the ceiling.
11. Write a book of recipes. Decorate the cover with vegetable printing.
12. Make musical instruments from scooped out, dried gourds.
13. Decorate wrapping paper with vegetable prints.
14. Embedded in clay, macaroni sculpture becomes an unearthly fantasy city.
15. Using bottles, odd objects and tissue paper fruits, make still life displays. Set them in shadow boxes.

The Human Body

As the boy stretches towards the sun in growth, thinking his muscles and freckles are miracles, so does the little girl, all curls and thick lashes, swoon with her reflection in the mirror. In this chapter, we are about to compare these features which make us alike, yet so different. All in fun, we'll kid ourselves with "Self-Portrait" caricatures and "Op Art Faces."

Shifting attention, we'll also check our innards with the "Inside Story Chart," then watch the "Grow Board" as passing months add inches to little bodies. Creeping into this amusing self-evaluation are some very solid drawing lessons, concealed in "Figure Scribbling" and "Body Building."

All we are doing here, is twinkling a small light to illuminate some of the abstract and complex fundamentals of the human machine; how it moves, how it looks, but mostly, what makes it tick.

FIGURE SCRIBBLING

MATERIALS

1. 18" x 24" newsprint
2. two crayons—different colors

BEFORE YOU BEGIN

Labeled "Daddy," the child's crayon can hatch a watermelon head atop outsize spidery legs, arms sprouting where ears should be. The proportions of the human form can quickly be put into perspective with this simple figure scribbling device.

Have the class stand and ask them to:

1. bend over. "Which part of your body is larger; from your waist to your head, or from your waist to your toes?"

2. touch their elbows to their sides—they land at the waist.
3. place their hands flat against their sides. Many never realized that the arm and hand extend to mid-thigh.
4. spread one hand over their face. Both are almost equal in size. Also point out that feet are larger than one's hands, never smaller.

Though today's lesson is unconcerned with facial details, use the opportunity to illustrate some relative proportions. Choose a model to stand before group, and "draw" an imaginary line from the top of his ear, across his face. It's eye level. A second "line," from the bottom of his ear, aligns approximately with the upper lip.

Often compounding his difficulty is the child's desire to show action rather than straight, stiff figures. With an assist from a cardboard Halloween skeleton, show how movement takes place at the joints; knees, elbows, and wrists. Combine this visual demonstration with actual movement by having the youngsters bend in varied positions. Try dancing poses, "throwing" a ball, and "swinging" a bat. Hold each position in a frieze. Consider the placement of the arms and legs in relation to the rest of the body as these action poses are assumed.

Armed with a new awareness, most will register surprise at their ability to scribble pose after pose. Demonstrate the scribbling technique on the board. Explain that each sequence will be timed. If unable to complete a particular pose, the children should forget it and go on to the next one. Later, allow time for the completion of the unfinished figures.

Though basically an exercise in drawing, the abstract results make compelling bulletin board displays.

PROCEDURE (Illustration 6-1)

1. Fold the newsprint in fourths. Each section of folded paper will be used for a new sequence. (step a)
2. Request a child to come to the front of the room. Ask him to assume some action pose; hopping, boxing, kneeling, etc. (step b)
3. Give the class a few seconds to study the posed figure. "Look at the model, and at one of the four boxes on your paper. Try to imagine the shape filling one entire box on newsprint. Choose a crayon. You have one minute to scribble in the figure and fill in the first box on your paper." (It may take one or two attempts for children to catch on, so allow time for several poses.) (step c)
4. Choose a new model for each pose. Go on to the next box and, using a second crayon, repeat the procedure. The activity may continue as long as both teacher and class wish. (step c)
5. (Optional) Delineate and define the scribble figures with a contrasting color crayon.

WHAT THE CHILDREN CAN DO AFTERWARD

1. Title the drawings and display them on a bulletin board.

ILLUSTRATION 6-1

2. Scribble figures without the aid of live models.
3. For a new twist, try "scribbling" inanimate objects around room.

RELAX WITH TIME SAVERS

1. Complete all the paper folding before the scribbling exercise. If time has been allowed for many poses, have additional folded sheets ready in advance.
2. Save time and space. Completed drawings should be placed beneath the blank sheets of newsprint, or placed carefully on the floor.
3. Tell the class to keep their eyes on the posed figures, not the clock. The teacher is the "timer." Most likely, a few will complete all the scribbling sequences. Dispel protests by assuring the children an opportunity to complete the unfinished scribble figures at the lesson's end.

BODY BUILDING DRAWINGS

BEFORE YOU BEGIN

All about, we see and hear advertising exhorting us to greater health and beauty. Whether we believe Madison Avenue's version or not, exercise is quickly becoming a national pastime. Young and old, in response to fashion, judgement, and mass media's advice, can be found skiing, jogging, jumping, golfing, skating, and leaping about tennis courts. Capitalize on the familiar trend in your next art lesson.

Reviewing the previous "figure scribbling" exercise provides a solid background for these detailed, realistic drawings. Ask each child to choose a particular "action pose" relative to a favorite game or exercise (some may wish pictures illustrating several poses at one time). One needn't select complex contortions. In fact, the simpler the pose, the easier it is for youngsters to concentrate on properly proportioned figures. Encourage your class to act out their ideas, or pose for one another, as they work. Those who still find figure drawing difficult may adopt the scribbling technique, outlining the completed shapes to add definition. Concentrate on figures only; such additions as tennis rackets or skis may be added later.

ILLUSTRATION 6-2

MATERIALS

1. drawing paper
2. crayons
3. large sheet of construction paper
4. small sheets of construction paper
5. scissors
6. paste

PROCEDURE (Illustration 6-2)

1. Hand out paper and crayons. Have the children draw and color action poses.
2. Where equipment additions (balls, nets, rackets) are desired or needed, cut them from colored construction paper and paste them in place. (steps a & b)
3. Staple the drawing to a larger background sheet of construction paper. (step b)

WHAT THE CHILDREN CAN DO AFTERWARD

1. Title each drawing. Display it on a bulletin board.
2. Start a physical fitness campaign. Write appropriate slogans to accompany the drawings. Display these in school halls.
3. Make a physical fitness mural. Have each child cut out his action pose and paste his contribution to a large sheet of mural paper. Construction paper cut-outs of equipment complete the picture.

RELAX WITH TIME SAVERS

1. Have small sheets of construction paper and paste available in the front of the room. Children may help themselves. Scraps should be shared to limit waste.
2. Set up a pasting station. All pasting should be done in this designated area.

SELF—PORTRAIT (Illustration 6-3)

MATERIALS

1. large sheet of drawing paper (about the size of a newspaper sheet)
2. black and white tempera paint
3. brushes
4. small mirrors from home

ILLUSTRATION 6-3

BEFORE YOU BEGIN

"Look in the mirror and what do you see?" No one is going to attempt anything beyond his ability, so what difference does it make if today's self-portrait turns out to be a caricature? More fun that way!

With eyes closed, feel for ears, nose and eyes. "What about the shape of the face—is it round? pear shaped? oval? "Use little hand mirrors and neighbor's observation to compare features. "Are your eyes round? almond shaped? large or small?" "What does your nose look like? Is it straight, aquiline, long or short?"

Now that the child has taken a few minutes for penetrating study of what he looks like, go on to the unusual characteristics. Consider singular hairstyles, glasses, even freckles.

Tell the children they are to fill their paper with one large face, using black and white tempera only. This focuses attention on the basic features previously discussed. Don't bother to have the class "divide" the face into equal parts, or go into detail about proportion. Do warn against tight little lines. Then, just give them free rein and watch for some hilarious self-portraits. Room is of essence here. If easels are unavailable, or impractical, move back the furniture and use the floor.

PROCEDURE

1. Distribute paper, paint and brushes.
2. Ask the children to reflect a moment on the previous class discussion, then paint a self-portrait.
3. Let the paintings dry thoroughly before hanging.

WHAT THE CHILDREN CAN DO AFTERWARD

1. Ask the children to select a classmate (don't tell who) and do his portrait. Hold up the finished paintings and ask the class to identify each one.
2. Write autobiographies.
3. As a follow-up, do full color portraits.
4. Hang the finished pictures along the hall, outside the room.

RELAX WITH TIME SAVERS

1. If the floor is to be used, spread newspaper before distributing materials.
2. Distribute paint cups—one white, one black, for two children to share.
3. Have additional paint available in plastic detergent squeeze bottles. Children may help themselves to refills.
4. Select two assistants to collect, wash and store paint cups and brushes.
5. To avoid running, don't lift paper until the paint is almost dry.

SILHOUETTES

ILLUSTRATION 6-4

MATERIALS

1. black construction paper
2. overhead projector
3. white chalk
4. white construction paper
5. paste
6. scissors

BEFORE YOU BEGIN

Ever make a shadow hand picture on a sun-soaked wall? Silhouettes are just as easy, and even more fun. We've seen our country's immortals portrayed in simple outline innumerable times, with no uncertainty about identification. Today we'll try silhouettes of our own.

Most important is a careful preliminary demonstration of the procedure. Select a child, and, following the suggested method, outline his profile. As you work, discuss distinguishing characteristics—nose, chin, hairstyle, etc. For recognizable results, every line must be followed with care.

Explaining that each will have a turn to draw his partner's silhouette, pair off children, giving each couple a number. The first couple, after completing their own outlines, calls the next "number" to take their places.

PROCEDURE (Illustration 6-4)

1. Tape a sheet of black construction paper to a wall or blackboard. (step a)

2. Set up the overhead projector at opposite end of room. Sit the child, in profile, in front of the black sheet of construction paper. Flash the light of the overhead projector toward the child, so that his silhouette appears on the paper. (step a)

3. Have a second child outline the image with white chalk. (step a)

4. When the silhouette is finished, have partners reverse roles and repeat procedure.

5. Ask each child to return to his seat with his own silhouette. Cut this out carefully.

6. Paste the cut-out to a sheet of white construction paper. (step b)

WHAT THE CHILDREN CAN DO AFTERWARD

1. Tack the profiles to a bulletin board and play a game of "Guess Who." Have the children identify their classmates in silhouette, pointing out their distinguishing characteristics.

2. Write autobiographies. Display these on the bulletin board with silhouettes.

3. Paste sticks to the cut-out heads and use them as puppets.

4. Use the silhouettes as covers for individual work folders. Have youngsters leave the folders on their desks for parents to review on Open School Night.

5. Paste the silhouette to a red construction paper valentine. Write a Valentine's Day greeting on the reverse side.

6. Frame the silhouettes and give them as gifts.

RELAX WITH TIME SAVERS

1. Since not all children may participate at once, try to set up the projector and work area where it will interfere the least with other class activity.

2. Assign the group some independent work, so that you will be free to guide those working on the silhouettes.

3. Set up a paste station in the back of the room. All pasting should be done here.

"OP—ART" FACES

MATERIALS

1. manila paper
2. two magazine "face" pictures
3. rulers
4. pencil
5. scissors

BEFORE YOU BEGIN

"Op" art has found itself a warm spot in the eyes of youth. Anything intriguing, puzzling, and loved by kids, is fair play for classroom exploitation. This unit's special emphasis on physical features suggests "op art" faces for starters. Since planning and execution demand care, save this one for the upper grades. Have several samples, in gradual stages of completion, to illustrate necessary steps.

Several days should be allowed for the class to gather appropriate pictures. Selections should be geared to large faces with ample borders (cosmetic ads and magazine covers are excellent sources). In choosing picture combinations, seek contrast (man-woman, light hair-dark hair, adult-child). Have "extras" available for use during the lesson.

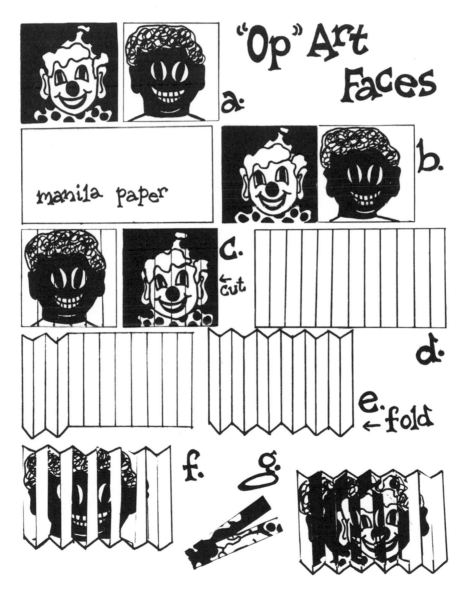

ILLUSTRATION 6-5

PROCEDURE (Illustration 6-5)

1. Trim two pictures so that they are equal in size. (step a)
2. Cut the manila paper so that it is exactly double the size of one picture. Test the measurements by placing the pictures, side by side, on top of the manila sheet; the two should equal the size of the manila. (step b)
3. With a pencil and ruler, measure across each picture, dividing it into equal width strips. If pre-planning finds it feasible, try using a 1/2" or 1" wide ruler (depending on size of pictures). Place the ruler at one edge of the paper and draw the first line. Then, place the ruler on the first line, automatically measuring a second line equal in width to the first. Continue until all the lines are drawn. Left-over space at the opposite end of the paper may be trimmed off. (Test this method first, as it only works when the picture has an adequate border which can be sacrificed. Otherwise, each strip width must be measured individually for accuracy before the lines are drawn.) (step c)
4. Mark off strips on manila using the above procedure. Remember, if each picture measures six strips, the manila must be sectioned into 12 strips to accommodate both pictures. (step d)
5. Using drawn lines as guides, fold the manila in an accordian manner. Make the folds sharp and definite. (step e)
6. Take picture number one. Using the pre-marked lines as guides, cut it into strips. These are pasted on alternate strips of the manila. Paste the first picture strip to the first manila accordian space. Paste the second picture strip to the *third* manila accordian space; the third picture strip to the fifth space, and so on. (step f)
7. Now, cut the second picture according to the pre-measured strips. Paste the strips from this picture on the remaining alternating manila spaces (the first strip goes on the second space, the second strip goes on the fourth space, and so on) until there are no more strips left. (step g)
8. If necessary, trim the completed op-art creation around the edges.
9. Stand at a slight distance. When viewed from left to right, the first face seems to predominate. From right to left, the second face emerges.

WHAT THE CHILDREN CAN DO AFTERWARD

1. Use the pictures as bulletin board decoration.
2. Have an "op art" art unit. Make an assortment of odd and mod creations. Invite other groups to the class exhibit.
3. Be on the look-out for "op" and "pop" art exhibits. If near-by, plan a class trip.

RELAX WITH TIME SAVERS

1. Complete all measuring before the paste is distributed. Children, often over-zealous, may try cutting and pasting before checking for accuracy. Assist and check each child's work, before permitting him to cut and paste.

2. Avoid complications. Cut one picture into strips at a time. If both pictures are cut out too far in advance, they're bound to get mixed up. In fact, the cut-out strips should be placed in sequential order, one next to another, and numbered on the reverse side. Its' proper sequence can be immediately placed.

3. Distribute paste in empty jar covers; one cover for two children to share. Have a helper collect and wash these at the lesson's end.

4. Apply paste with applicator sticks or brushes to avoid getting paste on the front surfaces of the paper strips.

TALKING HANDS

ILLUSTRATION 6-6

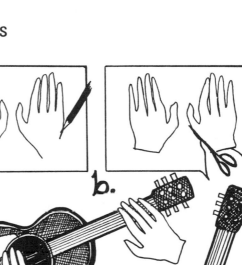

MATERIALS

1. colored construction paper
2. drawing paper
3. crayons
4. paste
5. scissors
6. pencil

BEFORE YOU BEGIN

Open class with "Let's make our hands talk." For those with question mark expressions, a quick demonstration—"admonishing," "caressing," "waving," "cooking"—immediately clarifies today's pantomime of hands. Class thespians, eager to get into the act, should be invited to "climb a rope," "catch a ball," "play cards," and generally "do their stuff." Portrayals are greater fun if demonstrations are "guessed" by others.

Similar to acting out, this lesson tells a story by using an object and hands only. Each child will draw a picture of, perhaps, a ball, bottle of milk, pencil, instrument—almost anything that must be manipulated will do. At this point, omit hands from the picture. To complete the "story," these will be added later.

PROCEDURE (Illustration 6-6)

1. Distribute a sheet of colored construction paper to each child, according to his choice.
2. Place one hand on the paper, and using a pencil, draw its outline. Repeat the procedure with the other hand so that you now have a right and left. (step a)
3. Cut out the hand shapes and save them. (step b)
4. With crayons, on drawing paper, draw some picture related to the use of hands. *Do not draw in hands.* Fill up the paper, but avoid tiny details (they are apt to be covered when the hand cut-outs are applied). (step c)
5. Paste the hand cut-outs appropriately to the drawing. (step d)

WHAT THE CHILDREN CAN DO AFTERWARD

1. Ask each child to hold up his drawing for class discussion.
2. Tack the pictures to a bulletin board. The varied array of subjects may prompt the class to compose a poem based on "hands." Invite other groups to a recitation.

RELAX WITH TIME SAVERS

1. Avoid mix-ups at pasting time by asking each child to write his name on the back of his hand cut-outs.
2. Collect scissors and clean up scraps before starting to draw.
3. Choose a table helper to bring the paste to his group. One portion of paste on a scrap of paper should suffice each table—remind the class that only a small amount is needed with which to apply the cut-outs.

THUMBPRINTS

MATERIALS

1. ink pad
2. paint and brushes
3. painting paper

BEFORE YOU BEGIN

Apart from smudging mother's wall, what's in a thumbprint? Can you imagine a cage of winking owls, fat pussy willows, and branches bursting with "leaves"? Illusion comes with a moment's hard stare. Then, with the apt assist of a quick brush stroke here and there, the thumbprint "suggestion" becomes a picture.

Take a moment to explain the individuality of each set of prints; like a signature, no two sets will ever match. If time permits, have the youngsters compare their prints for proof of such differences.

Demonstrate the technique, cautioning against excessive use of paint. Fingerprints, central to the picture, usually require only a few dabs or brush strokes to give them meaning.

ILLUSTRATION 6-7

PROCEDURE (Illustration 6-7)

1. Distribute paper. Ask the children to first think out their pictures with some "imaginary" prints. Then, hand out ink pads and paper.
2. Place a finger firmly on the pad (any or all the fingers of one hand may be used at a time), then stamp the fingerprints on painting paper. Continue to print a design for the basic result, replenishing fingers whenever necessary. (step a)
3. Add details with paint. (step b)

WHAT THE CHILDREN CAN DO AFTERWARD

1. Use the thumbprints as bulletin board decoration.
2. For once, mothers will be delighted to see a child's fingerprints. Frame these fantasies and give them as gifts.

RELAX WITH TIME SAVERS

1. Demonstrate how ink is applied to fingertips only. Do not stamp the entire hand or the picture will smudge.
2. Save desks by spreading newspaper in advance.
3. Distribute paint in plastic ice-cube trays; one tray for three or four children to share.
4. Have two children share one ink pad.
5. When finished, wash hands immediately.
6. Choose two helpers to collect and wash ice-cube trays and brushes. Ask a third assistant to collect and store ink pads.

FOOT FACES

MATERIALS

1. drawing paper
2. crayons

BEFORE YOU BEGIN

Oh, what to do on those dreary rainy days when classwork trickles slower than the rain rivulets on the window pane? Bring sunshine into the room with this zany brightener. One moment of thought, another crayoning, turns feet into the drollest faces. Lethargy evaporates as everyone enjoys a few good laughs.

PROCEDURE (Illustration 6-8)

1. Hand out large drawing paper and crayons.
2. Have each child remove one shoe (leave sock on), and draw an outline of his foot on drawing paper. (step a)
3. Ask the class to study this outline a moment. Then, using crayons turn it into a funny face. Or, should shapes remind one of some other subject, give the go-ahead to be original. (step b)

WHAT THE CHILDREN CAN DO AFTERWARD

1. Tack the pictures with whimsical titles, to a bulletin board.
2. Write amusing stories (Life With a Loafer, "Heels" I've Known)

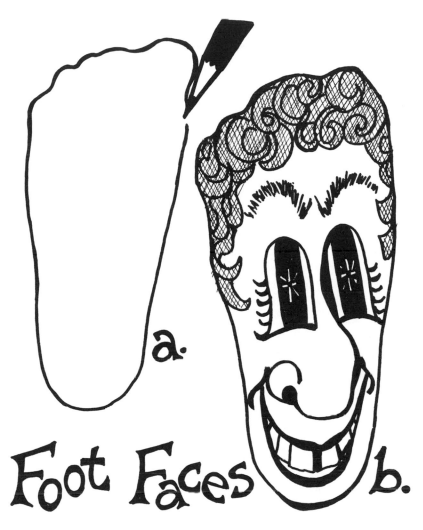

ILLUSTRATION 6-8

3. Cut out the decorated foot shapes and tape them "walking up" the wall.
4. Cut out the faces and use them as masks.

RELAX WITH TIME SAVERS

1. Have the children put their shoes back on as soon as the outline is complete.
2. Place paper on the floor to draw the foot outline.

WATCH ME GROW BOARD

MATERIALS

1. 5' x 2' piece of plywood
2. 5' x 1-1/2' sheet medium weight paper

3. pencils
4. rulers
5. paint
6. felt-tipped marker
7. scissors
8. mirror hanger

BEFORE YOU BEGIN

Here an inch, there an inch—how self-impressed is the boy who discovers himself a little bit bigger than he was only a few months ago. A "Watch Me Grow" board, as it builds egos, provides a vehicle for concrete lessons in linear measure.

Infant and toddler photos, precious momentoes of the school set, should be brought in for discussion, and, incidentally, admiration. Growth as a gradual process can be illustrated by a series of chalk lines. Draw a 20″ line on the board. "Many of you were about this size at birth." Then, measure a pupil, adding a second line to represent his height. Finally, illustrate adult height by a line for the teacher. Watch out for measure mania! This erupts even before there's a chance to explain how heights vary in people.

Grasp the opportunity to hand out rulers and yard sticks. First, let the children measure one another. Then try some measuring games. Expect each surveyor to come up with a different answer to "How many Andy's long is our room?" Discrepancies should point out the dire need for accuracy. Back at seats, study the ruler with special emphasis on fractional lines. Now, try measuring the room once more—this time expect a greater consensus of accuracy.

Divide the class and assign a number to each group. This measuring board represents six feet. But, since it will hang one foot off the ground, you need to select only five groups—one to work on each of the remaining five feet. Thus, each child will be assured an opportunity to add an inch or two of his own.

No ordinary marker, the board should be decorated with, perhaps, a tall flower, giraffe, or tree. Let the class decide. Try to give everyone a share in the designing and painting of the finished product.

PROCEDURE (Illustration 6-9)

1. If desired, paint the plywood a background color. Allow it to dry thoroughly.
2. Call group I to fill in the first foot of the measuring board. Place a ruler against the edge of the plywood. Pencil off half inches, inches, and feet. *Remember,* the board will be placed one foot above the floor. The first foot is therefore represented at the bottom of the board by the number "1". Each new group called should pencil off another of the remaining five feet. Have the children check one another's work for accuracy. (step a)
3. While groups work on the measuring board, others may design its decoration. Choose several children to make preliminary sketches. Put these choices up for a class vote.
4. Cut a piece of paper, equal in length and slightly narrower than the plywood

ILLUSTRATION 6-9

board, for the decorative pattern (decoration must not overlap numbers on board's yardstick). Have one or two children copy the chosen picture (giraffe, flower) onto the pattern paper. Carefully cut out the picture. (step b)

5. Tape the pattern to the plywood. Choose another group to outline the taped shape onto the wood with chalk. Errors may be dusted off. (step c)

6. Remove the pattern. Colorfully paint the picture, filling in the details. Let it dry. (step d)

7. Carefully go over the measured lines and numbers with a felt-tipped marker. If desired, the decoration may also be outlined for added definition.

8. Add a mirror hanger to the back of the grow board and attach it to a wall, one foot above the floor.

WHAT THE CHILDREN CAN DO AFTERWARD

1. Make a large class chart. Periodically measure the youngsters and record their heights.
2. Use measuring activities as a basis for arithmetic lessons (e.g., "Who is the tallest? shortest?" "What is the *difference* in their heights?" "If we made a 'people' tower of Mary, John, Anne and Tom, how tall would it be?")

RELAX WITH TIME SAVERS

1. Schedule independent work for children to complete while they are not actively involved in the project. This frees the teacher for necessary supervision.
2. Don't rush. It may be feasible to complete the measuring board over a two or three day period.
3. Have groups work in the back of the room where they will least disturb other class activity.
4. If the board is to be painted a background color, complete the procedure a day or so before initiating the rest of the activity.
5. Spread newspaper on the floor before any painting is begun.
6. Emphasize that all pencilling is to be done lightly so that errors may be erased easily.

Special Activity

Marvelous human machine, the body, yet children haven't the foggiest notion of the wonders encased within its epidermis. Mass media has the heart a valentine, the brain a sort of computerized walnut, and as one T.V. commercial documents, a stomach lever that regulates the speed of pain relievers.

With their inherent curiosity, children at all grade levels will enjoy putting their internal organs into perspective with this "Inside Story" idea.

"INSIDE STORY" CHART

MATERIALS

1. large sheet of oak tag
2. child model
3. pencil
4. felt-tip marker
5. red and blue roving
6. paste

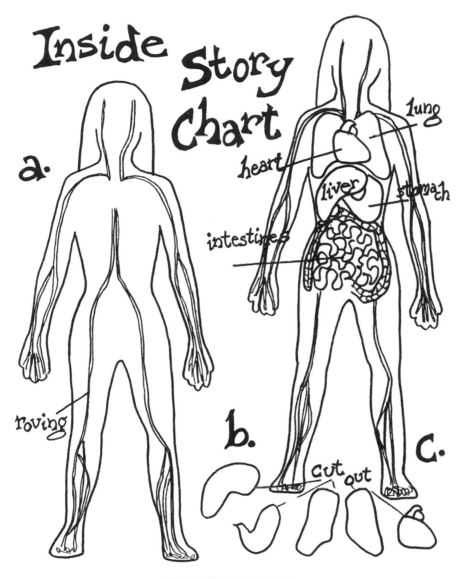

ILLUSTRATION 6-10

7. drawing paper
8. crayons
9. scissors

BEFORE YOU BEGIN

Launch this project mid-way into your study of the human body. Science room models, such as plastic hearts, lungs, and stomachs are a great help, as are pictures and films. If synthetic facsimiles are unavailable in your school, ask a local physician if he has office models he's willing to lend or contribute. These are frequently supplied to the doctor by pharmaceutical houses as a means of advertising, and are usually of no value to him.

Better still, invite him to visit your class to answer questions and explain the complex.

Don't rush completion. Many children profit from watching the life-sized model grow with each new learning experience.

PROCEDURE (Illustration 6-10)

1. Have the child model lie down on oaktag. Ask a second child to outline his shape. Define the completed figure with felt-tipped marker. (step a)
2. Paste red and blue roving in place to represent the major arteries and veins. (step a)
3. Draw, color and cut-out the necessary organs; heart, lungs, liver spleen, bladder, intestines and paste them in place. (steps b & c)
4. Write in the organ names with felt-tipped marker. (step c)

WHAT THE CHILDREN CAN DO AFTERWARD

1. Write reports on human organs and how they function. Attach the model and the reports to a bulletin board.
2. Display the model at a school science fair.
3. Invite other groups to see the model and listen to class explanations.

RELAX WITH TIME SAVERS

1. Divide the class into groups, each to work on some different aspect of the project.
2. Try to have life-sized models or pictures available to help children produce proportionate cut-outs.
3. Print all labels in pencil before applying the felt-tipped marker.

Bonus Ideas

1. Have each child make cut-outs of his hands and/or feet. Label the cut-outs respectively with the child's name using felt-tipped marker. Paste these cut-outs in a random pattern to a large sheet of mural paper. Attach the unusual mural to tack board.
2. Cut hand shapes from cloth. Applique to an apron and give it as a Mother's Day gift.
3. Make op art composites of animals, landscapes, or children's own original drawings.
4. Help kindergarteners make a "People Puzzle." Have a child lie down on an oak tag sheet and outline his shape. Cut this out "puzzle fashion." Apply felt backing. As they have fun putting the puzzle together, children are also learning about body proportions.
5. Use "Thumbprints" for original gift wrap paper and matching greeting cards.
6. Use the scribbling technique for making abstract land and city-scapes.
7. Have each child paint portraits of his family.
8. Assuming action poses before the overhead projector, have children outline one another's full body silhouettes. These may be painted and hung individually. Or, make a giant-sized physical fitness mural to display in the gym by pasting these body shapes to a huge sheet of mural paper.

Journey Through Space

Imagine what it must be like, way, way up in the heavens, to be weightless and floating in the company of stars. Space! What magic our times have given the very word; how it tantalizes our thoughts!

On July 20, 1969, when "Eagle" made its historic landing on the moon, children all over the world became part of a new era. At the gateway of this new frontier, where distance isn't calculated in terms of a paltry few thousand miles, but in light years, many of these very youngsters, and future generations like them, will be the pioneers in the endless space chasm. With space stations a possibility, how much longer to Mars, Venus, and Jupiter? Fascinating thoughts, to be sure.

As it reduces spectacular reality to child-size credibility, this chapter also invites imagination's trajectory to meet the challenge of the Space Age. Whether yours is a kingergarten or intermediate age group, the "Planet Mobile" and Planet Diorama" provide ample opportunity for the child to represent, in meaningful proportions, the wonders of the solar family. Then, our miniature "Rocket Ships" launch us to re-live that memorable July moon landing.

For fun en route, let's pause to gaze at "Stars in Abstract" and to acquaint ourselves with Pegasus, Big Bear, Scorpio, and those other personalities who wink at us from the evening sky. Some of these new friends escort us back to earth in the guise of "Constellation Nite Lites," Hole Punch" decoration, or "Zodiac Jewelry."

Playing host to wild young visions of what might be discovered in the land of "XLG" are "Imaginary Planet Mural" and "Space Creatures."

PLANET MOBILE

MATERIALS

1. oak tag circle 20″ in diameter
2. scissors

3. aluminum foil
4. string
5. tissue paper
6. white glue diluted with water
7. paint and brushes
8. wire hanger
9. transparent tape
10. stapler

BEFORE YOU BEGIN

As Earth and her sister planets have tirelessly floated around the sun, so has man's intelligence been spurred from time's beginning, to not only understand this performance, but to reach for worlds beyond. Infinity, as it tantalizes the adult brain, also makes the child ponder and fantasize about the starry spectacles in the vast theater of endless space.

Distances calculated in millions of miles, and planets many times larger than Earth, are, indeed, big bites for the very young to chew. For children to enjoy manipulative activities in connection with a unit such as this, it is necessary to reduce members of the solar system to rubber ball size. Thus, our "Planet Mobile."

Of course, this project must be accompanied by a study of the solar system. Before you begin, children certainly should understand that, with regard to size and distance, the model will be out of proportion. After all, considering that Pluto, for example, is forty times the distance from the sun than is earth, it would hardly be feasible to accurately represent or calculate space distances in the ordinary classroom. It should be explained that the models must simply be scaled from smallest to largest, and placed in relative order on these mobiles. As a guide, and to avoid recurrent questions as children work, have two lists on the board; one giving the order of planetary size, the other showing their respective distance from the sun.

In order of size (going from smallest to largest), are Mercury, Mars, Pluto, Venus, Earth, Uranus, Neptune, Saturn and Jupiter. Distances from the sun are as follows; Mercury (closest), then Venus, Earth, Mars, Jupiter, Saturn, Uranus, Neptune, and, finally, Pluto.

Upper graders can make individual mobiles. With small-fry, however, keep the lesson a class project, increasing the suggested dimensions for a larger model, and allowing each child to contribute an assigned share.

PROCEDURE (Illustration 7-1)

1. Push the curved portion of the hanger through the center of the oak tag circle. Straighten the remaining part of the wire hanger. (step a)
2. Flat against the underside of the oak tag circle, shape the wire into concentric circles. Tape the wire to secure it in place. Hang the "wired" circle from a fixture and adjust the wire frame so that the oak tag circle hangs straight, without tilting. The planets will later be suspended from this oak tag and wire form. (steps b & c)

3. Shape the planets, from smallest to largest, from aluminum foil. Tie each foil ball securely with string. Leave a long piece of string attached to each ball so that it may later be suspended from the oak tag circle. (steps d & e)

4. Applying with diluted white glue and brushes, cover each foil ball with tissue paper. Allow these to dry. Some children may wish to portray the sun, and several small planets in aluminum foil alone. If so, simply add a final layer of foil to cover the string. (step f)

5. Paint the planets and let them dry. The rings of Saturn may be added by wrapping a rolled piece of foil tightly around the planet. (step g)

6. The planets may now be added to the oak tag circle. To keep the mobile from tilting, hang the circle from a fixture, then add the planets. Start with Mercury and work outwards from the sun. Each attached piece of string is trimmed to vary the hanging length, then tied to the wire form, or taped to the underside of the circle. (steps h & i)

Planet Mobiles

ILLUSTRATION 7-1

WHAT THE CHILDREN CAN DO AFTERWARD

1. Prepare talks on the planets. Invite other classes to hear the presentation and view the display.
2. Write science fiction stories of what one might expect to find on different planets.
3. Find books related to space study. Have each child write a book report, and have the class compile a bibliography for future reference.
4. With children standing in for sun, Earth, and moon, show visually how our planet behaves in space ("Earth" child "spins" on axis as he also revolves around "Sun." "Moon" child revolves about "Earth" and so on).

RELAX WITH TIME SAVERS

1. Pre-cut oak tag circles well in advance of the lesson. Assist children with wire hangers, manipulating them so that mobiles handle properly. Trim excess wire with wire cutters when necessary.
2. Do not erase the blackboard lists indicating planetary size and distance from the sun until all have completed the project.
3. Dilute the glue with water in advance. Have one paint cup, filled with this solution ready for each child. Have a bottle of glue on hand near the sink so that youngsters may help themselves to re-fills.
4. When painting, let the background color of each planet dry before adding the details.
5. Provide a roll of foil for three to four children to share.
6. Distribute paint in plastic ice-cube trays; one tray for two children to share.
7. Distribute enough tissue paper for each table to share.
8. Select helpers to collect and store left-over tissue paper and foil; others to collect and wash paint cups, ice-cube trays and brushes.

PLANET DIORAMA

BEFORE YOU BEGIN

From the "Twinkle, Twinkle Little Star" stage on, wide-eyed youngsters are absorbed in the observation of a star-studded sky. A take-off on the "Planet Mobile," this project is geared to the ability of the lower graders, who, rather than leave a precious project suspended in school, prefer to tote it home.

Each child will choose one "favorite" planet and concentrate on its characteristics. Of course, pictures, films and discussions about the solar family are a preliminary must. Encourage each youngster to select "his" planet, work carefully, and include as many of its details as possible.

Demonstrate in advance how the tissue paper is applied to the model.

ILLUSTRATION 7-2

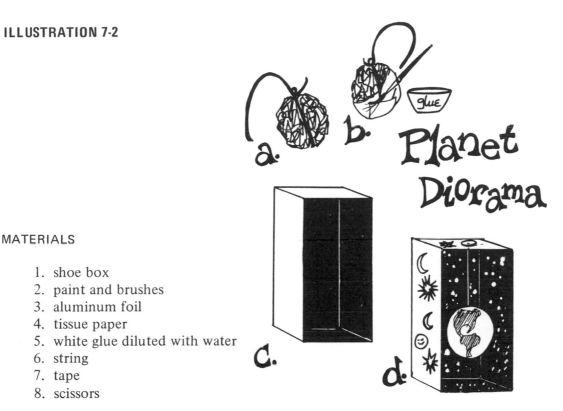

MATERIALS

    1. shoe box
    2. paint and brushes
    3. aluminum foil
    4. tissue paper
    5. white glue diluted with water
    6. string
    7. tape
    8. scissors

PROCEDURE (Illustration 7-2)

1. Shape a planet from aluminum foil. Allowing a long end piece to dangle, tie the string securely around the foil ball. (step a)
2. Apply layers of tissue paper using diluted glue and brushes. Overlap and smooth the paper sheets until the entire foil "planet" is covered. Let it dry. (step b)
3. While the tissue paper ball dries, paint the inside of a shoe box black. The outside of the box may be painted a solid color, even gaily decorated. Some may also choose to paint yellow stars against the blackened shoe box interior. Let the box dry. (steps c & d)
4. Paint the dried tissue paper balls; first a background color, then add details. Form the rings of Saturn by rolling a piece of aluminum foil and wrapping it securely around the circumference of the planet.
5. Trim the string to a desired length. Stand the shoe box vertically and tape the loose end of the string to the underside end of the box. (step d)

WHAT THE CHILDREN CAN DO AFTERWARD

1. Write simple informative paragraphs about the planets on chart paper. Tack it to a bulletin board and display the dioramas on a near-by table.

2. Display the shoe box planets along a window sill.
3. Display the projects in school showcases.
4. Invite other groups to a class exhibit, and have each child tell a few facts about his planet.
5. Have the children bring the planets home for use as room decoration.

RELAX WITH TIME SAVERS

1. Spread newspaper before distributing materials.
2. Help children tie the string to the aluminum foil balls. Have pieces of string cut in advance of the lesson.
3. Pre-mix a glue and water solution. Distribute one paint cup, filled with this glue solution for every two children to share.
4. Have a place where planets and painted shoe boxes can dry safely.
5. Distribute the paint in empty ice-cube trays; one for every two children to share.
6. Choose assistants to collect newspaper, scraps, and wash paint cups and trays.

IMAGINARY PLANET MURAL (Illustration 7-3)

ILLUSTRATION 7-3

MATERIALS

1. bulletin board paper
2. paint
3. large drawing paper
4. paste and glue
5. construction paper
6. assortment of collage scraps (fabric, buttons, costume jewelry, beads, glitter, thin wire)
7. scissors

BEFORE YOU BEGIN

In this, the age of the astronaut, is there a child who hasn't envisioned himself a ubiquitous space hero, braving all the perils of mysterious unconquered planets? Reverie propels him to weird planets, there to perform intrepid feats that might very well be as uncanny as the imagined land.

Combining language arts, imagery and collage, today's lesson will complete an unfinished story with words, crayon, paint and paste. Start off with something like this;

> While soaring smoothly through space, home and family light years away, the instrument panel amazingly becomes unhinged before your startled eyes. Tearing noises and debris are in horrible accompaniment, as you are catapulted from the pilot's seat and helplessly flung against a wall. Mighty thunderous, howling crash! Monitors no longer register and Earth contact is lost. Spiralling through the blindingly flourescent blaze of Galaxy X's wild color, the piercing screech of going down, down, down, seems to madden your brain and dissolve your ears. Finally, with a heaving tremble that quiets to a sickening crunch, your craft digs into what sounds like a soft sludge bank. Eerie calm. Gathering courage and whatever strength is miraculously left, you try to see through the porthole. Nothing. . . view completely blocked. With no alternative you fearlessly squeeze through a damaged escape hatch of the hopelessly damaged craft. Outside . . . you behold and gasp at the sight of what must be the strange land of . . .

Distribute drawing paper, crayons, paste and a multitude of collage materials with which to create the story's end. Give a quick demonstration lesson, showing how paper may be scored and cut; wire twisted and spiralled, to give a three dimensional effect. Ask for volunteers to conjure a painted background mural scene of unearthly flora and fauna.

Then let imaginations fly. Only one rule—make planetary creatures large, almost as large as the drawing paper. Small, tight figures will surely be lost on such a mural.

PROCEDURE

1. Draw a space creature on the large drawing paper. Cut it out.
2. Show how to achieve 3-D effects by scoring, curling, and accordian folding construction paper (and heavy aluminum foil) to make outlandish eyes, ears, hair, and limbs. Thin wire may be curled around a pencil and used as antennae, or when attached to bits of paper, as springs for "pop out" features.
3. Using paper and wire as described above, as well as an ample assortment of other available collage scraps, have each child paste and crayon his own fantastic space creature.
4. Tack the bulletin board paper in place. Select a committee of three or four to plan and paint a large imaginary background scene.
5. Have each child tack or staple his completed figure to the painted scene.
6. With collage materials and/or paint add "homes, "transportation vehicles," and the like.

WHAT THE CHILDREN CAN DO AFTERWARD

1. Discuss the mural. Choose a name for the imaginary planet.
2. Ask each child to write the balance of the story the teacher has begun, explaining what life might be like in this fantasy world, or the fate of our space hero.
3. Give each figure a cardboard backing, add manipulating sticks, and have a puppet show.

RELAX WITH TIME SAVERS

1. Give a demonstration lesson before distributing materials.
2. Provide an ample assortment of collage scraps for each table. Have construction paper scraps available for children to help themselves.
3. Distribute paste in empty jar covers; one for two to three children to share.
4. Tack the bulletin board paper in place in advance of the lesson.
5. Spread newspaper on the floor before painting the bulletin board background.
6. Choose helpers to collect and wash paste receptacles; collect and store collage scraps; and pass wastebasket.

CRAYON AND PAINT A PLANET (Illustration 7-4)

ILLUSTRATION 7-4

"Saturn and some of its moons"

Crayon and Paint a Planet

MATERIALS

1. painting paper
2. crayons
3. black paint and brush

BEFORE YOU BEGIN

To launch a space study program, add verve with an array of planets, brilliantly crayoned to come gleaming through a black painted background. As guides for planet details, use pictures or filmstrips. A word of advice; for best results press down hard with crayons and do not leave open spaces.

PROCEDURE

1. With crayon draw and vibrantly color a planet.
2. Add the background by applying black paint (diluted slightly with water) across the entire surface of the picture. The paint will not adhere to the waxy crayoned portion. Let it dry.

WHAT THE CHILDREN CAN DO AFTERWARD

1. "Frame" the pictures by stapling them to larger sheets of construction paper. Tack them to a bulletin board.
2. Use pictures as covers for space study work folders.

RELAX WITH TIME SAVERS

1. Spread newspaper before painting.
2. Distribute one cup of black paint for two children to share.
3. Choose helpers to collect, wash and store paint cups and brushes.

MOON LANDING DIORAMA

MATERIALS

1. cardboard box (shoe box for individual projects, larger cartons for group work)
2. plaster of Paris bandage rolls
3. bowl of warm water
4. black paint
5. aluminum foil
6. pipe cleaners
7. string
8. wire
9. toothpicks
10. tempera paint
11. small bowl of sand
12. pebbles and small rocks
13. small cardboard rectangle

BEFORE YOU BEGIN

For all the songs ever sung about the romantic moon, few people thought anyone would, or could, really get there! Then, on July 20, 1969, even in the remotest corners of the globe, eyes were riveted to television screens as the world watched man cast his first earthly footprints on the moon's surface.

Children who witnessed the incredible moon walk, or saw re-runs, will surely be armed with facts of this extraordinary accomplishment. Personal memories, plus special magazine editions, newspaper clippings, even long playing records, provide excellent reviews of this, the first manned lunar landing.

Today's lesson is meant to recapture the enthusiasm of this amazing historic moment. The diorama suggestion may be an individual or small group project, depending on age level. Older, more adept children, should be able to work the plaster of Paris swiftly and easily. Collect the necessary boxes in advance—shoe boxes for individual projects, and larger cartons for group work.

Demonstrate how the plaster and sand are worked to represent the lunar surface, and how plaster can be used to model figures.

PROCEDURE (Illustration 7-5)

1. Paint the outside of the box in any decorative color.
2. Paint the inside of the box black on three sides; leave the bottom bare. Let it dry. (step a)
3. Sculpt the lunar landing module from aluminum foil. Its size should be proportioned to the size of the diorama box being used. Insert toothpicks, pins, and the like in the model to achieve the irregular aspects of the odd looking vehicle. (step b)
4. On the cardboard rectangle, paint in the details of the American flag. Let it dry, then thread the flag through a pipe cleaner (or thin wire) "pole." (step b)
5. Make pipe cleaner figures of the two astronauts. For larger dioramas, sculpt these figures from aluminum foil. (step b)
6. Dip a plaster of Paris bandage roll in warm water. Squeeze it slightly. Work the roll carefully around the pipe cleaner (or foil) armature, giving the figure shape and dimension. Use pictures of astronauts in space suits as modelling guides. Let the plaster models dry. (step c)
7. Form a small plaster ball to represent the Earth. Suspend the ball from a piece of string. Let it dry. (step c)
8. Paint in the details of the space suit on each plaster astronaut. Press an aluminum foil helmet around the head of each model.
9. Paint the Earth details, as they appear from outer space, on the plaster "planet." Let it dry.
10. Form a lunar surface from plaster. Make the first layer by working the plaster roll back and forth along the bottom of the box. Then, work in several

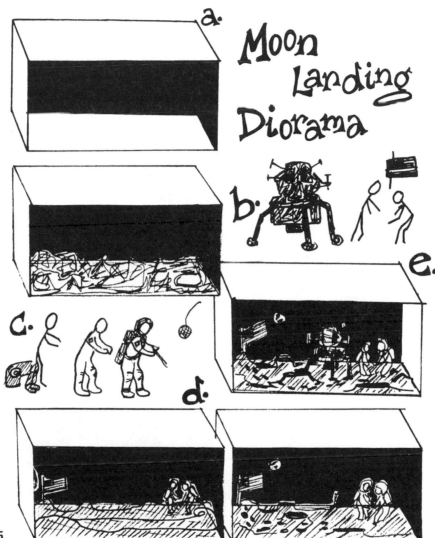

ILLUSTRATION 7-5

circles, molding "craters" with fingers. For a granular surface, sprinkle small amounts of sand on the wet plaster, working it into the moonscape. Imbed pebbles and "moon rock." With toothpicks, etch in booted footprints. (steps c & d)

11. Secure the flag and the astronaut figures into the lunar surface with additional plaster bandage. Allow these to dry. (step d)

12. Place the aluminum foil landing module inside the diorama. Suspend the distant "Earth" from the top of the box with tape. Attach wire or pipe cleaner probes to the arm of each astronaut. If desired, tape a tiny plastic bag filled with rock samples to the other arm. (step e)

WHAT THE CHILDREN CAN DO AFTERWARD

1. Display the completed dioramas on a table beneath a bulletin board. Make a bulletin board collage of headlines and pictures commemorating the moon walk.
2. Display the models in school show cases.
3. Research, then write reports of the events leading up to Apollo 11.
4. Have the children act out the moon walk.

RELAX WITH TIME SAVERS

1. If this lesson is to be a group project, assign several small committees a task in the project's completion (painting, making models, sculpting lunar surface).
2. Set up a plaster station in back of the room. Spread it with newspaper and have all the necessary supplies on hand. The children may take turns working in small groups.
3. Have paint cups and paint in liquid detergent squeeze bottles, available. When the children are ready, they may pour the required paint colors into cups and work individually at their seats.

STARS IN ABSTRACT (Illustration 7-6)

ILLUSTRATION 7-6

Stars in Abstract

MATERIALS

1. black construction paper
2. iridescent paint, diluted with water
3. toothbrush
4. newspaper

BEFORE YOU BEGIN

Disguised as tiny yellow flecks against the night's sky, incredibly bright galaxies blaze like electrified jewels. Spacemen of the future may feast their eyes on stellar abstracts bursting with flaming reds, blues, throbbing violets.

Use movies, filmstrips, books, and "special edition" magazines for pictures of the milky way and galaxies beyond. Given the general idea, a special brush and some paint will lead each child to conjure his own starry abstract.

Demonstrate how paint is splattered with a brush before distributing materials.

PROCEDURE

1. Spread newspaper on the desks.
2. Distribute black paper, paint and a toothbrush to each child.
3. Dip the bristles of the brush into a desired paint color. Only a small amount is necessary. Holding the brush toward the paper, rub your thumb lightly over the bristles, splattering paint in a random pattern. Try the first splatter on a piece of newspaper to gauge the proper amount. Too much paint will form unwanted "blobs." Make such test splatters with each new paint application. To avoid runs, allow each color to dry before adding a new one.
4. Continue to paint in this manner until the paper is filled.

WHAT THE CHILDREN CAN DO AFTERWARD

1. Staple the abstract to a larger sheet of construction paper and use it as bulletin board decoration.
2. Make work folders for space study units. Starry abstracts make attractive covers.

RELAX WITH TIME SAVERS

1. Dilute the paint with water in advance of the lesson. Distribute "water paint" in plastic ice-cube trays; one for two children to share. Fill some sections of the tray with water so that the brushes may be rinsed before each new paint application.
2. Wear smocks to avoid splattered clothing.
3. Choose a helper to collect and dispose of newspaper. Ask two or three others to collect, wash and store paint trays and brushes.

ROCKET SHIPS

MATERIALS

1. 3 cylindrical cans, proportionately sized (e.g., 3 lb., 2 lb., 1 lb., coffee cans; large, medium and small sized cylindrical oatmeal boxes, frozen juice cans)

2. white glue
3. oak tag circle
4. masking tape
5. paint

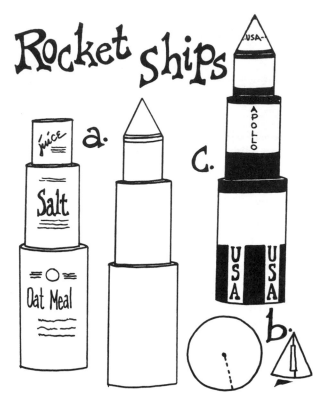

ILLUSTRATION 7-7

BEFORE YOU BEGIN

Centuries ago, when man in a merry holiday mood, sent rockets through the sky, he little knew the soaring, fire-cracking invention would one day point the way to the moon. From early Chinese inventors to Goddard's use of liquid fuel, to present day satellites, the history of rocketry, in this the space age, demands attention.

Supply films, read and discuss the subject with special emphasis on the many types of satellites and their functions. Then, with an abundance of appropriately shaped containers on hand, each child can make a rocket of his own. Start collecting these early in the unit.

Container size will depend on the model's ultimate use. For small dioramas, use different sized frozen juice cans. Ideal for larger displays are coffee cans, oatmeal boxes, or the large and jumbo variety of snack cannisters.

If the group enjoys doing so, let them work in committees, with respective groups producing rocket replicas from Explorer I to Apollo 11. Each group is then responsible for researching the historical developments and discoveries related to his particular ship's history.

PROCEDURE (Illustration 7-7)

1. Starting with the largest and finishing with the smallest, glue three proportionately sized containers one atop another. (step a)
2. Form the oak tag circle into a cone shape. Tape the cone to the top container. (step b)
3. Paint the entire rocket white. Let it dry.
4. Using magazine or text pictures as guides, paint in the accurate detailed markings. (step c)

WHAT THE CHILDREN CAN DO AFTERWARD

1. Use the rocket models as part of a diorama display.
2. Display and label the models on a large table beneath a bulletin board. Make a bulletin board time table chart, giving the names, dates and details (e.g., manned-unmanned, American-Russian) concerning each launch represented in the table display.
3. Invite other groups to an informative presentation, and to view the display.

RELAX WITH TIME SAVERS

1. If cardboard containers are being used, strip the outside paper label. Fewer coats of paint will then be required. If metal is being used (or containers which are difficult to peel), let the first coat of paint dry thoroughly. If the advertising shows through apply additional coats of paint.
2. Spread newspaper before painting.
3. Since drying time will probably vary for each project, set up a painting station in the back of the room where details may be added and projects left to dry.

SPACE CREATURES

MATERIALS

Cardboard Box Collage
1. any empty foodstuff or detergent box
2. cut-out sections from molded egg boxes
3. aluminum foil, available collage materials
4. scissors
5. paint and brushes
6. construction paper
7. wire and/or pipe cleaners

Plaster Collage

1. aluminum foil
2. plaster of Paris bandage rolls
3. copper wire
4. pencils
5. dress maker pins with colored tops
6. available collage materials
7. polymer acrylic medium or white glue
8. brushes
9. paint
10. bowl of warm water

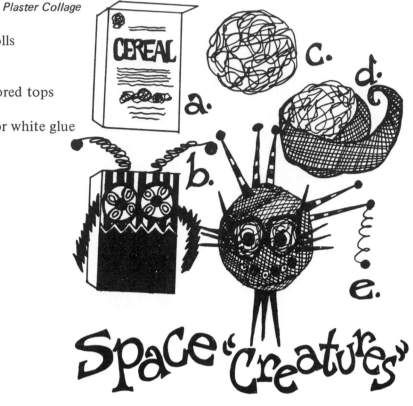

ILLUSTRATION 7-8

BEFORE YOU BEGIN

Via young whimsey, let imaginations transport us from the scholarly studies of space to a world of extra-terrestrial creatures. Two procedures for making unearthly beings are included here. Fast and uncomplicated, the cardboard box collage is best for the primary youngsters. More challenging, unusual and colorful plaster creatures are better suited to the upper grades.

Each child can make several plaster forms. Those which are not completed in school may be decorated at home and used to adorn mobiles.

Before distributing materials, demonstrate how unusual effects are achieved with paper, wire, and foil.

PROCEDURE I — CARDBOARD BOX COLLAGE (Illustration 7-8)

1. Trim the open flaps from a cardboard box. Paint the box and let dry. (step a)
2. Cut out sections from molded egg boxes. Make eerie eyes, ears, noses. Paint these weirdly and let them dry.
3. Paste the egg box sections in place. Apply further decoration with available collage scraps. (step b)

4. Wire or pipe cleaners may be twisted or curled around a pencil to form antennae. Pierce these through the outside of the box. If necessary, secure them with tape from the inside. (step b)
5. Make hair by fringing or curling strips of aluminum foil and pasting them in place.
6. Accordian fold strips of construction paper, if desired, and paste, as limbs, to the cardboard box. (step b)

PROCEDURE II – PLASTER COLLAGE

1. Form the aluminum foil into a ball (make several such balls in varying sizes). (step c)
2. Bend, twist and curl the wire into weird shapes for antennae.
3. Dip a plaster of Paris bandage roll in a bowl of warm water. Squeeze it slightly. Wrap the plaster around the aluminum foil ball, smoothing it in place as it is worked. (step d)
4. Insert desired wire or pipe cleaner "antennae" and/or pins into the ball while the plaster is still wet. Insert a long, straight piece of wire securely into the wet plaster from which to suspend the completed creature. Let the plaster ball dry. (step e)
5. Colorfully paint each dried plaster ball.
6. Apply available collage materials by brush with polymer acrylic or white glue diluted with water (polymer acrylic coats with a permanent glaze). (step e)
7. Allow all the decoration to dry.

WHAT THE CHILDREN CAN DO AFTERWARD

1. Have each child give his creature an unusual name and homeland. The extra-terrestrial visitor should receive an impormptu introduction to classmates.
2. Give a puppet show. Manipulate the creatures by placing a hand inside the box. Use plaster figures marionette style.
3. Suspend space creatures at varying lengths from fixtures about the room.
4. Give these creatures as gifts to brothers and sisters.
5. Attach space personalities to wire forms and use them as mobiles.

RELAX WITH TIME SAVERS

1. Set up a plaster station in the back of the room. Spread this area with newspaper. Allow the children up several at a time to complete the plaster work.
2. Distribute paint in plastic ice-cube trays; one tray for three children to share.
3. Distribute a varied assortment of construction paper, and assorted collage materials for each table to share.
4. Distribute paste in empty jar covers; one for two children to share.
5. Appoint "plaster," "paint," and "collage," helpers to collect, store and clean these supplies at the lesson's end.

ZODIAC JEWELRY

ILLUSTRATION 7-9

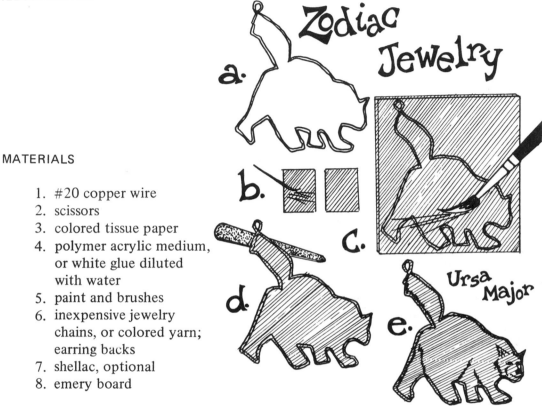

MATERIALS

1. #20 copper wire
2. scissors
3. colored tissue paper
4. polymer acrylic medium,
   or white glue diluted
   with water
5. paint and brushes
6. inexpensive jewelry
   chains, or colored yarn;
   earring backs
7. shellac, optional
8. emery board

BEFORE YOU BEGIN

Before the advent of astronomy, pseudo-science astrology was such a powerful influence that great men seldom risked decisions without first considering the propitious positions of planets and stars. Surely, in ancient history, this was one of the most enveloping of superstitions amongst Egyptians, Hindus, and Chinese. It even had a firm grasp in Europe at the beginning of the Christian era.

Today, though mostly for fun, those in search of a decision maker may turn to horoscopes. Some believe that the stars, in relation to one's birth date, can even describe personality. For real or make-believe—whether one "sees" things in the stars or not—zodiac jewelry is a close cousin to the lucky protective amulets of a by-gone time.

Inject some tongue-in-cheek astrology along with myths of stellar heroes. Everyone will want to know his personal horoscope. With the wealth of publications on the subject flooding the book stalls, this is an easily filled request.

With a special member of the zodiac in mind, show how these capricious charms are made. Once familiar with the procedure, the children may complete several pieces, making in addition to pendants, charm bracelets and matching earrings. Man in the moon, flaming sun, and other members of the zodiac may be included.

PROCEDURE (Illusrtation 7-9)

1. Bend and twist a piece of copper wire into a desired zodiac shape. Form a twisted loop at the top of the charm. Flatten the wire shape as much as possible against a hard surface. (step a)
2. Cut two tissue paper squares, slightly larger than the size of the charm. With a brush, coat one side of each square with polymer acrylic medium (or white glue, diluted with water). Coat the copper wire charm outline with the same solution. (step b)
3. Place the charm between the coated squares of tissue paper. Gently press out any air bubbles. Coat the outside surfaces of the tissue paper with the acrylic medium. Should the paper tear, simply place another piece of tissue paper over the charm, and re-coat it with polymer acrylic. Let it dry thoroughly until the tissue paper is shiny and hard. This may require several hours. (step c)
4. Cut any excess tissue paper overlapping the wire frame, and from inside the loop. If necessary, use an emery board to file away remaining "fuzz." (step d)
5. Decoratively paint in zodiac details. Let dry. (step e)
6. If white glue has been used, shellac the finished pieces.
7. Thread yarn or chain through the loop of the charm. Smaller, matched pieces, may be glued to earring backs.

WHAT THE CHILDREN CAN DO AFTERWARD

1. Give the jewelry as gifts, or wear as personal adornment.
2. Suspend each zodiac charm from a thin wire or nylon thread, and attach it to a class mobile.
3. Attach the charms to windows. The sun will shine through the charm, giving the effect of stained glass.
4. Use the charms as Christmas tree decoration.
5. Use the charms as window shade pulls.
6. Sell this zodiac jewelry at a school fund raising fair.

RELAX WITH TIME SAVERS

1. Polymer acrylic is now used in many schools. For making the jewelry described here, it is ideal, for it produces a translucent, plastic-like product. However, if this material is unavailable, white glue and water works almost as well, especially when varnished. If the latter is to be used, pre-mix the solution in advance. Distribute either medium in paint cups; one for two children to share.

2. Work on a hard, non-paper surface, such as scrap wood. Dried polymer acrylic, should it adhere to class furniture, may be removed with denatured alcohol.
3. Provide a safe place where the objects can dry.
4. Distribute the paint in plastic ice-cube trays; one for every two or three children to share.
5. Spread newspapers on desks before painting.
6. If shellac is used, apply it in a well ventilated area of the room. Clear nail polish may be substituted.
7. Choose helpers to collect, wash and store paint trays, cups and brushes.

CONSTELLATION NITE—LITE

MATERIALS

1. medium size gift box
2. yellow, black and white paint
3. brushes
4. hole puncher, or small pointed scissors
5. aluminum foil
6. 25 watt bulb in socket, with cord
7. construction paper
8. pencil
9. scissors
10. fire proofing spray

BEFORE YOU BEGIN

Thousands of years ago, many a lost traveller blessed the stars for faithfully guiding him across land and sea. Sages then were unaware that stars are suns, blinking because of the presence of vapor and dust in the atmosphere. Instead, they read those "diamonds in the sky" as outlines, or constellations. Dubbed with names like Pegasus, Great Dog, Big Bear, and Pisces, each stellar pattern became woven into myths and legends which have been handed down to the present time.

If the science teacher will lend a telescope and, perhaps, his assistance, plan a star-gazing session one night for children and parents. Then, bring a stellar personality indoors—Leo, Taurus, Scorpio, Aquarius, or any of the others crossing the night sky, can adorn our constellation nite-lite.

Ask for boxes (almost any medium size box will do, provided it stands firmly on its side) and necessary electrical equipment from home several days in advance of the lesson.

PROCEDURE (Illustration 7-10)

1. Spray the entire box with fire proofing spray.
2. Remove the box cover and paint the entire outside surface black. Let it dry. (step a)
3. Draw a pattern of a desired constellation figure on construction paper. Cut out this pattern. (step b)
4. Line the inside bottom half of the box with aluminum foil. Cut a small hole, for the cord, passing through the foil and the back of the box. (step c)
5. Using the pattern as a guide, outline the constellation shape on the painted box cover. (step d)

ILLUSTRATION 7-10

6. Remove the pattern. Pencil in small dots wherever stars should be. Make sure this placement is accurate.
7. Using a fine paint brush and white paint, go over the pencilled outline shape, adding desired details. Let it dry. (step e)
8. Using a hole puncher, or small pointed scissor, cut small circles for stars wherever dots have been placed. With yellow paint and a brush join the basic star clusters, conforming to the constellation pattern. (step g)
9. Place a light bulb in a socket inside the box. Thread a cord through the back opening of the box. Replace the decorated box cover. (step f)
10. Plug the lamp into a wall. The foil reflects light as it shines brilliantly through the cut out stars.

WHAT THE CHILDREN CAN DO AFTERWARD

1. Collect and read myths about stellar personalities.
2. Use star boxes as part of a solar system unit exhibit.
3. Bring the project home for use as a night lamp.

RELAX WITH TIME SAVERS

1. Spread newspaper before starting to work.
2. Make sure the construction paper patterns are smaller than the box tops, yet not so small as to "get lost" on the box cover.
3. Test each new application of paint on scrap or newspaper to make certain it does not "blob."
4. If scissors are used, cut-out stars should be about the size of a hole made with a standard hole puncher. If sufficient light does not shine through a particular opening, it may be made larger after the project has been completed and tested.
5. Distribute enough white, black and yellow paint in cups for two or three children to share.
6. Choose two helpers to collect, wash and store paint cups and brushes. Ask a third to dispose of newspaper.

HOLE PUNCH CONSTELLATIONS

MATERIALS

1. black construction paper
2. yellow construction paper
3. white and yellow paint, and brushes
4. hole puncher
5. pencil
6. stapler

ILLUSTRATION 7-11

Hole Punch Constellations

BEFORE YOU BEGIN

Pure pleasure for the teacher, this lesson is quick, simple, and winds up with results. For the child, it's learning with a gimmick. The ingenious gadget here is nothing more than teacher's hole puncher—a device for which the schoolboy seems to have an affinity. Our scholar will be able to punch out the patterns of stellar constellations, after a brief demonstration on procedure.

With a short introduction to the Dippers, Leo, Taurus, and their astral neighbors, the class is ready to "perforate" and paint away!

PROCEDURE (Illustration 7-11)

1. With white paint and a brush, paint the outline of a desired constellation on black construction paper. (step a)

2. Dot in the accurate placement of stars with a pencil. Punch out holes wherever these dots have been placed. (step b)
3. With yellow paint, join the "stars" to show a basic stellar pattern. (step c)
4. Staple the painting to yellow construction paper. "Stars" will "shine" through. (step d)

WHAT THE CHILDREN CAN DO AFTERWARD

1. Use the pictures as a bulletin board decoration.
2. Collect and read myths about stellar personalities.
3. Use hole punch constellations as greeting cards for astrology enthusiasts.

RELAX WITH TIME SAVERS

1. Spread newspaper before painting.
2. Distribute paint in plastic cups for children to share.
3. Choose helpers to collect, wash and store paint trays and brushes.

Bonus Ideas

1. Convert your room into a space museum. Suspend cardboard rockets, planet mobiles and space creatures from the fixtures. Display dioramas along the window sills. Adorn your bulletin boards with fantasy murals, colorful galaxies and constellation pictures. Invite other groups to view the display.
2. Make an animated movie of a rocket launch from take-off to lunar landing (see index—film making).
3. Fire proof heavy cardboard, bend it to the proper shape, and make constellation lamp shades.
4. Use the hole punch suggestion to design a city skyline lit up at night. Cut buildings from black construction paper, punch out "windows" and back each hole with colored paper. Tack these pictures to a bulletin board.
5. Splatter a galaxy on large mural paper. Tack this to a bulletin board and use the abstract as a background for class reports pertaining to space study.
6. Summoning all available research and imagination, model dioramas of unexplored planets.
7. Make dioramas of space stations on the moon. In addition to plaster, use oddly shaped boxes, large pasta noodles, and folded construction paper for the lunar structures.
8. Try making a relief globe of the Earth from plaster of Paris.
9. Using magazine cut-outs and newspaper headlines chronicle the historic moon landing in eye-catching collage.
10. Make space helmets from paper bags. Add paint, wire and other imaginative collage effects.
11. Plaster of Paris balls are an excellent basis for many themes; try adorable Easter bunnies and colorful Christmas decorations.
12. Make outer space creatures by substituting gourds for plaster.
13. Adapt the "Zodiac Jewelry" suggestion to Christmas, Valentine's Day and other holiday themes.
14. Make a simplified "Moon Landing Diorama" for primary grade youngsters. Eliminate the plaster of Paris. Instead, sculpt the lunar surface from aluminum foil. Use pipe cleaner figures for astronauts, and portray the distant earth with a magazine cut-out or drawing pasted to the diorama background.

Around The World 8

Come on aboard for a guided world's tour! With the trusty aid of scraps, paint, and crayon, we'll travel to seek out cultures and learn native crafts. This chapter is geared toward giving the child a glimpse of customs, some long gone, in his own, as well as distant lands. Through examples of painting, sculpture, mosaic, and costume, each new country will begin to gently unfold the full flavor of its heritage and "personality." With "Mexican Masks," "Tepees," and "Totem Poles" we'll delve into and participate in mock ceremonial rites of the Mexican and American Indian. With "Button Wind Chimes" we'll emulate the Japanese love of nature's subtle gifts.

What's most important here, is that youngsters learn to question the seemingly simple and complex. Why, for example, is the "Chinese Hat" everlastingly popular? Or, what vestiges of Viking culture are still evident today?

You needn't search the globe for materials with which to "internationalize" classroom walls and display areas. In fact, many items are those which usually find their way into home and school wastebaskets! Broken egg shells become delicate flower cups! Cardboard rolls are naturals for stringing Japanese style wind chimes and sculpting totem poles. Dimestore and broken strands of beads make perfect tesserae for "Florentine Mosaic Jewelry." So, why delay? Let's start packing for our unforgettable trip "Around the World."

FLORENTINE MOSAIC JEWELRY

MATERIALS

1. jewelry clay: Mix 1 part table salt with 3 parts flour. Gradually blend in small amounts of water until the mixture acquires a clay-like consistency. Knead on a board before using.
2. small bottle caps

3. tesserae: small glass
   or plastic beads
   (Mother's broken
   costume necklaces).
4. small tweezers
5. toothpicks
6. shellac
7. glue
8. pin backs, earring
   backs, inexpensive
   chains

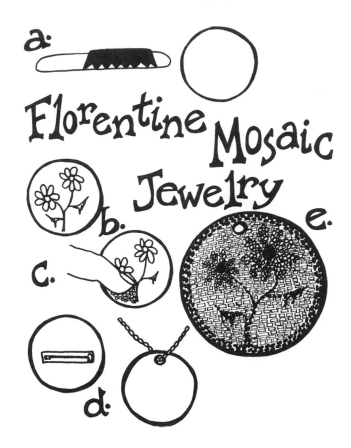

ILLUSTRATION 8-1

BEFORE YOU BEGIN

The fine art of mosaic had its dawn in Egypt. Later, Greeks geometrically patterned the floors of their homes and courtyards in mosaic. Romans employed the art form to duplicate earlier Greek paintings which otherwise would have been lost to our world when the originals disappeared. Byzantines, at least from the 6th to 12th centuries, used pieces of colored glass to create mosaics as the main decoration in their architecture.

Mosaic, or surface decoration, can be made by inlaying any kind of tesserae; colored stones, marble, glass, or seeds. Born of this venerable art and known as "Florentine Mosaic," various stone-like materials, including mother-of-pearl, have for centuries been used by Italian artisans to fashion personal and household ornaments.

For tesserae we'll use beads by the bottle, or from Mother's discarded and broken costume jewelry. Unlike working with tiles or glass, we'll do no cutting or gluing. For younger groups, stick to colorful abstracts and large figures without minute details. Bugle beads and large beads handle so well for beginners that it's a good idea to use them exclusively at the start.

PROCEDURE (Illustration 8-1)

1. Follow the recipe (as listed under "Materials") for the necessary amount of dough.
2. Work on a floured surface. Flatten a small amount of dough (not too thin), then use a bottle cap to cut out a pin, earring, or medallion shape. (step a)
3. Using a toothpick, "draw" a desired design in the cut-out dough. Errors may easily be rubbed off and the picture re-done. (step b)
4. Fill in the design using assorted beads. Make certain to mosaic the entire jewelry piece—the background as well as the picture or abstract. Use tweezers to facilitate handling. Each bead should be imbedded securely in the dough so that it can be easily seen, but not "buried" beneath the surface. Where large areas are to be covered with a single color, beads may be sprinkled, then gently pressed into place with a finger. (steps c & e)
5. Force a hole through the top of each medallion piece for stringing later. Let the completed dough mosaic dry and harden. This may take a day or two. Should breakage accidentally occur, repair it with white glue. (step d)
6. Coat each hardened piece with shellac. Let it dry.
7. Glue appropriate backings to pins and earrings. Thread a chain through the medallion opening. (step d)

WHAT THE CHILDREN CAN DO AFTERWARD

1. Make matching jewelry sets to sell at a school fund raising fair.
2. Include mosaics in a display of Italian crafts.
3. Give the jewelry as gifts.
4. Larger mosaic pieces may be glued to a velvet backing and framed for wall decoration.

RELAX WITH TIME SAVERS

1. Encourage children to bring in their respective "special stones," or beads.
2. Dough may be made in advance, refrigerated over night in plastic and used the next day. If time permits, allow each group of children to measure and prepare their own dough.
3. Provide a small cup of flour for each table. The dough is managed best when it is worked on a floured surface. Use small amounts of flour to avoid an unnecessary mess.
4. Distribute beads, sorted as to color and shape, in plastic ice-cube trays or cupcake tins. Allow one tray for two children to share.
5. Provide a safe, dry area where mosaics may harden.
6. Set up one area of the room for varnishing. Use spray shellac, or clear nail polish.

MEXICAN FLOWERS

MATERIALS

1. package of crepe paper—one package makes two flowers
2. flower "stems"—choose tomato sticks, dowels, thin branches, or straightened coat hangers
3. thin floral wire "stamens"
4. string
5. floral tape
6. stapler
7. scissors
8. crepe paper scraps for flower centers

BEFORE YOU BEGIN

   Spilling out of planes from Mexico, vacationers return with armloads of double and triple blossomed flowers. Some resemble giant anemones and huge poppies, others are shapes still unbred, but all shame nature for not being first to invent such dazzling combinations.

   These paper flowers come home as gifts, or warm reminders of a holiday amidst blue waters and sun washed plazas. With only a few paper folds and scissor snips, anyone can make flowers as charming as those beckoning irresistibly from vases in shops and carts of Mexico. Realistic or fake, each flower shape begins with such simple folds that even second graders turn out beauties!

   Demonstrate the procedure, emphasizing that the trick is in the folding. As to colors, though subtle pastels are lovely, the theme here is "South of the Border." Mix a sizzling fiesta for authentic "Mexicania."

PROCEDURE I (Illustration 8-2)

1. Cut a package of crepe paper in half. Each half produces one flower. (step a)
2. Holding 1/2 of the paper package vertically, cut the desired petal shape (e.g., pointed, oval, jagged) between the two folds. (step a)
3. Unroll the paper. Horizontally, fold the entire paper length in half and seam the ends together with a stapler. (steps a & b)
4. Fold the paper in half two more times. (step c)
5. Gather the paper at the bottom. Insert any desired contrasting inner decoration, or thin wire stamen.
6. Insert a flower stem (dowel, tomato stick, branch) through the bottom opening. Secure the stem to the gathered flower parts tightly with string or thin floral wire. (step d)
7. Beautiful floral effects depend on time and care taken in separating and

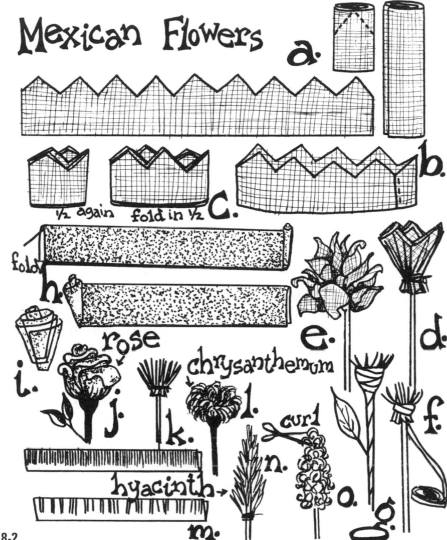

Mexican Flowers

a.

b.

½ again   fold in ½ C.

fold

h.

rose

i.

j.   k.

chrysanthemum

l.

curl

n.

o.

e.

d.

f.

g.

hyacinth →

m.

ILLUSTRATION 8-2

shaping the flower petals. Begin with the bottom layer, gently separating it from the others. Carefully contour each petal, slightly stretching the crepe paper into a desired form. Work each inner layer in the same manner. (step e)

8. Wrap floral tape around the flower base to conceal string and form a calyx. Continue to tape along the stem. If desired, cut crepe paper leaves, score, and attach them to the stem with additional floral tape. If branches are used, you may wish to maintain the natural look and forego taped stems. (steps f & g)

PROCEDURE II — ROSES

1. Use 1/2 of a crepe paper package for each rose. Unroll the entire width of this

1/2 package. Fold the paper in half vertically, but *do not make sharp crease in the fold.* (step h)

2. Starting at one end of the folded sheet, roll the paper into concentric circles. Make each paper rotation a bit wider than the previous one, using a hand to separate new layers and guide the rose shape. Roll the paper more tightly for opening buds. (Note—this procedure produces a rather large rose. For smaller flowers cut smaller strips from the crepe paper package.) (steps h & i)

3. Gather the flower tightly at its base and proceed as in Procedure I. Gently stretch the paper at the upper edges. (step j)

PROCEDURE III — CHRYSANTHEMUM

1. Lengthwise, fold 1/3 of a crepe paper package into a narrow strip. Cut even fringes. (step k)

2. Open the width of the fringed paper, seam the ends and proceed as in Procedure I. (step l)

PROCEDURE IV — HYACINTH

1. Follow the directions for a chrysanthemum, but cut a *randomly* spaced fringe. (step m)

2. Attach the fringed strip to one end of a "stem" with tape. Wind the remainder of the strip down 1/3 the length of the stem. Carefully curl each paper fringe around a pencil or blunt edge of a scissor. (steps n & o)

WHAT THE CHILDREN CAN DO AFTERWARD

1. Collect large vases and arrange attractive floral displays.
2. Use the flowers as favors for parents invited to a class Latin American party.
3. Sell the flowers at a school fund raising fair.
4. Use paper flowers as stage decoration for a play or sing.
5. Give these Mexican flowers as gifts.
6. Imbed the flowers in green styrofoam for a "Mexican" garden.
7. Use the paper flowers as centerpieces for a PTA or other school function.

RELAX WITH TIME SAVERS

1. Halve each crepe paper package in advance of the lesson.
2. Distribute a sufficient color selection of crepe paper materials to each table.
3. If coat hangers are used as stems, straighten them before the lesson.
4. One stapler can be shared by four to five children.
5. Supervise individuals as the flowers are gathered and secured with string; they must be tied securely.
6. Have two children share a roll of floral tape and wire.

TEPEES AND TOTEM POLES (Illustration 8-3)

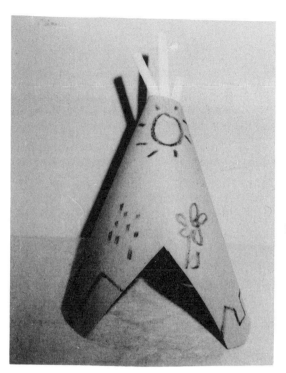

ILLUSTRATION 8-3

MATERIALS

Tepees
1. construction paper
2. crayons
3. paste
4. stapler
5. drinking straws

Totem poles
1. cardboard roll from waxed paper
   or aluminum foil package
2. aluminum foil
3. masking tape
4. poster paint and brushes
5. varnish

BEFORE YOU BEGIN

If today we are going to be Indians, we should surely know something about the impressive totem pole that towers over and protects our village of tepees. Totem poles held such importance in Indian culture that families took their surname from the carved animal, fish, or bird. If the clan symbol, or totem, was an animal, then this mythical ancestor was to be forever protected, and, of course, never eaten!

Imagine the party that went along with the raising of a totem pole! Here's a chance to exhaust excess energy playing Indian, by building a village around which to whoop and dance.

As almost every natural phenomenon was explained by some lovely legend, such tales should surely be heard along with tribal songs and chants that accompanied dance. Young braves and maidens should also learn how Indian forefathers survived through food preservation, tracking skills, and alertness to forest sounds. Dye making that colored so much of their lives is still another facet of culture children love investigating.

Two procedures are described below; one for making tepees, the other for totem poles. Both are easy. Make totem poles first, then, as paint dries, complete a village of colorfully designed tepees.

PROCEDURE I — TEPEE

1. Cut semicircles from the construction paper (size will depend on available display space).
2. With a crayon, decorate each semicircle with an Indian design.
3. Fold the decorated semicircle into a cone shape and staple it in place.
4. Cut out a V-shaped opening in front of the tepee.
5. Cut two drinking straws in half; flatten and color them with a crayon. Insert the straws through the opening at the top of the tepee. Paste the straws in place inside the model.

PROCEDURE II — TOTEM POLE

1. Cover a paper roll with several layers of aluminum foil, molding the totem pole features as you work.
2. Cover the foil-wrapped roll completely with masking tape. The foil should not show through.
3. Decoratively paint the taped surface. Let it dry.
4. Complete the totem pole with a coat of varnish.

WHAT THE CHILDREN CAN DO AFTERWARD

1. Use a large table or floor for a village panorama. Attractively group the tepees and totem poles. Add plastic Indian figures, horses, fences, and the like brought in from home. Or, model these from clay.

2. Have each child use his model inside a shoe box for an individual diorama.
3. Learn Indian songs and dances. Invite other groups to view the display and listen to a class presentation.

RELAX WITH TIME SAVERS

1. Pre-cut semicircles for tepees in advance of the lesson.
2. Let each table share a stapler.
3. Distribute paint in plastic ice-cube trays; one for two children to share.
4. Have two children share a roll of tape and one roll of aluminum foil.
5. Set up a spray station in a well ventilated area of the room. One at a time, have the children varnish the totem poles in this area.

BUTTON WIND CHIME

MATERIALS

1. small cylindrical cardboard roll (larger ones may be halved)
2. paint
3. varnish
4. embroidery yarn
5. assorted flat buttons

BEFORE YOU BEGIN

In legend and art, the Japanese people give testimony to their love of flowers, birds, and countryside. Devotion to nature extends to the murmuring running waters and whispering winds. Indeed, barely a garden is without the gurgling water and tinkling music of a wind chime. Like the Japanese, let us hang chimes in the garden or window for a breeze to play its song.

Materials for this simple wind chime are usually abundant in every household. Begin to collect these, however, a week in advance. Though this lesson will hold the interest of most children, it is of special advantage to the lower grades where small manipulative skills are being developed. Show your class how to string and overlap the buttons. Guide their first attempts during the demonstration lesson.

PROCEDURE (Illustration 8-4)

1. Decoratively paint the cardboard roll and let it dry. (step a)
2. Varnish the painted roll. Let it dry.
3. Thread a needle with an extra-long piece of embroidery yarn. Knot it at the bottom. (step b)
4. String the first row of buttons, double looping them, so that they overlap slightly against one another. (step b)
5. When the desired number of buttons have been strung, push the needle

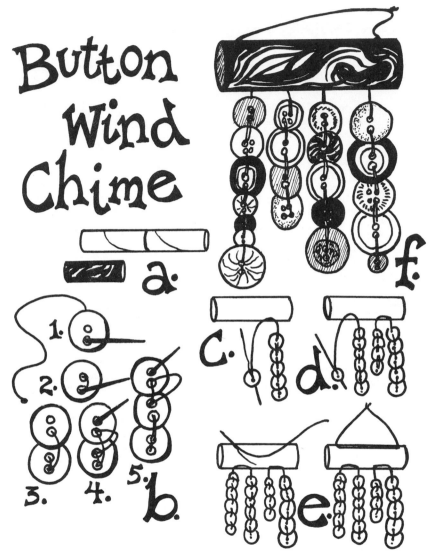

ILLUSTRATION 8-4

through the paper roll (beginning about 1/4″ from the edge). Approximately 3/4″ from first row of buttons, pass the needle out through the paper roll. (step c)

6. Working down this time, proceed to string the buttons. Knot the thread after the last button has been added. (steps c & d)

7. Thread and knot a second piece of embroidery thread. String this row of buttons in same manner as the first, attaching it 3/4″ away from the preceding row. Make the fourth row in the same manner as the second. (steps d & e)

8. Opposite the hanging buttons, about 1/2″ from the cylindrical opening, pass a threaded needle through the roll. Repeat the procedure 1/2″ from the second cylindrical opening. Tie the two string ends together, forming a loop from which to suspend the completed wind chime. (step e)

WHAT THE CHILDREN CAN DO AFTERWARD

1. Hang the chimes outdoors in a tree nearest the classroom.
2. Bring the chimes home as gifts for mother's garden.

RELAX WITH TIME SAVERS

1. Pre-cut large cardboard cylinders to size prior to the lesson.
2. Distribute paint in plastic ice-cube trays; one for two to three children to share. Spread newspaper before painting.
3. Set up a varnish station in a well ventilated area of the room. Have the youngsters complete this job in small groups at this station.
4. Distribute a sufficient supply of buttons for each table to share.
5. While varnished cardboard rolls dry, clean and store the paint supplies and discard the newspaper.

MEXICAN MASKS (Illustration 8-5)

ILLUSTRATION 8-5

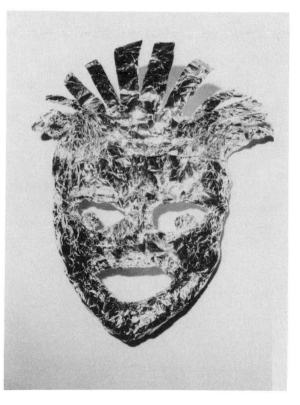

MATERIALS

1. heavy aluminum foil
2. stapler
3. scissors
4. construction paper scraps
5. glue
6. string

BEFORE YOU BEGIN

Yanqui Indians of Mexico wore masks on the backs of their heads! Masks that are used today to decorate were then part of ceremonial rites. Long before the arrival of the Spanish, Indians had talent for superb craftsmanship. Modern Mexicans, still in that same intricate and imaginative manner, use the metallic minerals abundantly mined in their country to produce magnificently designed works of art.

Whether the mask we make will be for costuming or wall decoration we would do well to imitate the Mexicans. A little originality of our own will, of course, add immeasurably to an afternoon of unique learning.

Give some time for research. "When were masks worn?" "By whom?" "What did they represent?" Any related literature and photos should provide a glimpse into this exotic aspect of another culture.

Do a quick demonstration before handing out materials. Encourage classmates to help each other with initial sculpting.

PROCEDURE

1. Tear off three equal size sheets of heavy aluminum foil, slightly larger than the size of a child's face.
2. Place the foil sheets together and press them against the face, carefully molding the features. Have the children assist one another if necessary, making certain that the nose, eye sockets, and mouth are well defined.
3. Remove the mask from the face. Each child may now re-shape the impressions for unusual effects. Cut out the eye openings. Add any other decorative cut-outs.
4. Neatly fold and press the edges to the back of the mask.
5. Shape additional foil for an elaborate headdress, fringed eyelashes, and so on. Staple these in place.
6. Cut small colorful construction paper "jewels." Glue them to the headdress, as well as to the lower edge of each eye.
7. Staple string to the back of the mask.

WHAT THE CHILDREN CAN DO AFTERWARD

1. Use the masks as hanging wall decorations.
2. Wear the masks as part of a play costume.
3. Use them as Halloween masks.

RELAX WITH TIME SAVERS

1. Pre-cut aluminum foil sheets in advance of the lesson. Clip three sheets together and have one set ready for each child.
2. Have a roll of foil for each table to share when making additional decorations.
3. Provide a stapler for every three children to share.
4. Distribute two to three paint cups filled with glue for each table to share.
5. Provide a box of construction paper scraps for each table to share.
6. Choose helpers to collect scraps in a wastebasket, and clean and store paint cups and brushes.

INTERNATIONAL SHOW DOLLS

MATERIALS

1. thin wire for armature
2. small mound of clay
3. plaster of Paris bandage (or regular plaster of Paris)
4. fine sand paper
5. paint
6. varnish
7. assorted materials for making costumes: fabric scraps, construction paper, tissue paper, crepe paper, ribbon, buttons, yarn
8. white glue and brushes
9. needle and thread, optional
10. scissors
11. small bowl of warm water

BEFORE YOU BEGIN

What better way to salute the United Nations than with a parade of show dolls resplendent in traditional costume? Dolls costumed to represent member nations help add a touch of cheer and color to the world's age old ills of politics and disease.

Ask each child to select a country (perhaps from his own ancestry), research traditional costumes and begin collecting scraps which would appropriately dress his mannequin. Pictures, as well as dolls from home collections are helpful for preliminary study. Compare these styles to note similarities and differences.

Count on several working sessions. Leave the exact costuming methods to the children. Though most will prefer developing their own ideas, and should, suggestions described below might well be demonstrated for starters. Point out that the fabric scraps and tissue paper can be glued directly to the doll. Provide a needle and thread for the more patient and adept costumier.

It might be noted that plaster of Paris bandage rolls are preferred to the traditional plaster technique, though the latter may be substituted. Bandage rolls enable children to work more neatly and faster, by cutting small amounts of plaster material as needed.

PROCEDURE (Illustration 8-6)

1. Form an armature for the doll shape from thin wire. Imbed the armature in a clay base so that the doll stands without wobbling. (step a)
2. Cut off several inches of plaster bandage as needed. Dip each strip into warm water, squeeze it slightly, and wrap it around the wire armature. Sculpt and encase the entire doll, including the clay base, in plaster. Allow it to dry thoroughly (this will take only several minutes). (step b)
3. Gently sand any rough spots until smooth.

ILLUSTRATION 8-6

4. Paint the doll. If a long, elaborate costume is required, it may only be necessary to paint the face and hands. Let the paint dry thoroughly.
5. Varnish the painted areas. Let them dry.
6. Choose attractive collage scraps for the desired costume. Using white glue and brushes adorn the doll in traditional native attire.

Some Suggestions:

a. *Norwegian Peasant*—Make a colorful full-length skirt from tissue paper or fabric. Crayon or embroider a traditional design along the hem. Glue the skirt in place. Use sheer white fabric for a peasant blouse (cut the front, back and sleeves separately, then glue them in place). Add a vest in the same color as the skirt. Cut a stiff white fabric apron and tie it around the waist. Braid yellow yarn for hair. Tie a colorful scarf around the doll's head. (step c)

b. *Hawaiian Native*—Paint the entire plaster body. Choose a colorful patterned fabric and tie it, sarong style, around the doll's waist. String small multi-colored tissue paper circles together, and crumple them between your fingers for a flower effect. Place this paper lei around the doll's neck. Glue on black yarn for the doll's hair. Cut a cardboard surf board for the doll to carry in his arm. (step d)

c. *Spanish Senorita*—Make a full length skirt from a construction paper semicircle. Secure it in place around the doll's waist. Glue strips of red crepe paper, in tiers, around this skirt shape. Ruffle the edges by gently stretching the paper between your fingers. Glue on the dress bodice. Glue on black yarn for "upswept hair," and adorn it with a nylon lace "mantilla." Place a construction paper fan in the doll's hand. (step e)

WHAT THE CHILDREN CAN DO AFTERWARD

1. Have each child introduce his doll to his classmates, telling how one might spend a typical day in the country this doll represents.
2. Learn ammenities in a foreign language (hello, good-bye, thank-you, come again). Ask the children to learn these phrases for the country his doll represents. Print these on a bulletin board display.
3. Display the dolls in school show cases during United Nations Week.
4. Ask the children to give a travelogue type talk about the countries their dolls represent.
5. Learn traditional songs and dances from other lands. Invite other groups to a musicale and doll exhibit.
6. Display the dolls against a background of class made travel posters.
7. Display the dolls beneath a bulletin board world map. Tie one end of string to each doll's hand; attach the other end to its native country on the map.

RELAX WITH TIME SAVERS

1. Set up work areas so that children may conveniently rotate from one step to the next. First, complete all the wire work at seats. Proceed to a plaster station, complete with necessary supplies in the back of the room. Do all sculpting in this area.
2. Wash hands of all plaster when the sculpting is completed.
3. Proceed to a painting and varnishing area. While painted dolls dry, youngsters may choose their desired materials from available scrap boxes.
4. Provide an assortment of additional decorative materials, such as yarn, buttons, thread, and the like for each table to share.
5. Choose class helpers to clean each work area; table assistants to collect and discard (or store) scraps on the desks.

EGGSHELL FLOWER CUPS

MATERIALS

1. egg shell
2. soda bottle cap
3. glue

4. wax shavings
5. candle
6. paint and fine brush
7. thin wire, tissue paper, floral tape; or small artifical plastic flowers

ILLUSTRATION 8-7

BEFORE YOU BEGIN

Handed down through generations by the Amish, these delicate flower cups are a fine example of American folk art. Couple a little care in handling with some supervision with the melting wax process and your class can make traditional reproductions of these, as well as some highly acceptable originals. If no one in your class can bring one of these "Hex" land souveniers for "Show and Tell," then a sample will have to be made for study.

Eggshells, appropriately broken, wrapped in cotton and boxed, should be brought from home in advance of the lesson. Do have plenty of extras on hand for expected emergencies.

PROCEDURE (Illustration 8-7)

1. Cut a small hole in the top of the eggshell. Carefully empty the egg from the shell. Gently widen the hole, removing about 1/3 of the shell. Edges may be left jagged. Wash the inside of the shell and let it dry. (step a)
2. Glue the bottom of the eggshell to the inside of a large soda bottle cap. The egg will now stand securely. (step b)
3. Fill the shell about 1/4 full with was shavings. Light a long candle and tip it toward the inside of the wax-filled shell, allowing the wax to melt. Let the melted wax firm and harden. (step c)
4. Decoratively paint the outside of the shell. Let it dry. (step d)
5. Make small colorful flowers from tissue paper attached to thin wire. Cover the wire stems with floral tape. Gently insert these flowers into the wax-filled shell. Small artifical flowers may be substituted. (steps e & f)

WHAT THE CHILDREN CAN DO AFTERWARD

1. Use the flower cups as part of an American art display.
2. Flower cups make decorative party favors.
3. Give flower cups as gifts, especially at Easter.

RELAX WITH TIME SAVERS

1. Help the children glue the eggs to bottle caps. Hold the egg in place until the glue dries.
2. Set up an area in back of the room where wax may be melted. This job requires close supervision. Work with one child at a time.
3. Set the decorated eggshells safely aside while making the flowers.
4. Distribute an assortment of pre-cut wire stems, tape and tissue paper (cut into small squares and circles), for each group to share.
5. Have the children bring flower cups home after completion.

CHINESE HAT

ILLUSTRATION 8-8

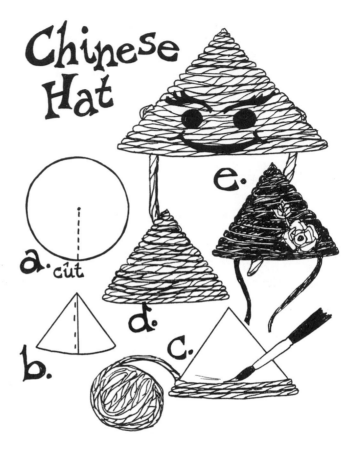

MATERIALS

1. 15″ cardboard circle
2. yellow yarn
3. white glue and brush
4. stapler
5. yarn and needle
6. paste, paper, collage scraps, optional

BEFORE YOU BEGIN

Though it looks like a collapsing tent, there are few head coverings as practical the year round as this Chinese hat. What other head gear takes into consideration all of the elements? With a crown that peaks above the very top of the scalp, an insulating air space is formed, protecting the head from direct heat in summer, and cold in winter. Just as it's shape forms a sunshade, so is it an umbrella that permits rain to wash along its sides, without trickling down the neck, or drenching one's face. So simple! So ingenious!

Use these simple hats for costumes. Then, in late spring, with the advent of warm summer days on the beach and in the sun, we do well to embellish this clever Chinese hat idea with creative collage.

PROCEDURE (Illustration 8-8)

1. With a pencil, draw in the radius of the cardboard circle. Cut along this line. (step a)

2. Over-lap the cut-out sides, forming the circle into a cone shape. Staple the cone in place, making certain it fits the child's head securely. (step b)

3. Working in concentric circles, from the bottom of the hat surface upwards, apply small amounts of white glue at a time with a brush. Wind the yarn into place over the glued area, pressing each new layer closely and firmly against the previous one. Continue to glue, then wind the yarn, until the entire hat is covered. (steps c & d)

4. To make tying strings, thread a long piece of yarn and attach it with a button-hole stitch to each side of the hat. Tie the strings under the chin. (step e)

5. Optional—Paste or sew an assortment of collage materials to the simple peasant hat. Make whimsical faces from felt cut-outs, add tissue paper flowers, or try a summer collage of sea-shells, construction paper fish and fish net. (step e)

WHAT THE CHILDREN CAN DO AFTERWARD

1. Wear the hats as part of an oriental costume.
2. Sell the decorated hats at a school fund raising fair.
3. Coordinate beach bags to match the decorated hats. Wrap any suitable, empty box with yarn and adorn it in the same way as the hat.

RELAX WITH TIME SAVERS

1. Pre-cut the cardboard circles in advance of the lesson.
2. Help the children fit the cone shapes to size before stapling them closed.
3. Provide a paint cup, filled with glue for each child.
4. If sun hats are being made, distribute an assortment of collage materials for each table to share.
5. Choose helpers to collect and store usable scraps.

Special Activities

There are never enough glorious hours in the day for a boy, his kite, and an open field. Some breezy, clear noon surprise your class, Japanese style, with these eye-catching box kites. Excitement reaches a fever pitch with the promise of kite flying contests and a chance to "wow" schoolmates with unusual, original creations.

BOX KITES

MATERIALS

1. four 18" balsa sticks
2. four 8-1/4" balsa sticks

3. 25″ long white shelf paper or brown paper
4. thread (button sewing thread)
5. kite string
6. white glue
7. crayon

BEFORE YOU BEGIN

Amongst the many kites loved by the children of Japan is the box kite we're about to construct. As we watch a paper and cloth kite float over the horizon, we think of the contrivance as a delightful toy. So it is, but facts take us further. Precede the lesson with some fascinating background about kites in general.

Kites have been used in photography, radio, to measure wind velocity, and in advertising. A kite was employed to carry the first lines across the gorge to build the Niagara Falls suspension bridge. As for the box kite in particular, it has been sent aloft by men stranded at sea to signal their position.

So enthusiastic about kite flying are the children of Japan, that May 5th of every year the sport highlights the country's "Boy Festival." On that day one "carp kite," symbolizing manly courage and strength, is flown for each boy in the family. Imagine a sky filled with a huge school of fish, jumping and swimming upstream in the wind!

Once they've experimented with the kites suggested here and have read a bit of intriguing history, children may well decide to construct other types of kites to whirl come another windy day.

For today's lesson, have a sample kite on hand, as well as a set of necessary materials. Explain the basic steps. Once the kite designs are finished, complete the remainder of the activity as a demonstration lesson, with the class following the teacher's step by step instruction. Have all materials cut to size and compiled in individual ready-to-assemble sets in advance of lesson. Keep additional replacement materials available.

PROCEDURE (Illustration 8-9)

1. Color a picture or design on the shelf paper. (step a)
2. Make a 1″ fold along the length of one end of the 25″ paper. Fold the remaining 24″ in quarters. Each quarter will measure 6″ across. (steps b & c)
3. Fold down the paper in half and cut along the fold. The two resulting identical pieces will form the top and bottom sections of the box kite. (step d)
4. Separate the paper sheets and lay them out on the desk, one beneath the other. Keep the respective fold marks in line. At this time the child may write his name on the 1″ fold. (step e)
5. Place 18″ sticks along the outer edge of the sheets and each of the three folds (exclude the 1″ fold). Each stick should extend approximately 1″ beyond the upper sheet, and 1″ below the lower sheet. (step e)

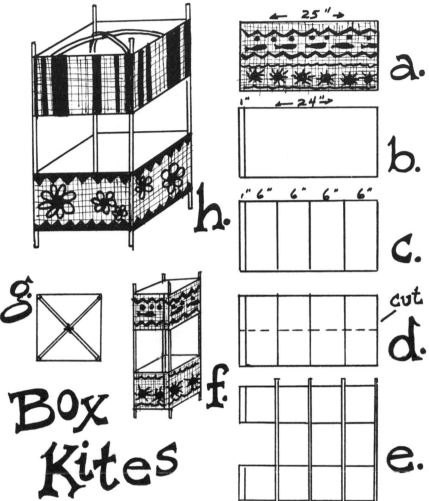

a.

b.

c.

d.

e.

f.

g.

h.

Box Kites

ILLUSTRATION 8-9

6. When the sticks have been satisfactorily placed, remove them, one at a time, apply glue and replace them, securing them firmly to the paper.

7. Place glue on the inside of the 1″ fold and attach it to the end of the stick, forming a collapsible square. Let the glue dry. (step f)

8. Cross sticks must now be made from the 8-1/4″ balsa sticks. Two such sticks are needed for the top of the kite, and two for the bottom. Start at the upper kite section, with one 8-1/4″ cross stick. Approximately 1″ from the top edge of the kite, insert a stick diagonally and secure it with thread to the two opposite kite sticks. Similarly, place a second 8-1/4″ cross bar and attach it to the remaining sticks at the top of the kite. Secure the cross sticks at the center with string (exercise greatest care, for it is here that breakage most often occurs). (steps g & h)

9. Repeat the process on the bottom half of the kite.
10. Attach a kite string to a side stick.

WHAT THE CHILDREN CAN DO AFTERWARD

1. Naturally, take these kites outdoors and practice flying. The time and care which went into the making will be rewarded, since the box kites will go up with little difficulty and do not require as much wind as their conventional counterparts. A few precautions should be reviewed before flying; stay away from transmission towers and electric wires; do not attempt to retrieve a kite from wire; stop flying should it start to rain.
2. Have a flying contest. Invite other classes and ask the teachers to be judges.

RELAX WITH TIME SAVERS

1. Have all the materials pre-cut in advance, with plenty of extras on hand.
2. Distribute a bottle of glue and a sufficient supply of thread to each child. It should not be necessary to interrupt the demonstration lesson to search for additional materials.
3. Proceed in a step-by-step manner. Circulate about the room often, making certain that all understand the directions.
4. Carefully supervise the children as the cross bars are ties. Many will require assistance. Explain that the cross pieces are tied, rather than notched, so that the sticks will "bow" slightly should the kite hit an object. When notched, and rigid, they are apt to break.

STICK PUPPET VIKINGS

MATERIALS

1. cardboard sheet
2. scissors
3. crayons
4. paste
5. aluminum foil scraps
6. tissue paper
7. white thread
8. tongue depressor
9. stapler
10. corrugated cardboard box
11. paint
12. long strips of blue construction paper
13. oaktag sheet

BEFORE YOU BEGIN

To "go Viking" once literally meant to go forth on an expedition of plunder. So it was that the Scandinavians (Norwegians, Danes and Swedes) were known as Vikings as they marauded lands and dared unknown seas in the 250 years before the Christian millennium.

ILLUSTRATION 8-10

During their career of pillaging and piracy, the "Northmen" or "Norsemen" would often find a new country attractive enough to remain. In their travels they left settlements in the Orkney and Shetland Islands, Hebrides, Iceland, Greenland, and Finland. It is interesting that in all the world, only Iceland's language closely resembles that of the original Vikings. As most school children already know, Vikings, braving formidable waters in fragile ships, were actually the first to step ashore in North America—several hundred years before Columbus set sail!

Surrounding these fierce warriors and their sleek ships are many legends, as well as historical facts. Take time to investigate the Viking heritage. Delve into saga, religion, and custom.

Pictures of Viking ships are helpful in both discussion of ornate vessel carvings and in our own puppet construction. As models, use Viking type dolls and pictures from home or library.

The resulting stage and stick figures, an excellent approach to informal puppetry, make compelling class displays when not in use. You may wish children to work in small groups, each creating puppets and stage sets to coordinate with aspects of Norse life.

PROCEDURE — PUPPETS (Illustration 8-10)

1. Draw the Viking ships and warriors on stiff cardboard. Each drawn figure creates a new puppet, and should be adequately sized in proportion to the cardboard box stage.
2. Color each figure with crayon and cut it out. (steps a & b)
3. Cut the ship's sail from tissue paper or striped gift paper and paste it in place. (step b)
4. Attach "ropes" from the mast to the body of the ship with heavy white thread, secured in place with paste. (step b)
5. Make Viking shields from aluminum foil backed cardboard. Paste these in place. Etch a shield design with a pencil point or toothpick. (step a)
6. Staple the completed figures to tongue depressors. (steps a & b)

PROCEDURE — STAGE

1. Remove the box flaps.
2. Paint a scene on the inside back of the box. Let it dry. (step d)
3. Cut slits along the bottom of the stage. The puppets will be inserted and manipulated along these slits. (step d)
4. Make a raised sea from long strips of blue or green construction paper. Cut "waves" along one edge of each paper strip, then fold back the opposite edge so that the waves "stand." Make three such wave strips and paste them, one behind the other, to the cardboard stage foreground. (steps c & d)
5. Make raised ground from a folded sheet of oaktag. This should extend halfway across the stage. When attaching, make certain that the slits in the oaktag align with the slits at the base of box. (steps c & d)
6. Place the stage on a table. Put two or three large books beneath each end of the completed box stage. Insert the puppet figures through the slits so that the tongue depressors protrude from the base of the stage. The children work behind the stage by slipping their hands under the box and manipulating the stick puppets from side to side. If desired, hands may be concealed by means of a crepe paper skirt stapled around the base of the box. (step d)

WHAT THE CHILDREN CAN DO AFTERWARD

1. Working two at a time, have the children present informal puppet shows.

2. Store the puppets in the box slits when they are not in use. Place the stage on a table for class display.

RELAX WITH TIME SAVERS

1. Have some groups work on the cardboard stage in back of the room while others make puppets. The roles may later be reversed.
2. Distribute a sufficient assortment of necessary puppet-making materials for each table to share.
3. Carefully supervise the youngsters as the slits are cut across the stage surface.
4. Spread newspaper before painting the cardboard stage.

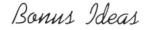

Bonus Ideas

1. Make early American show dolls for a panorama of colonial life.
2. Learn about primitive homes around the world. Make classroom models.
3. Learn and experiment with the art of candle dipping as part of a study about early American life.
4. Paint or crayon a display of international flags.
5. Try Indian picture writing, on bark if possible. Have children translate one another's messages.
6. Make a colonial hornbook.
7. Stencil Pennsylvania Dutch hex signs on wooden circles or paper plates.
8. Learn about heraldry. Ask each child to reproduce, or invent, a family coat of arms.
9. Add foreign flavor to this year's Christmas party with a Mexican piñata.
10. Embroider felt belts and suspenders with Tyrolean designs.
11. Make stick figures and a stage to represent a Thai floating market, or the gondolas of Venice.
12. Have an international hat show. Make traditional hats from paper and fabric.
13. Disguised as dragons in the sky, Chinese kites promise novel flying fun.
14. Find some simple international recipes. With parent's help, plan a round-the-world smorgasbord.
15. Make small "Mexican flowers" for Easter bonnet decoration or Mother's Day bouquets.
16. Make a life-size Indian village.
17. Make Hawaiian grass skirts and leis from crepe paper.
18. Have very young children make "wind chimes" by stringing a variety of pasta shapes; or use beads from discarded costume jewelry.

Mood, Music

and Dance

9

To experience the blending of mood, music, and dance is like watching the enactment of some almost forgotten dream—often lovely, sometimes terrifying, always with an intangible mystique. As music seems to lift and sway the unbelievably graceful ballerina on its every note, so do our emotions breathlessly rest on every cadence. How do we verbalize the excruciating beauty of such a moment? It's so abstract. We're so inhibited.

Instinctively, the very young do know how, and express these feelings best with paint, brush, or a lump of clay. Utilizing such familiar media, the lessons which follow help the child relate more closely to music and dance. At the same time, here is a chance to refreshingly explore these two art forms from primitive beginnings to modern day "rock."

Transcending the limits of age and individual creativity, each child feels a measure of success when his painted or sculpted reactions are the unique personification of his own emotions and dreams.

PAINTING TO MUSIC (Illustration 9-1)

MATERIALS

1. phonograph and two records; choose selections with contrasting moods, preferably long playing
2. two large sheets of painting paper
3. paint and brushes

BEFORE YOU BEGIN

Picture for a moment mankind's first conductor. What genius it took to synchronize those crude musical instruments to create harmony! Whether his primitive scores

Painting to Music

ILLUSTRATION 9-1

commanded the brave to war, or frightened devils away, music, then as now, was one of early man's strongest emotional catalysts.

We see these spontaneous effects of music as the youngest child struts to a march, glides with the waltz, and "monkeys" to the beat of rock. For today's lesson, responses will be expressed somewhat differently, through paint and brush.

To more clearly enable children to perceive the different effects of music, it is suggested that two recorded selections, contrasting in mood and "new" to young listeners be used. Directions should emphasize freedom of choice, with each child painting that which he interprets.

As music conducts imaginations, expect a wide assortment of colorful lines and abstracts. Though class interpretations may abound with similarities, you're also apt to find some rather fascinating expressions of those listening to the beat of another drum.

PROCEDURE

1. Start the first recording while you are distributing the materials. Tell your class they are to listen, then paint, whatever they feel in response to the selection.
2. Midway through the record, change the selection, replacing it with another, distinctly different in mood. Distribute a second sheet of paper and ask the children to again paint what they feel.
3. Ask the children to study their completed paintings as they listen once more to the two recordings. Then have them discuss their painted reactions to the musical selections.

WHAT THE CHILDREN CAN DO AFTERWARD

1. Have each child title his paintings with a word or short phrase.
2. Let the children explain their pictures. Help the class discover what effects the music had on their choices of color, line, or painted theme.
3. With the actual song titles as headings, prepare a bulletin board display of the painted interpretations.

RELAX WITH TIME SAVERS

1. Do not initiate the activity when the class is over-stimulated. Choose, instead, a moment of relative calm.
2. Have children clear the area around their desks so that the first completed painting may be safely placed on the floor to dry, while the second selection is being played.
3. Distribute each sheet of painting paper separately immediately before the respective recordings are played.
4. Fill each ice-cube tray with a generous choice of tempera colors. Two children can share a tray. Re-fill these supplies, if necessary, as the children work.
5. Discourage talking and "comparing notes" while painting.

ILLUSTRATE A SONG (Illustration 9-2)

ILLUSTRATION 9-2

MATERIALS

    1. drawing paper
    2. crayons

BEFORE YOU BEGIN

When you recall your favorite song, what pictures and patterns meander through your mind? As the notes play upon your ears, is some memory revived to live again? For something new in pictures, let's draw these moods and daydreams.

Have some children hum or sing their favorite melodies. Each performing youngster should tell why his own selection happens to be so special to him. Just what does he "see" in that particular tune? Feelings, "happenings," reveries—verbalize them all. Then, distribute materials and have each child use only one tune for his crayoned illustration.

Since this lesson is not aimed at the spontaneous expression of emotions as in "Painting to Music," no records should be played while the class works. Here, instead, the youngster will reflect upon his personally "special" song or melody.

PROCEDURE

1. Distribute the drawing paper and crayons. As materials are handed out, ask each child to consider a favorite song, especially one which sparks a significant memory, dream, or feeling.
2. Each child represents his chosen song with a crayoned illustration. Fill the entire paper.

WHAT THE CHILDREN CAN DO AFTERWARD

1. Have the children display their pictures, allowing their classmates to guess the titles of the songs.
2. Appropriately title the drawings and display them on a bulletin board.
3. Another day, allow time for children to bring in records. Display the drawings, without titles, and ask the class to match the played selections with the crayoned results.
4. Look for doubles—two or more children who have illustrated the same song. Compare these drawings for similarities and differences.

RELAX WITH TIME SAVERS

1. Ask your class to avoid discussion once the materials have been distributed.
2. To encourage careful planning, remind the children that they will receive but one piece of paper for this activity.
3. As youngsters work, walk around the room encouraging them to completely fill the paper.

"WHO WE ARE" NOTES (Illustration 9-3)

ILLUSTRATION 9-3

MATERIALS

1. bulletin board paper
2. roving
3. stapler
4. construction paper or drawing paper
5. scissors
6. crayons

BEFORE YOU BEGIN

Oh, that first day of the new term! How the stoutest little heart trembles! All new kids. A strange teacher. What desolation!

Let 3R reviews wait while children sing their way to friendship. Besides being a happily unorthodox method of introduction, this is also a first lesson music. Use available musical instruments, as well as the services of anyone in your new class knowledgeable enough to introduce the recognition of whole, half, quarter notes, and so on, and their placement to make up the musical scale.

Then, to loosen tension, sing together—old favorites, school songs. Better still, make up a new tune. Try to have the class "write" a song by placing their decorated and labeled "notes" along the roving bulletin board "staff."

Older groups can do the lesson in its entirety. Younger children fare better if the background has been prepared in advance and a choice of notes cut out for them to colorfully personalize.

PROCEDURE

1. Staple the background bulletin board paper in place.
2. Stretch the roving across the length of the board for a music staff. Staple it in place. Similarly, design a roving treble clef.

3. At their seats, have the children draw, color, and cut out a single note. Each name is clearly crayoned on the oval portion of the symbol. (Or, draw a face on the oval, and print the name on the note stem.)
4. Staple or tack these notes along the music staff in a random pattern, or so that they represent the first line of a musical favorite.

WHAT THE CHILDREN CAN DO AFTERWARD

1. Have each child staple his work to the staff, explaining the note it represents and its value.
2. Place the notes so as to represent a familiar tune. Without musical accompaniment have the children try to hum, then name the song.
3. As each child contributes his labeled symbol, have him introduce himself to his classmates.

RELAX WITH TIME SAVERS

1. Choose a committee of two or three to help complete the roving background.
2. The crayoned names should be large and neat. Rule in lines for primary youngsters to guide their printing. Caution them against obliterating the name with any crayoned decoration.

FILM PAINTING

BEFORE YOU BEGIN

"Do your own thing!" Art, always a mirror of changing times, reflects this cry of today's generation. With following precedent "out" and expressing any idea "in," the "own thing" business also stretches to include literature, music, and films. So then, as creativity defies the commonplace, we, too, can flee familiar pigeon holes to go along with change.

All of us harbor a desire to dare to be different, even at the expense of conventional, comfortable lessons that have worked without a snag for years. We've all seen movies, we've all doodled in color. Now let's combine the two. Like magic, the ingredients for setting lines and squiggles into blazing psychedelic motion include only a roll of film, some felt-tipped markers and mood-setting music.

Since most children are unable to visualize or pre-plan the completed film-music abstract, it is necessary to explain the importance of background music. Underscore how dramatic effects are accentuated through musical accompaniment by varying musical selections as the children work.

Leader, or clear film may be purchased from most any camera store, or perhaps ordered from the school audio-visual aids department. Though any size may be used, clear 16 millimeter film produces the best results.

ILLUSTRATION 9-4

MATERIALS

1. felt-tipped marker—assorted colors
2. leader film or clear film and projector (make sure the film size fits the projector)
3. record
4. pins
5. India ink and/or pencil
6. ink pens and/or fine brushes

PROCEDURE (Illustration 9-4)

1. Start a record playing, then unroll the film and distribute an assortment of materials (felt marker, pins, brushes). (step a)
2. Have the children scribble felt color along the entire length of film. For special effects, and as the music dictates, poke small holes throughout the design with pins and "scratch out" portions of color. (step b)
3. Other effects are achieved by pencilling in fine lines over the colored film, and/or adding pen and brush strokes of India ink. *Fill in all space with color or a design.* (step b)
4. Both sides of the film may be used—try a solid color on one side, and a design on the reverse side.
5. Allow the painted film to dry thoroughly. Roll up the film and view it through a projector with the music playing in the background.

WHAT THE CHILDREN CAN DO AFTERWARD

1. If more than one background selection was played during the lesson, study the varied colorful effects. See if the class can pinpoint where the recorded selections were changed.
2. Choreograph a dance around each abstract and its musical accompaniment.
3. Compose an original class poem to music. Tape record the recitation to music, and use it as a soundtrack for the abstract film.
4. Be certain to solicit "What To Do" ideas from children. The lesson lends itself to a host of creative suggestions.

RELAX WITH TIME SAVERS

1. Unroll as much film as the room permits. Assign children to groups; three or four members each. Lightly pencil off sections on unrolled film assigning each child in a group a marked-off portion to decorate. In this way, three or four children may work, unhampered, at a time.
2. Allow one fully decorated length of film to dry thoroughly before exposing any more of roll for next group to paint.
3. Each child, when finished, should arrange his materials neatly on the floor, for use by his other classmates.

BALLERINA MOBILE

MATERIALS

1. clothespins with large round heads
2. crayons
3. small paper doilies
4. rubber bands
5. paste
6. pipe cleaners
7. wire hanger

BEFORE YOU BEGIN

Tiny winsome ballerinas who pirouette on the wisp of every fluttering breeze, are charming "any time" decorations in kindergarten or first grade. Just for fun, or to educate little fingers to manipulate, dress these leaping, twirling dolls with paste and crayon.

Do you want to switch from the classics to peasant polka? Well then, simply change costumes with some of those marvelous bits and pieces sitting in the class collage scrap box.

ILLUSTRATION 9-5

PROCEDURE (Illustration 9-5)

1. Crayon in hair on the ball portion of the clothespin (or make the hair from yarn, pasted in place). (step a)
2. Draw the eyes, nose and mouth on the upper main portion of the clothespin. Color in dancing shoes at the base. Crisscross lines for ballet slipper laces. (step b)
3. Lift out the center circle of a doily and apply a ring of paste to one side of the remaining lacy portion. Slip the doily through the clothespin opening and press the open ring about the pin for a ballerina skirt. (step c)

4. To form arms, wind a pipe cleaner around the clothespin, twisting it in back to secure it in place. Trim the "arms" to size with a pair of scissors. Bend the pipe cleaners to form "elbows" and "hands." (step d)
5. Cut a small circle from another doily for a lace hat to match the skirt. Paste it in place. (step d)
6. Slit the rubber bands. Tie one end around the doll's head at the clothespin indentation, and tie the other end to a wire hanger. (steps e & f)

WHAT THE CHILDREN CAN DO AFTERWARD

1. The mobiles may be suspended individually from fixtures. More attractive, attach several wire hanger mobiles in a random pattern (secure them in place with transparent tape).
2. Use the ballerinas as informal puppets. Play music and have groups of children, bobbing their dolls from rubber bands, take turns "dancing" them around their desks.
3. Use the clothespin dolls as Christmas tree ornaments.

RELAX WITH TIME SAVERS

1. Demonstrate the procedure before distributing materials.
2. Prepare the materials in complete, individual sets before the lesson. Allow enough materials for each child to complete three or four dolls.
3. Distribute paste in empty jar covers; one for two children to share.
4. Choose helpers to collect and wash the paste receptacles and pass a wastebasket.

BALLET COLLAGE (Illustration 9-6)

MATERIALS

1. heavy drawing paper
2. crayons
3. collage materials—crepe paper, tissue paper, fabric scraps, construction paper, glitter, buttons.

BEFORE YOU BEGIN

To tell a story, to express mood with dance and music — that's ballet. Beautiful art form that it is, few children are fortunate enough to attend a professional theater performance. To expose youngsters then, we must turn to television's special programs. Check local educational networks, as well as other station "specials" for future dance presentations, and alert your class as to the channel and time of such programs. Whereas modern ballets sometimes confuse the very young, story-book types bring so much enthusiasm, it's wise to stick to the latter. Look for televised productions of such favorites as "Swan Lake," "Nutcracker Suite," and, perhaps "Billy the Kid"—these are often seen during holiday seasons.

Some background preparation is essential. First, set aside time to listen to a ballet recording and learn the story. Then, go over terms such as: "fouette," "battement," "elevation," "jete pirouette," "plie," "rond de jambe." Fortified with definitions, it would be fun to see how many can execute one of these!

Of course, little girls are completely enchanted with the ballerina; her arabesque and tutu. As for the boys—it should be pointed out to them, that the ballet dancer who does his "entrechat" is no sissy. His training is more exhausting, more exacting, than if he were readying himself for the Olympics. Indeed, he is all muscle. Superior intelligence, sensitivity, and control must be his if he is to interpret an idea, story, or mood. How perfect he must be, for if this sinewy dancer makes one little mistake, he can look pretty silly!

ILLUSTRATION 9-6

Now we are ready for our collage follow-up. Each youngster can choose his favorite ballet scene for reproduction. Stress that results are not to be a mere collection of ballerinas. Instead, each collage should recapture a graceful movement as well as some aspect of the story. Steer children away from recreating an entire stage "set" and towards the selection of dominant characters of the ballet. Those who encounter frequent difficulty with figure drawing will benefit from lessons in this area (consult the index on "Figure Scribbling" and "Body Building Drawings").

PROCEDURE

1. On heavy drawing paper, crayon a chosen ballet scene. Make the figures large, distinct, and, most of all, expressive.
2. Costume the figures and adorn the background accordingly by cutting, folding, then pasting available collage scraps to the drawn scene.
3. Add finishing touches and fine details with crayon.

WHAT THE CHILDREN CAN DO AFTERWARD

1. The finished collages make excellent covers for "Music and Dance" work folders.
2. Tack the completed pictures to a bulletin board.
3. Ask the class to write short essays describing their collages and expressing their reactions to the ballet.
4. Ask the gym instructor to teach the children some basic ballet positions, and perhaps, a simple dance.

RELAX WITH TIME SAVERS

1. If possible, have the children first sketch out their drawings on scrap paper.
2. Distribute an ample supply of collage materials for each table to share.
3. Distribute paste in empty jar covers; one for every two children to share. Have a paste jar available so that youngsters may help themselves to refills.
4. Appoint helpers to collect and store usable supplies, wash the paste receptacles, and pass a wastebasket for scraps.

THE KALEIDOSCOPE (Illustration 9-7)

BEFORE YOU BEGIN

When Sir David Brewster patented the kaleidoscope in 1817, he probably never imagined that musical comedy directors and choreographers of the next century would exploit his invention to put together dance sequences! This idea is especially employed in conjunction with overhead cameras to catch the full, startling effect of dancers changing positions in unison.

ILLUSTRATION 9-7

The Kaleidoscope

MATERIALS

1. large pieces of mural paper, taped together to form one huge sheet
2. pencils
3. paint

In a way, we are about to do something of the same with our mammoth mural. We will replace multi-hued specks with human figures, choreograph our own symmetry of design, then capture the effect with paint and brush! Though a challenge to accomplish, our result will be bizzare and alive with color.

Enlist the aid of the gym teacher as the class arranges a dance recital for the next assembly performance. The repertoire can include a selection choreographed, at least in part, by the children. Available musical comedy films that illustrate the kaliedoscopic effect will certainly leave no doubts as to what is to be accomplished.

With rehearsals under way, some cooperation is required to plan and execute the mural layout; an excellent scenery prop for the coming performance. Consider first, a feasible mural size. Decide how many children it will accommodate, then plan the kaleidoscope pattern within this limit. Larger groups can very well work on two or three designs to be used separately, or taped together. Designs should be sketched on the blackboard, tested on taped mural paper, then modified on the board diagram before actual work begins. Incorporate only two positions within each kaleidoscope design.

With preliminaries out of the way, pair children in opposite positions within the design. Push back the furniture to make a clear working area and ask the children to assume their positions on the mural paper which has been placed on floor. Explain that at a given signal half the supine group will rise (leaving the second half of the "human pattern" lying on the paper) to trace the outlines of their partners. Check work before giving a second signal for the partners to reverse their roles.

Understandably, this is an activity best left to upper grades. Whether used to enhance a total music and dance study, or just for the fun of it, success hinges on cooperation and planning with the utmost care.

PROCEDURE

1. Tape enough mural paper together to make one huge sheet, large enough to accommodate all the children in the group (mural size will depend on class size). Where numbers overwhelm it is best to make two or three designs.
2. Turn the paper over, tape side down.
3. Have the children work in pairs. Ask them all to lie down on the paper forming the total desired design. Then, ask the first half of the group (half of the total pattern) to rise and trace the outlines of their partners left on the paper.
4. Reverse roles. The second half of the group now lies on the paper, assuming the design's complementary position, as the first group rises to outline their shapes.
5. Select two or three children to pencil over the completed outlined design and add definition.
6. The Kaleidoscope design, now complete, may be painted. Let it dry.

WHAT THE CHILDREN CAN DO AFTERWARD

1. Use the mural as a backdrop for a play or dance recital.
2. Use it as a permanent decoration along an entire classroom wall, or in the school lobby.

RELAX WITH TIME SAVERS

1. Request that the girls wear slacks.
2. Make certain to have the entire group assume their positions on the paper and check their placement before asking the first group to start outlining their partner's shapes.
3. Avoid congestion by having the "outliners" take turns; it is not necessary that all complete this task at the same time. Since the actual procedure is quick and simple, it is far more feasible for children tracing their partner's shapes to do so one or two at a time. As soon as a child's outline has been completed, he and his partner should go to their seats. They may return when it is time to reverse roles for completion of the second phase of the design.
4. Allow no more than three or four children to paint at a time. Individual figures should thoroughly dry before the adjacent ones are painted.

MOOD SCULPTURE (Illustration 9-8)

ILLUSTRATION 9-8

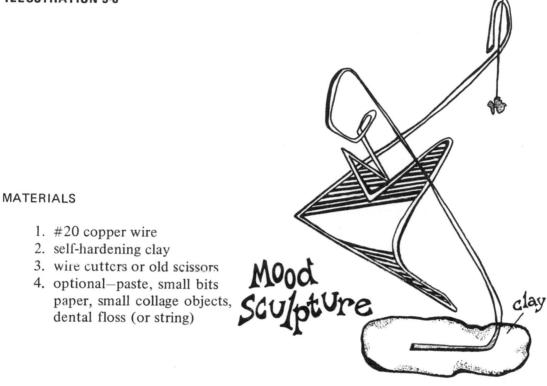

MATERIALS

1. #20 copper wire
2. self-hardening clay
3. wire cutters or old scissors
4. optional—paste, small bits paper, small collage objects, dental floss (or string)

BEFORE YOU BEGIN

Thus far, this chapter has centered on helping youngsters interpret mood as it relates to music and dance. For the most part, imaginations should have received a directive boost from musical accompaniment and visual aids. See if aesthetic senses are now keen enough to go it alone. In children's hands, amorphous media will be bent, twisted and spiralled to shape a wire representation of rhythm, mood, and movement.

Children should receive minimal instruction. Say only that they may choose any sensation, be it sadness or joy; recollection of melody; a particular dance or game stance. Let the children dwell on the basic wire shape, achieving form and balance. Then distribute any optional materials.

PROCEDURE

1. Distribute the wire and a small amount of clay. Ask each child to think a

moment, then select some movement, rhythm or emotion. Interpret these feelings by sculpting the wire; bending, twisting and shaping it in place. Trim the sculpture with the wire cutters or old scissors.

2. Imbed the basic wire form in a self-hardening clay base. Where appropriate or desired, paste bits of paper or collage materials to dental floss (or string), then suspend these additions from the wire sculpture.

3. Allow the clay to harden around the base of the sculpture.

WHAT THE CHILDREN CAN DO AFTERWARD

1. Ask each child to display his sculpture. Invite class conjecture and interpretation. Finally, have those who wish to do so, explain their creations.
2. Ask each child to title his sculpture to use in a class display.
3. Study the sculptures of those who have interpreted the same feeling, mood, or emotion. Have the class point out the similarities and differences.
4. Display the wire sculpture in school showcases.
5. Study and interpret pictures of famous abstract sculpture.

RELAX WITH TIME SAVERS

1. If wire cutters are unavailable, go through your scissor collection and distribute those which are old and worn; new scissors may suffer premature wear if used on wire.
2. Distribute boxes of optional materials for each table to share.

WORD-FEELING PICTURES (Illustration 9-9)

BEFORE YOU BEGIN

If the printed word has punch for us, it is derived from our own conditioned learning. The novice reader, however, sees merely a series of perplexing lines and curves. As long as we've been so engrossed in "moods," "feelings," and "emotions," it's fitting that we abandon the "type" of conventional manuscript and apply some artistic interpretation to our meaningful friend the written "word."

At all grade levels teachers find the word-feeling approach a well received gimmick for boosting vocabulary and word recognition for new and slow readers.

Discuss how many words may be "drawn" to convey meaning, illustrating with board samples. For starters, try writing "fat" with wide curved letters; "tall" with vertically elongated letters, and "electric" with jagged strokes. You'll have little chance to continue alone, for everyone will want to shout some novel addition. Permit groups to experiment with fun words on the board, but caution against overflowing contributions with "*Save* the good ones."

MATERIALS

    1. newsprint
    2. crayons

ILLUSTRATION 9-9

PROCEDURE

    1. Distribute newsprint and crayons.
    2. Ask each child to select five or six words which can be illustrated as to

meaning. Write (or "draw") these words on newsprint using crayon. Avoid tiny letters. Place the words in an attractive pattern, spacing them so that each word stands out clearly.

WHAT THE CHILDREN CAN DO AFTERWARD

1. Ask each child to hold up his word-feeling picture for the class to see. Ask others to read the words as the teacher writes them on the board in conventional form. Later, read the entire board list — see how many new words the children have learned.
2. Use the "word pictures" as bulletin board decoration.
3. Compose, or copy, a short descriptive paragraph on chart paper. Incorporate the word-feeling approach wherever possible.

RELAX WITH TIME SAVERS

1. Have dictionaries available so that children may check for proper spelling.
2. Guide the children as they work, encouraging colorful, readable results.

MAKE-IT-YOURSELF RHYTHM BAND

MATERIALS

BONGO DRUMS
1. two coffee cans with removable plastic lids
2. wood-textured shelf paper, or paint
3. two 1" strips of dark brown construction paper or leather strips
4. small block wood
5. paste
6. nuts and bolts

TOM-TOM DRUM
1. jumbo snack container with removable plastic top
2. white paint
3. tempera colors
4. dowel stick
5. child's large wooden bead
6. optional—scrap leather

BUTTON CASTANETS
1. two buttons, same size
2. 3/4" wide elastic
3. needle and thread

GONG
1. large aluminum jar cover
2. leather strip
3. large wooden bead and dowel to fit
4. paint—white and colors

SHAKERS
1. small aluminum pie tins (individual portion size)
2. two tongue depressors
3. polymer acrylic medium (or white glue diluted with water)
4. stapler
5. dried beans or pebbles
6. tissue paper
7. tempera paint

SAND BLOCKS
1. two wooden blocks
2. sand paper
3. white glue
4. large spools
5. paint

BEFORE YOU BEGIN

Gathering in the fire-lit cave how they exulted the day's successful hunt! Grunting in unison and with joy for their bravery, they stamped their feet and clapped their hands in great thumping, smacking rhythmic beats. For rhythm, primitive man had only to borrow from that very day: dripping water on forest leaves, measured strides of prey and pursuer, and, through it all, the quickening lub-dub, lub-dub of his heart.

So compelling were these sounds, so intrigued was man, that it was only natural for him to combine and embellish any and every raw material capable of imitating nature. A hide-covered tree stump — where could one find a more perfect imitator of that thing that throbbed in the chest? A few of these drums, a banging together of bones, stones and wood, and hence, in the dawn of the world, we have, unwittingly born, the first rhythm band.

That same love of rhythm and challenge of invention is still very much alive today. Put on the right track, almost any child can match that cave man when it comes to turning up an enterprising array of materials for making shakers, drums, gongs, and whatever else might thump, rattle, and boom. Empty tin cans, especially those which thoughtful manufacturers have supplied with plastic tops, sewing chest treasures, discarded toddler toys, and all that might wring out a tone, should be collected and sorted a week or so in advance.

Materials and procedures needn't be limited to those suggested here. Once they've begun, most children will insist upon testing their wealth of debris for musical and rhythmic possibilities.

Divide the class into groups and areas according to the instrument being made (bongos, shakers, and so on). Supply each area with the necessary materials, as well as a sample or two for reference. Pre-arrange a drilling and bolting session with the shop teacher.

PROCEDURE I — BONGO DRUMS (Illustration 9-10)

1. Cut the shelf paper to fit the size of each coffee can. Glue it in place. (Drums may be painted instead, if desired.) (step a)
2. Paste construction paper strips around the top and bottom of each can to give the effect of leather trim. If possible, substitute genuine leather strips. (step b)
3. Drill a hole at two opposite ends of the wooden block. Match these against the coffee cans, drilling corresponding holes through cans. (step c)
4. Place the block between the two cans and secure them in place with nuts and bolts. (steps c & d)

PROCEDURE II — TOM-TOM DRUM

1. Remove the plastic top from the can.
2. Give the can several coats of white paint to obscure the advertising. Let it dry.
3. Add a colorful background coat of paint, let it dry, then brush on additional decoration. (step e)

ILLUSTRATION 9-10

4. Replace the plastic top.
5. To make a drumstick, glue the dowel inside a large wooden toy bead. Paint, or cover the head with a piece of scrap leather, glued in place. (steps f & g)

PROCEDURE III — BUTTON CASTANETS

1. Cut two small pieces of elastic, just long enough to stretch securely around child's thumb and index fingers respectively. (step h)
2. Sew each piece of elastic into a loop. Choose two colorful buttons, and sew a loop to one side of each button. (steps i, j & k)
3. To wear, slip thumb and index finger of same hand through elastic loops, attaching one button (castanet) to each finger.

PROCEDURE IV — GONG

1. Drill a hole through a jar cover lip. (step l)
2. Apply several coats of white paint to the jar cover to obscure any advertising. Let it dry, then decorate it with tempera paint. (step m)
3. Loop a thin leather strip through the hole and tie it in place. (step n)
4. Make stick by gluing a wooden dowel inside a large wooden bead. Paint it and let it dry. (step f)
5. To play, hold the gong by the leather strip and strike it with the stick.

PROCEDURE V — SHAKERS

1. Staple two pie tins together around the edges. Leave one small opening through which to fill the pie tins with beans or pebbles. (steps o & p)
2. Glue two tongue depressors together, and insert them through the pie tin opening. Staple, sealing the beans between the two tins, and securing the tongue depressor handle in place. (steps q & r)
3. Using polymer acrylic medium (or diluted white glue) cover the aluminum tins with colored tissue paper. Let it dry. (step s)
4. Decorate the shakers with tempera paint. (step t)

PROCEDURE VI — SAND BLOCKS

1. Glue a spool "handle" to one side of each wooden block. (step u)
2. Decoratively paint the spool and the block. Let them dry. (step w)
3. Glue a sheet of sand paper to the bottom of each decorated wood block. (step v)
4. To play, hold each sand block by the spool handle and rub the sand paper surfaces against one another.

WHAT THE CHILDREN CAN DO AFTERWARD

1. Experiment with percussion sounds. Test the possibilities of each instrument, then combine them for a percussion musicale.
2. Accompany favorite recordings with the class made instruments.
3. Use class made instruments as part of an assembly performance.
4. Invite other groups to a presentation. Have each youngster demonstrate his instrument and explain how it was made.
5. Play the recordings and ask the children to listen for individual instrument sounds.
6. Visit a museum and examine the instruments of early man.
7. Collect and display pictures of musical inventions from primitive times to present day.

RELAX WITH TIME SAVERS

1. Make certain each group and work area is supplied with sufficient necessary

materials. This frees the teacher to circulate about the room, uninterrupted, giving constructive help where needed.

2. Have a painting station, in addition to work areas, set up in back of the room. Have the children complete all painting in this area.
3. Try to have all necessary shop work done in one session. Send only those who require the assistance to the shop teacher.
4. Don't rush; good results are surely worth the two or three necessary work sessions.

Bonus Ideas

1. Paint a large abstract mural to music. Assign several groups a portion of mural paper. Each group takes its turn painting to a different musical accompaniment.
2. Correlate a rhythm band to an American Indian study. Decorate the instruments accordingly.
3. For fun, try incorporating word-feeling when writing short stories. Have the children write original stories using as many words as they can which lend themselves to the "word-feeling" technique.
4. Wire sculpt to music.
5. Watch vocabulary grow with a "word-feeling" mural. Add new words whenever opportunity or whim permit.
6. Watch for television opera performances. Listen to recordings and the libretto. Then follow-up the story in collage.
7. Have the class arrange a rhythm band presentation. Select a group name for the band, then design record album covers.
8. Study traditional dances of other nations. Portray these classical movements and costumes in paint or collage.
9. Compose a rhythm band accompaniment to abstract painted film.
10. Make an abstract kaleidoscope by overlapping human figures.
11. With younger groups make a spontaneous kaleidoscope. Take a long sheet of mural paper and ask several children at a time to lie down in a random pattern. Have others trace their outlines, then paint the mural.

Potpourri

10

So now we come to this final chapter and on the desk is still a potpourri of materials and techniques! An ingredient common to this left-over catch-all is that each lesson yearns to give new flavor to tired old schoolroom practices. If your faded bulletin boards need luster, or you're searching to sparkle with a novel gift idea, or tunneling through rainy day blues, you'll surely find a solution among the lessons which follow.

For bulletin boards with "class" try all-in-one lessons with double the display power, such as "String Painting and Collage" and "Collagraphs." To find splashes of color with that art gallery look, little garners more enthusiasm than "Tissue Paper Water Colors." For those who prefer the stark dramatic effects of black and white, unusual "Scratchboard" is an absolute must.

Any of the above, especially when framed, make perfect holiday gifts or permanent wall hangings. If, however, the occasion is truly unique, you'll want to take time for "Shoe Box Sand Casting" and the current craze amongst yarn enthusiasts, "Carpet Tack and Yarn Pictures."

On woeful rainy days, for a touch of unanticipated fun, "unfinish" a "Take-Away Picture" or find out "What's in a Doodle?"

Special are those activities which promote basic skills. "Newspaper Designs," for example, help the young reader develop eye-reading coordination and aid manuscript practice. Another day the same lesson becomes the basis for teaching the number of objects in a set!

What you'll like best is that this chapter, regardless of the activity you choose, is not only adaptable to all age levels, but is also a fresh approach to that which has become familiar and easily understood.

STRING PAINTING AND COLLAGE (Illustration 10-1)

ILLUSTRATION 10-1

MATERIALS

1. painting paper
2. tempera paint
3. several pieces of string
4. painting paper
5. construction paper
6. clear drying glue
7. newspaper to work on

BEFORE YOU BEGIN

Just as mother works kitchen magic with left-overs, turning them into second day feasts, so does today's lesson with string and tempera cook up two distinct abstracts from the same ingredients. Using identical materials, but varying the "recipe" slightly, we see how a little ingenuity adds new flavor and variety to classroom art galleries.

Show how string is dipped, then swirled along the paper to produce the first effect. Remember not to discard those painted bits of string. Let them dry in squiggles for our "left-over" collage.

PROCEDURE I — STRING PAINTING

1. Dip the string in paint. Pull painted string in lines and swirls along the paper. Or, for a more definite line, lay the string on the paper in a curled fashion, press it lightly with your fingers and gently lift it off. Use a new piece of string for each desired color.
2. Allow the painted abstracts to dry.

PROCEDURE II — STRING COLLAGE

1. Form each piece of painted string into an interesting shape. Let it dry against a sheet of newspaper. The dried string will maintain its shape.
2. Carefully apply clear drying glue to the back of each dried string shape. Press it in place on a piece of construction paper, making an attractive abstract arrangement. Let it dry.

WHAT THE CHILDREN CAN DO AFTERWARD

1. Frame the work by mounting it on a larger sheet of construction paper. Display it on a bulletin board, alternating the painted and collage abstracts.
2. Bring the completed projects home for use as wall decorations.

RELAX WITH TIME SAVERS

1. Spread newspaper before starting to paint.
2. Distribute paint in plastic ice-cube trays; one for two or three children to share.
3. Provide extra paint in detergent squeeze bottles. Children may help themselves to refills.
4. Pre-cut string to a reasonable size; allow about five pieces for each child.
5. Use glue containers with control-flow tops. Two or three children can share one bottle.
6. Choose helpers to pass a wastebasket and collect scraps. Ask others to collect, wash and store ice-cube trays.

COLLAGRAPHS (Illustration 10-2)

MATERIALS

1. cardboard sheet
2. assorted collage materials (various strength and textures of string, corrugated cardboard scraps, discarded keys, play coins, sponges)
3. glue
4. scissors
5. tempera paint and brush
6. 3-4 sheets newsprint paper
7. spoon or brayer

BEFORE YOU BEGIN

Wary of complex methods and of materials difficult to come by, those who have shied away from lessons in printing will find collagraphs a painless approach to a most exciting technique.

ILLUSTRATION 10-2

This introductory method begins with familiarly simple collage, adds a bit of paint, then prints with hardly any effort. No carved potatoes, no special inks! Thus, perfect for every grade. Oddly enough, simplicity also has its bonus, as each initial collage is as much a "work of art" as are the resulting prints.

You may find that older groups have already successfully experimented and enjoyed themselves with linoleum, wood, and vegetable printing. Those who have not will so want to treat themselves as a follow-up to today's lesson.

Try to have a professional print or two available for class study. Explain, not only how it was made, but how the artist values his work. Prints are usually sold by number. Out of, say one hundred, the first is most highly valued while the last brings a considerably lower price. Why? Have class find the answer by printing several collagraphs from the same inked collage.

PROCEDURE

1. Choose an assortment of collage scraps. Experiment, arranging these attractively on the cardboard sheet. Pieces of sponge, string, corrugated cardboard, and the like may be cut to the desired size and shape.
2. When pleased with the arrangement, glue the collage scraps in place.
3. Generously coat the entire collage surface with tempera paint.
4. Place the first sheet of newsprint over the painted collage before it has a chance to dry.
5. Using the back of a spoon (or brayer), firmly rub it over the paper, pressing it against the raised objects.

6. Carefully lift the paper, look at the first print and set it aside to dry. Take a second newsprint sheet and quickly repeat the process. Make the third and fourth prints in the same manner.

WHAT THE CHILDREN CAN DO AFTERWARD

1. Have the children number their prints. See how textures are reproduced by having the children study one another's prints and guess the objects or collage material used.
2. Have several youngsters display all three or four results and ask the class to determine which was done first, second, third, last.
3. Display the original collages and the resulting prints on a bulletin board.
4. Compile a class book of numbered prints for parents and visitors to enjoy.

RELAX WITH TIME SAVERS

1. Spread newspaper before distributing additional materials.
2. Distribute an assortment of collage materials for each table to share.
3. Have two children share a cup of paint and a bottle of glue with a controlled-flow top.
4. Provide a convenient area where collagraphs may safely dry before hanging.
5. Choose helpers to collect, wash and store paint cups and brushes. Have others collect the remaining scraps and pass a wastebasket for newspaper.

SCRATCHBOARD (Illustration 10-3)

MATERIALS

1. scratchboard or oaktag
2. paint brush
3. India ink
4. straight pins, compass, or other pointed tool
5. optional—water-color paint

BEFORE YOU BEGIN

A sheet of scratchboard and a simple everyday tool are all you need for a double lesson in etching and texture. Dramatic in black and white, this quick and easy process may be varied to include delicately hued pictures and abstracts. Note that oaktag may be substituted for scratchboard. The latter, available in art supply stores, is sturdier and produces longer-lasting results. Pre-coated scratchboard is also available in black as well as colors.

Begin the lesson by talking about the inherent texture of everything about us. Then demonstrate how to capture this quality by etching into inked paper.

If destined for the bulletin board, give the display added appeal by having youngsters etch on an assortment of scratchboard shapes. Let them choose oblongs, circles, and other shapes, all cut to size in advance.

ILLUSTRATION 10-3

PROCEDURE

1. Using a brush, evenly coat one side of the oaktag with India ink, *brushing in one direction only*. Let it dry. (Omit this step if scratchboard is being used.)

2. Scraping away the black ink with a pointed tool exposes the white paper below. In this manner have the children scrape or "etch" a desired picture or design.
3. Optional—for a colorful variation, coat a white sheet of oaktag with a water-color wash (or use pre-colored scratchboard). Let it dry, then add a coat of India ink. Proceed as described above. This time, a color will show through instead of the white natural background.

WHAT THE CHILDREN CAN DO AFTERWARD

1. Group the etchings attractively for a bulletin board display.
2. Bring the etchings home for framing or use them as wall hangings.

RELAX WITH TIME SAVERS

1. Spread newspaper before distributing the materials.
2. Have all children wear smocks.
3. Distribute the ink in paint cups; one for two to three children to share. As soon as the scratchboard sheets have been properly inked, collect the paint cups.
4. Choose an assistant to pass a wastebasket and collect the newspaper at the lesson's end. Select another child to wash and store the brushes.

CARPET TACK AND YARN PICTURES

MATERIALS

1. small wooden board (exact dimensions depend on the desired size of picture)
2. sand paper
3. pencil
4. multi-colored yarns
5. carpet tacks and hammer
6. scissors
7. optional—paint or wood stain
8. tracing paper

BEFORE YOU BEGIN

Once upon a time, art yarn work was considered the creative outlet for genteel ladies and grannies. How things have changed! Presently this is one of the ever growing hobbies in our country. So much so, that, according to the *Wall Street Journal,* suppliers of knitting and crewel yarn can hardly keep up with public demand.

Every spring, when outdoor art exhibits sprout as quickly as flowers, we see more and more intricately woven yarn wall hangings displayed in the distinguished company

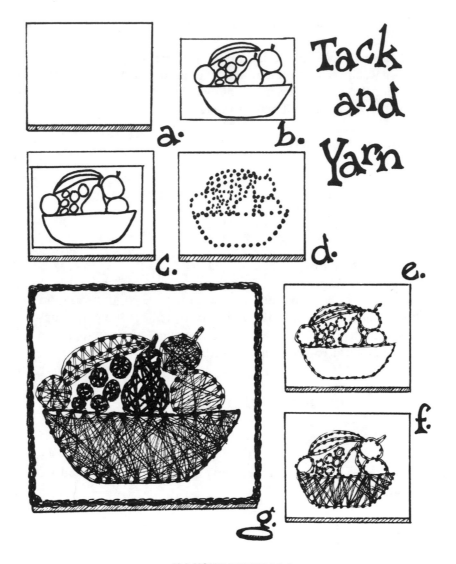

ILLUSTRATION 10-4

of oils and water colors. These yarn pictures are very much like the ones we are about to make.

Though increasingly popular, the carpet tack and yarn craft may well be new to the school youngster. Therefore, it is wise to have a sample on hand and take time for a demonstration lesson. Remember, the degree of detail will depend on age level. Older groups can attempt composite designs, while primary graders, using more widely spaced tacks, should be guided along the path of simplicity. These youngsters should choose a single object or shape (flower, bird, tree) as the basis for yarn designs.

PROCEDURE (Illustration 10-4)

1. Sand the rough edges of a wooden board smooth. If desired or necessary, stain or paint the board. (step a)
2. In pencil, sketch a desired object or picture on tracing paper (e.g., bowl of fruit, flower, boat, dancer, tree). (step b)
3. Transfer the design onto the board. (step c)
4. Using a hammer, nail carpet tacks to the board along the entire outline of the completed picture. Tacks should be evenly spaced (use judgement, not ruler). Many tacks are not needed, though older children may use closer spacing if desired. Be certain to place a tack wherever drawn lines meet. (step d)
5. Choose an appropriate yarn color to outline each color area of picture (e.g., green for leaf and stem, yellow for flower petals). Knot the yarn securely around the first tack, wind it once around the next tack, and so continue until a given portion of the picture or design has been completely outlined. Now, choose a second color—yellow, perhaps, for some flower petals. Outline this area in the same manner as the first. When the yarn is to be ended, tightly tie a small knot to the tack and trim it closely with scissors. Be certain to make a yarn outline of the entire picture or design. (step e)
6. With the outline complete, each area may be "filled-in" with corresponding yarn colors. Attach the yarn to a tack and wrap it in a crisscross fashion, completely filling each inner section of the outlines picture. If necessary, or if the yarn around some tacks becomes too bulky, additional tacks may be hammered into the design. (step f)
7. Make a braid frame from long strands of yarn, and glue it around the edge of the wooden board. (step g)

WHAT THE CHILDREN CAN DO AFTERWARD

1. Display yarn creations at a yearly exhibition of school crafts.
2. Bring the pictures home for use as wall hangings.
3. Give these carpet tack and yarn pictures as gifts.

RELAX WITH TIME SAVERS

1. If the board is to be painted or stained, complete this job a day or so in advance.
2. Have children complete the pencilled sketch before distributing additional materials.
3. Supply a large assortment of colored yarn for each table to share.
4. Each child should have his own small container of carpet tacks and a hammer. Review the proper use of a hammer during the demonstration lesson.
5. Sweep well under the desks at the lesson's end, collecting any stray tacks.

TOOTHPICK SCULPTURE

ILLUSTRATION 10-5

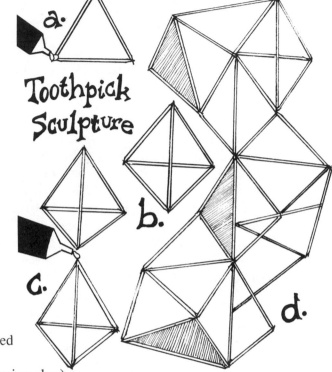

MATERIALS

1. box of round, multi-colored toothpicks
2. airplane glue (extra-fast drying glue)
3. manila paper to work on
4. optional—colored cellophane

BEFORE YOU BEGIN

Toothpick sculpture, for older, more adept children, inspires the latent engineer to design tomorrow's space station, towering high riser, or fantasize a delicate sculpture of line and shape.

A day or so in advance, ask each child to bring in a box of round, multi-colored toothpicks. Demonstrate how to initiate the sculpture by building a base from two or three separate pyramids, then attaching them. Once begun, you may choose to have children complete their projects during leisure time or free periods.

PROCEDURE (Illustration 10-5)

1. Lay the manila paper on a desk. Using glue, form two or three toothpick triangles. Let these dry against the manila. (step a)
2. Glue additional toothpicks to each triangle, forming separate pyramids. (step b)

3. When the pyramids have dried, glue them together. Now, working quickly with glue and toothpicks, add on to the basic shape building as large a tower, shape, or design desired. (steps c & d)
4. If desired, or for variation, glue on cut-out pieces of cellophane to complete the sculpture. (step d)

WHAT THE CHILDREN CAN DO AFTERWARD

1. Display the sculptures on a table in the room. Have each child print a title for his creation.
2. Suspend each sculpture from the ceiling.
3. Use it as a Christmas tree decoration.
4. Combine the sculptures to form a giant class spatial sculpture.

RELAX WITH TIME SAVERS

1. Try to provide a separate box of toothpicks for each child.
2. Each child requires his own tube of glue. Show how to squeeze out small amounts at a time.
3. Provide a safe place for storing incomplete projects.
4. If glue must be bought from the store, the teacher should make all purchases a day or so in advance.

GEOMETRIC DESIGNS (Illustration 10-6)

MATERIALS

1. pencil
2. rulers
3. compass, or assorted bottle caps
4. scissors
5. drawing paper

BEFORE YOU BEGIN

Take a simple line, add another. Soon the first "line" leads to full-blown design, and the youngster has opened the lid to plane and solid geometry!

Initiating this lesson poses little difficulty since, today, even a kindergartener can rattle off and identify an impressive list of common shapes: square desk, rectangular bulletin board, or round reading table. Enliven routine responses by signaling a search for shapes within shapes: small square panes in a rectangular window, individual tiles on classroom floor, and so on. Finally, branch out of the room for ice-cubes, cylindrical cans, cones, trapezoids, parallelograms—in short, the "geometrical works."

On the board, draw and appropriately label a sample of each named shape as you quickly discuss its properties.

Tell the class they are now to make a full page design, starting with one basic figure and adding lines to form a geometrical abstract. Give a brief board demonstration as you review the uses of the compass and ruler.

ILLUSTRATION 10-6

PROCEDURE

1. Distribute the materials. Ask each child to draw a basic shape on any part of paper, using a ruler or compass (small, medium and large size bottle caps may be used in place of compass). Add other lines and shapes to the first until the entire paper is filled with a geometric abstract.
2. Color in the abstract with crayon.

WHAT THE CHILDREN CAN DO AFTERWARD

1. Play a game of "How Many Shapes Can You Find?" Have classmates exchange their abstracts and count the number of different shapes included in his partner's drawing. Let the top three "winners" display their creations for class study.

2. Use the geometric designs as bulletin board decoration.
3. Use the abstracts as covers for geometry unit folders.
4. Bring the completed pictures home for framing.

RELAX WITH TIME SAVERS

1. Use assorted bottle caps in place of a compass in the lower grades. Have a variety of caps for each table to share.
2. With older groups, distribute a ruler and compass to each child.

NEWSPAPER DESIGNS

MATERIALS

1. page from classified section of newspaper
2. crayon

BEFORE YOU BEGIN

Everlastingly in search of a new twist to "reading, 'riting and 'rithmetic"? If so, classified sections of daily newspapers may well be this year's versatile, inexpensive and lucky find.

Those boxed ads turn out to be natural building blocks for boosting basic skills! Take reading for example. Unaware of true intent, any child will happily crayon away a repeated design as he really develops left to right coordination. The newspaper's marked guidelines may also be employed to take the tiring edge off manuscript exercise. Choose two letters and review them in captivating color. Likewise, as described below, practice those numerals as they relate to number of objects in a set.

Used in combination with the above, or for fun, each completed "exercise" merits display as compelling, creative design.

PROCEDURE (Illustration 10-7)

1. Distribute a classified sheet of newspaper to each child. Point out how several ads are boxed in larger squares or "frames." Though some of these frames may vary in size it is really quite easy to visually re-proportion them so that they align with other boxes across the printed page. Those who have difficulty seeing this can lightly pencil in a line within the larger ad boxes, reducing them in size so that they conform with the others across the page. Once the first line of squares, or frames, have been marked, the rest is easy; simply pencil in the corresponding lines down the remainder of newspaper.
2. Choose two objects to alternate in design; one figure or object will appear in each newspaper frame. Some suggestions:
   a. Review two manuscript letters, such as "B" and "Z". Have children

practice these by alternating the two letters in bright crayon across the page. Fill the paper. Contrasting colors may be used for each letter. (step a)

b. Select two different shapes or figures as part of a repeated design. Alternate these on the newspaper frames, making sure to work from left to right.

c. Drill the number of objects in a set. For example, write the number "2" in the first frame, then draw two objects in the second frame (e.g., two circles). Again, place a "2" in the third frame and draw two objects in the fourth. Continue on each line until the page is filled. (step b)

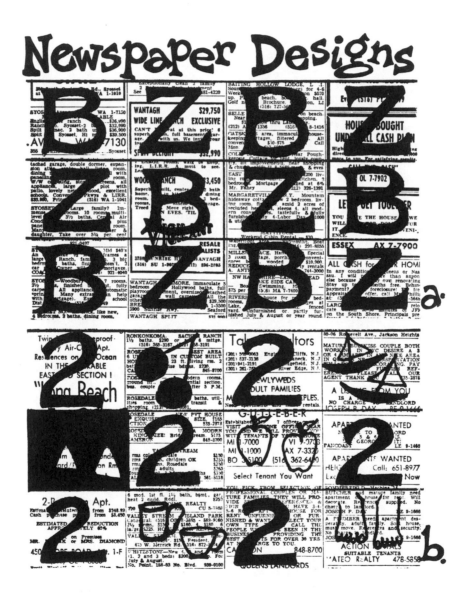

ILLUSTRATION 10-7

WHAT THE CHILDREN CAN DO AFTERWARD

1. Mount the newspaper designs on construction paper for display on a bulletin board.
2. Make extra-large sized designs for use as gift wrap paper.
3. Make a set of note cards. Cut each signed sheet into smaller squares and paste these to folded sheets of construction paper. These may be given as gift sets, or used individually for invitations and greetings.

RELAX WITH TIME SAVERS

1. Circulate about the room, making certain that the children are working from left to right across the page.
2. When necessary, help younger children gauge the size of the frames by pencilling in the first row of paper guidelines in advance of the lesson. That first line acts as a guide for the second, the second for the third, and so on.

3—D PAPER COLLAGE

MATERIALS

    1. construction paper or plain brown paper
    2. manila paper
    3. scissors
    4. paste

BEFORE YOU BEGIN

That crayoned masterpiece so proudly borne home by mother's budding artist usually has a humble beginning as a rather ordinary piece of construction paper. Since much of classroom art hinges on the intricacies of folding and cutting, the lone sheet of paper deserves its day.

Aim for a striking 3—D collage. Here children sharpen basic manipulative skills as they fold and coax paper strips into a variety of swirls, curls, chains, and fringes. Demonstrate these effects, invite suggestions and, most important, encourage "instant" invention from youngsters as they collage their own paper fantasies.

PROCEDURE (Illustration 10-8)

    1. Demonstrate how to cut, curl, fold, and score construction paper to make odd shapes (see illustration for just a few suggestions).
    2. Decoratively paste these forms to a sheet of manila paper.

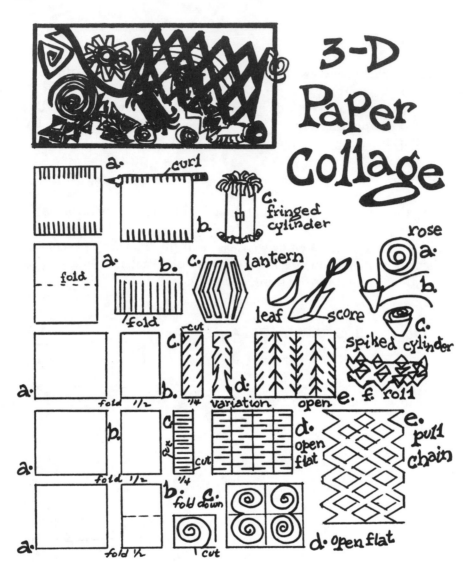

ILLUSTRATION 10-8

WHAT THE CHILDREN CAN DO AFTERWARD

1. Create a paper spatial environment by cutting huge shapes from brown paper and suspending them from the ceiling.
2. Display the 3–D pictures on bulletin board.
3. Color or paint the paper figures and use them as Christmas tree decoration.

RELAX WITH TIME SAVERS

1. If construction paper is used, distribute a large assortment for each table to share. Have the children utilize and share scraps.

2. If brown paper is used, cut it to size in advance of the lesson and distribute 3-4 sheets per child.

3. Distribute paste in empty jar covers; one for two children to share. Have a paste jar available for refills.

4. At the lesson's end, have helpers collect scraps, wash and store paste receptacles.

WHAT'S IN A DOODLE? (Illustration 10-9)

ILLUSTRATION 10-9

MATERIALS

1. crayons
2. large drawing paper

BEFORE YOU BEGIN

Frequently embellishing the corners of a bedraggled notebook are a rare assortment of zig-zag lines and an array of pointillism. How many a schoolboy, past and present, doodled his way to eye to eye confrontation with an exasperated teacher? If thumbing through such animated margins tests your mettle, control yourself and capitalize on this irritant! A touch of humor may conquer waning interests and turn idle scribbles into what may yet pass as young abstract art. Unexpected, it all ends up as fun when line and color explode into a new surprise.

PROCEDURE

1. Distribute crayons and drawing paper. Each child selects a crayon, closes his eyes, then scribbles a design over the entire paper. Make large sweeping movements, not tiny, tight lines! Lines may curve, swerve, zig and zag, provided the doodle is not over-done.
2. Ask the children to open their eyes and study the scribbled designs. With assorted crayon colors, fill in all the spaces of the doodle with crayons. In addition to filling these spaces with solid color, the children may also incorporate the use of lines, in added long strokes, dots, and simple pattern to achieve varied effects.
3. If necessary, delineate the original scribble design by going over the doodle lines with a dark colored crayon.

WHAT THE CHILDREN CAN DO AFTERWARD

1. Look for a picture within a picture. The completed abstracts often contain hidden faces, flowers, birds. Have each child study his own picture from every angle to discover such concealed figures. Then, ask his classmates to find these concealed surprises.
2. In conjunction with the above, ask the children to write short paragraphs titled "What's in a Doodle?" Display the pictures and creative writing on a bulletin board.
3. For a giant sized class abstract, staple the doodles one next to another on a bulletin board, or large mural paper.
4. Staple each picture to a larger sheet of construction paper. Have the children title their doodles and display them on a bulletin board.

RELAX WITH TIME SAVERS

1. Time the children during the initial scribbling part of the lesson, to insure against too many tiny spaces. Instruct your class as to procedure, then allow 15-20 seconds for them to complete the basic design with their eyes closed.
2. Distribute a box of crayons for two children to share. Encourage the class to fill the spaces neatly and attractively, pressing hard with their crayons for a well colored abstract.

TAKE—AWAY PICTURES (Illustration 10-10)

BEFORE YOU BEGIN

How do we "unfinish" a picture to finish it? To work out this riddle, children of any age can, of all things "subtract" from their paintings! It sounds strange, but here is a way to novel, spontaneous fun. For a double answer to today's enigma, try both of the following methods.

ILLUSTRATION 10-10

MATERIALS

1. rubber cement or masking tape
2. water colors or crayons
3. painting paper

PROCEDURE I

1. Have the children randomly drip rubber cement on paper, or apply strips of masking tape. Make the "globs" or strips vary in size. If glue is used, allow it to dry.
2. Apply paint or crayon over the entire glued or taped paper. Do not let the children labor at adhering paint or crayon to the covered section, since the glue or tape will later be removed.
3. If paint has been used, allow it to dry thoroughly.
4. Gently peel off all glue or tape. The unpainted paper beneath comes out forming an abstract pattern.

PROCEDURE II

1. Use masking tape or glue and apply it as described in step one above.
2. Pretend the glue or tape does not exist and crayon a picture or scene, filling the entire paper.
3. Peel off the tape. The resulting picture is now abstract.

WHAT THE CHILDREN CAN DO AFTERWARD

1. Display the pictures on a bulletin board.
2. Frame the abstracts and bring them home for use as wall hangings.

RELAX WITH TIME SAVERS

1. Distribute one tube of rubber cement to each child, or a roll of tape for two children to share.
2. If paint or glue is used, spread the desks with newspaper.
3. Distribute paint in plastic ice-cube trays; one for two or three children to share.
4. Have an assistant pass a wastebasket at the lesson's end to collect scraps of tape or glue. Choose others to collect, wash and store paint trays and brushes.

GLITTER PICTURES (Illustration 10-11)

ILLUSTRATION 10-11

MATERIALS

1. clear drying glue
2. construction paper
3. assorted colored tubes of glitter
4. crayon
5. newspaper to cover desks
6. cupcake tins
7. small bottle caps

BEFORE YOU BEGIN

Dimestore tubes brimming with colorful glitter are just too irresistible to children for us to ignore. Among the probable rewards for indulging young temptations, expect an array of gilded owls, dazzling ballerinas and glowing floral displays.

Show how glitter is used with minimal waste by filling a small bottle cap with a desired color, applying it to the glued area, then shaking the excess into newspaper. The paper is then folded up at the sides and the glitter is poured back into the cupcake tin for re-use.

PROCEDURE

1. With crayon, draw an outline of a desired picture or object to be filled in with glitter.
2. Distribute glitter colors in cupcake tins. Give each child a small bottle cap. Explain that the cap is filled with a desired color from the cupcake tin. Unused glitter can easily be returned.
3. Apply a little glue to a small portion of the outline. Fill a bottle cap with the needed amount of desired color. Sprinkle the glitter from the cap over the glued area. Continue working until the picture outline is covered.
4. Working a small area at a time, fill in the rest of the picture.
5. After each new color application, shake off the excess and return it to the appropriate section of the cupcake tin for re-use.

WHAT THE CHILDREN CAN DO AFTERWARD

1. Display the glitter pictures on a bulletin board.
2. Use the pictures as greeting card decorations.

RELAX WITH TIME SAVERS

1. Have two or three children share a cupcake tin of assorted glitter colors.
2. Provide small craft sticks or folded pieces of scrap paper for spreading glue.
3. Use glue bottles with control-flow tops.
4. Choose helpers to spoon any left-over glitter from the cupcake tins into their original tubes.
5. Dump all excess glitter into newspaper and funnel it into an extra tube or empty bottle. Have each child contribute any left-over glitter remaining on his newspaper to this new multi-colored addition.
6. Choose helpers to pass a wastebasket and collect newspaper. Ask one person from each table to sweep the area around desks.

SHOE BOX SAND CASTING

MATERIALS

1. shoe box
2. wet sand
3. objects to be pressed into sand (bottle caps, buttons, spoons, pencils, shells cookie cutters)
4. plaster of Paris
5. heavy wire or piece of bent wire coat hanger
6. tempera paint and brushes
7. varnish
8. clean, dry brush for dusting excess sand

BEFORE YOU BEGIN

In winter, when children's daydreams of sun and surf seem as remote as castles in Spain, we might, for the sake of fun and reverie, recapture a bit of last summer. Carving personal momentoes in drenched sand may be done most anytime, anywhere.

Remembering the enchanted days listening to the sea, let's carry illusion one step further and imagine our room as the seashore. As we imbed our careful patterns in soaked sand we needn't fear the tide to wash it away. Instead, our plaque designs will be preserved as reminders of summer by the sea.

PROCEDURE (Illustration 10-12)

1. Fill a shoe box with approximately 2″ of wet sand. (step a)
2. Press objects into the sand so that they leave deep impressions. Or have the children use their fingers to "draw" a favorite object, shape or design. (step b)
3. Prepare the plaster of Paris to the consistency of thick sour cream. Pour the mixture into the shoe box over the wet sand, filling the box at least 1/2″ above the depressed shapes or design. (step c)
4. After the depressions have been filled, loop a piece of coat hanger (or other piece of wire) in the partially dried plaster to serve as the plaque hanger. Allow the plaster to harden thoroughly. (step d)
5. Remove the plaque from the shoe box and dust away any clinging sand from the surface with a dry brush. (step e)
6. Paint the dried plaster plaques with tempera. Varnish may be applied when the paint has dried. (step f)

WHAT THE CHILDREN CAN DO AFTERWARD

1. Write poems about the seashore and summer.
2. Hang the plaques around the room for wall display.
3. Bring the sand casting designs home as gifts.

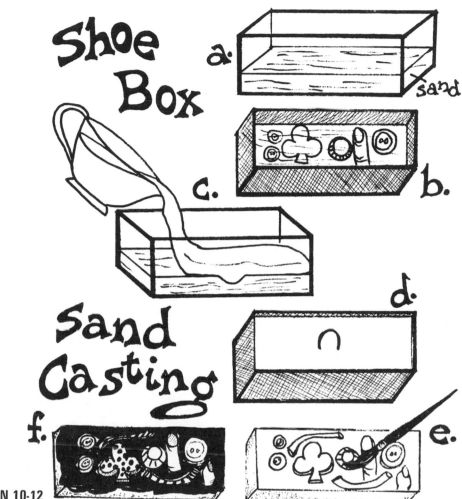

ILLUSTRATION 10-12

RELAX WITH TIME SAVERS

1. Spread newspapers before distributing the materials.
2. Have sand available in one area of the room. Allow small groups of children to take turns filling their shoe boxes. Provide small shovels or large spoons for this purpose.
3. Distribute a varied assortment of items with which to create designs for each table to share.
4. Set up one or two plaster stations. Pour all plaster at these areas. Wet plaques may also be left to dry at these stations.
5. Distribute the paint in plastic ice-cube trays; one for two or three children to share.
6. Set aside another area of the room for varnishing.
7. Provide a large wastebasket, lined with a paper bag, where youngsters may discard their sand-filled boxes. Eliminate any unnecessary mess by disposing of the sand as soon as the plaster plaques have dried and been removed from their boxes.

8. Choose helpers to collect, wash and store paint trays and brushes. Have others pass a wastebasket for newspaper to be discarded.

TISSUE PAPER WATERCOLORS

MATERIALS

1. white paper
2. assorted colors of tissue paper
3. bowl of water and small sponge
4. India ink and pen (or fine brush)
5. newspaper to work on

BEFORE YOU BEGIN

Delicate and lovely water-colors, how do we manage them? Since watercolors can test the ability of a professional artist, think how it can frustrate the young novice! Because such paint dries in minutes, mistakes are difficult, sometimes impossible, to correct. On the other hand, watercolors must be carefully controlled lest extra droplets run on the picture to render it irreparable.

We can at last meet, with only small invention, the challenge of this popular type of painting. Here's a technique which eliminates the twin disasters of "too wet" and "too dry." Tissue paper regulates and provides splashes of color, while pen and ink delineate the details. Even devoid of ability, whether the painting is to be realistic or abstract, each child is assured of a soft pastel palette.

Show the children how to tear strips of paper to approximate the size and shape of sections within the picture. Still-life arrangements are excellent for a demonstration lesson. Experiment with displays. Then, have several youngsters help tear paper to represent a bottle, bowl, lemon, or whatever was included in the sample set-up. Emphasize how the tissue paper is then dampened with a sponge and allowed to "set" until the color is absorbed by the paper beneath. Finally, add just touches of detail with a pen and India ink. Here, heavy-handedness can be deadly! Caution that only a few outlines and strokes will be needed to complete the "painting."

PROCEDURE (Illustration 10-13)

1. Spread newspaper on the desks, then distribute materials.
2. Tear strips of tissue paper to represent the size and shape of each section of the picture (bowl, bottle, tree, flower) The torn pieces should merely approximate these shapes. (step a)
3. Place each piece of torn tissue paper in its appropriate position on white background paper. Dab each piece of tissue paper with a wet sponge. Let the tissue paper color soak on page for approximately five minutes, or until each color has been absorbed on the white paper beneath. Add more water as needed. (step b)

Tissue Paper Watercolors

ILLUSTRATION 10-13

4. Carefully peel off the paper, making certain the color does not smear where it is not wanted. (step c)
5. Using India ink and pen, add the details. Let the painting dry. (step d)

WHAT THE CHILDREN CAN DO AFTERWARD

1. Use watercolors as bulletin board decoration.
2. Frame the paintings and give them as gifts.
3. Use the technique to make gift or greeting cards, and matching gift-wrap paper.
4. Use the paintings as wall hangings.

RELAX WITH TIME SAVERS

1. Distribute one bowl of water for every three children to share.
2. Distribute a varied, colorful assortment of tissue paper sheets for each table to share.
3. Dampened tissue paper may be dried and saved for future collage projects.
4. If possible, provide a bottle of ink for each child.
5. Have a helper pass a wastebasket to collect newspaper and other scraps.

Bonus Ideas

1. Make novel gift-wrap paper by painting on large sheets of newspaper.
2. Decorate odds and ends cans with string collage. Use polymer acrylic medium or white glue diluted with water to adhere the string to painted juice or coffee cans.
3. Try linoleum, wood, and vegetable printing.
4. Make holiday plaques by sand casting. Imbed (or carve) Christmas trees, Valentines, Easter bunnies in the moistened sand. Add plaster, then decoratively paint the dried plaques. As another gift variation, have children cast their own hand prints.
5. Make jewelry boxes by decorating papier-maché egg cartons with glitter.
6. Use the glitter technique for lettering posters advertising school elections, and special fund raising sales.
7. Make tissue paper and ink collage. Using white glue diluted with water, apply tissue paper strips to paper. Then, follow the technique for "Tissue Paper Water Colors," adding India ink for definition.
8. Use a tissue paper collage as a background for bulletin board displays.
9. Make a class mural using the technique described in "Tissue Paper Water Colors."
10. Paint in vertical columns of classified newspaper sections so as to represent a cityscape.
11. Use polymer acrylic medium to adhere colorful tissue paper to inexpensive wastebaskets, tissue boxes, picture or mirror frames. When the paper has dried, ink on a simple abstract or sketch. These accessories make perfect gifts for use in a bathroom or bedroom.

Index